LINCOLN

LINCOLN
A PRESIDENT FOR THE AGES

Edited by Karl Weber

PUBLICAFFAIRS
New York

Book Design by Cynthia Young

The Library of Congress has cataloged the printed edition as follows:

ISBN 978–1–61039–263–1 (PB orig.)

ISBN 978–1–61039–263–9 (EB)

First Edition

10 9 8 7 6 5 4 3 2 1

CONTENTS

ABOUT THIS BOOK

"Now he belongs to the ages." When a grief-stricken Edwin M. Stanton, secretary of war, uttered those words at 7:22 on the morning of April 15, 1865, it marked the end of Abraham Lincoln's nine-hour death-struggle against an assassin's bullet and the beginning of an epoch of mourning, memorializing, pondering, and debating the enormous historical legacy of our sixteenth president—an epoch that, it sometimes seems, has continued unabated for a century and a half. Every generation rediscovers and reinterprets Lincoln, in the process redefining what it means to be American, so central is he to our national story.

Today, the motion picture is perhaps the single most powerful medium by which we repurpose the past—"writing history with lightning," as President Woodrow Wilson is supposed to have said about *Birth of a Nation*, one of the first, and most controversial, cinematic efforts to define the legend of Lincoln. So when one of our era's greatest directors—Steven Spielberg—joins forces with one of our leading playwrights—Tony Kushner—and a cast of eminent performers, headed by the brilliant and versatile Daniel Day-Lewis, to offer a new interpretation of Lincoln's story, it's likely that millions of Americans will seize the opportunity to take a fresh look at his legacy and to ask what new meanings it may have for us today.

Hence this book. In the wake of so many thousands of literary attempts to distill the essence of Lincoln, it may seem futile to try to offer a new version of the familiar story. In an effort to meet this challenge—and to take seriously, even literally, Stanton's encomium of Lincoln as a man who "belongs to the ages"—we approached a collection of today's most eminent historians, journalists, and students of Lincoln with a novel assignment: to offer their own best judgments, admittedly speculative but solidly grounded in historical fact and generations of scholarship, as to how Lincoln might have responded to the political, social, economic, and military crises of times not his own.

We were delighted when these notable Lincoln scholars accepted the task. The results appear in the pages that follow. You'll read the thoughts of Henry Louis Gates Jr., as to how Lincoln (had he lived) might have managed the enormous challenges of race relations during the period of Reconstruction and beyond, Jean Baker's fascinating (and somewhat counterintuitive) assessment of how the Great Emancipator might have responded to the movement for women's suffrage, and Daniel Farber's insightful comparison of Lincoln and Franklin D. Roosevelt as historical reshapers of the role of federal power in American democracy.

You'll read thoughtful discussions by the eminent historians and authors James Tackach, Allen C. Guelzo, Douglas L. Wilson, Richard Carwardine, and Harold Holzer on such topics as Lincoln and the use of atomic weapons, Lincoln and the creation of a new global order in the wake of World War II, Lincoln and modern communications and celebrity culture, and Lincoln and the religious right. And you'll read journalist James Malanowski's surprising (and surprisingly convincing) portrait of Lincoln as an "outlaw hero"; a penetrating analysis by Frank J. Williams, former chief justice of the Rhode Island Supreme Court, of how Lincoln might have approached today's controversial War on Terror; and a lively interview with journalist Andrew Ferguson, author of the acclaimed *Land of Lincoln*, on what he discovered about Lincoln's many meanings during a year of traveling the country to meet some of the sixteenth president's most passionate admirers—and detractors.

Each of these chapters introduces, in a sense, a *new* Lincoln; yet the cumulative effect, we think, will be to deepen your understanding of and appreciation for the political genius, spiritual wisdom, and profound integrity of the man so many consider the greatest and most representative American.

We're also delighted to be able to include in this book some other features that we hope will enhance your insight into the Lincoln legacy. Gloria Reuben, a noted actor and political activist, describes the very personal journey she took as one of the performers in the Spielberg *Lincoln* film. Reuben brings to remarkable life a little-known yet fascinating figure in the story of Lincoln and his family: Elizabeth Keckley, a mixed-race woman who was born a slave and raised herself, through talent, tenacity, and courage, to become a talented dress designer, entrepreneur, and the chief confidante of First Lady Mary Todd Lincoln. We think you'll agree that Reuben's chapter is a very special highlight of this book.

Finally, we've also sought to give Lincoln the opportunity to speak for himself. Widely regarded as the greatest writer among American presidents and one of the supreme prose stylists in American history, Lincoln authored many of the most memorable documents written in this country. We've selected a handful of the most significant and revealing examples, which you'll find interspersed among the chapters. We invite you to study these excerpts from Lincoln's own writings (which you'll notice retain the original nineteenth-century spelling, punctuation, and grammar) and enjoy the opportunity to immerse yourself, for at least a while, in the spiritually and intellectually invigorating currents of Lincoln's mind. It's a plunge that we think every citizen should take periodically, because from these springs have flowed some of the strongest, freshest streams of American freedom.

Karl Weber
Irvington, New York
September 2012

The earliest known photo of Lincoln, probably taken in Springfield, Illinois, by Nicholas H. Shepherd (1846). *Library of Congress*

THE FACES OF LINCOLN

KARL WEBER

Karl Weber is a writer and editor based in Irvington, New York, who specializes in politics, public affairs, and business. He has coauthored such books as Creating a World Without Poverty, *with Nobel Peace Prize–winner Muhammad Yunus,* Demand: Creating What People Love Before They Know They Want It, *with Adrian J. Slywotzky, and* Citizen You: How Social Entrepreneurs Are Changing the World, *with Jonathan M. Tisch. He edited the Participant Media Guides* Food, Inc. *and* Waiting for "Superman."

Among the many unique distinctions borne by the sixteenth president of the United States, Abraham Lincoln is the first major historical figure to be known to us through photography. Every previous giant of history, from Nebuchadnezzar to Cleopatra, Charlemagne to Elizabeth I, has an image that is more or less vague, based purely on contemporary descriptions and depictions of doubtful accuracy. By contrast, we know Lincoln the same way we later came to know Churchill and Hitler, Elvis and Marilyn, Ali and Oprah— through photographs that capture the concrete reality of the human face with a vividness, nearness, and objectivity previously impossible.

What's more, as with those later representatives of twentieth-century celebrity culture, we know Lincoln through a series of specific, iconic photos—images that somehow capture not just the reality of a moment in time but the historic context within which a life took shape and meaning. Close your eyes and the familiar images of Lincoln flash by on a mental screen: The senate candidate, young and beardless, with rumpled collar, a gently lopsided smile, and an untamable shock of hair slightly askew. The president on the battlefield at Antietam, impressively lean, towering in his stovepipe hat over his officers. The father, seated in an armchair, casting a gentle, bespectacled glance at an album spread open on his lap for the benefit of young Tad standing at his side. The aging statesman, his visage deeply care-creased, his eyes sunken as if haunted by the carnage of war, just days away from his own death (as we know, though he does not).

The faces of Lincoln, which we know through the mystery of photography; fragments of unmediated reality that are unmistakably alive yet somehow distant and untouchable, like the man himself.

About 130 authenticated Lincoln photos are now known. (You'll find reproductions of a number of them scattered through the pages of this book.) From those photographic images evolve the other familiar faces of Lincoln—the many Lincolns that pop up in people's minds when the name is mentioned: the portraits on the penny and the five-dollar bill, the disembodied granite head on Mount Rushmore, the nineteen-foot-tall figure of Georgia white marble grandly enthroned in Washington, and the filmed embodiments by actors from Walter Huston and Raymond Massey to Henry Fonda, Gregory Peck, and Sam Waterston—and now, of course, Daniel Day-Lewis in the new film, scripted by Tony Kushner and directed by Steven Spielberg, that is the occasion for the publication of this book. And let's not exclude such pop-culture incarnations as the audioanimatronic figure stiffly reciting excerpts from Lincoln speeches to entertain tourists at Disney World or the bearded, semi-comic pitchmen in a hundred television commercials promoting Presidents' Day auto sales. These, too, are faces of Lincoln—low-brow tributes to the national obsession with our greatest president and arguably our single greatest historical figure.

Every American president has multiple meanings—that's in the nature of politics and history, particularly in a country as vast, diverse, and eternally contentious as ours. But the amazing multiplicity of Lincolns is unique among presidents. Scholar Merrill D. Peterson has boiled them down to five core archetypes: Savior of the Union, Great Emancipator, Man of the People, First American, and Self-Made Man.[1] From these five, as Peterson amply documents, flow countless variants.

Some of these multifarious Lincoln images were current in his own day and were fodder for his political campaigns, as well as his opponents'. Sobriquets like the Railsplitter, Woodchopper of the West, and Honest Abe were concocted as slogans; so were insults like the Black Republican and the Illinois Baboon, often accompanied by cartoons depicting Lincoln not just as ugly, buffoonish, and dimwitted but as harboring a secret lust for Negro women. (Images like these are worth recalling when the media declares the latest presidential race "the dirtiest ever"—as they do like clockwork, every four years.)

Other Lincolns have proliferated in the public consciousness during the century and a half since his death. Many have solid grounding in historical fact, others a mere toehold. Most of us have at least a passing acquaintance with many of these Lincolns from a school history class or a Ken Burns documentary.

There's Lincoln the frontiersman, the enterprising but largely unsuccessful businessman, the comic-opera warrior (leader of a tiny company of Illinois militia that served—and saw no combat whatsoever—during the short-lived Black Hawk War of 1832), and the aspiring inventor. (Lincoln remains the only president ever to have obtained a US patent, although the gadget he designed for lifting boats over shoals in riverbeds was never manufactured.)

There's Lincoln the shrewd self-taught attorney, the cracker barrel philosopher, and the indefatigable teller of stories, some downright obscene. (During his own lifetime, books purporting to collect Lincoln's favorite jokes and anecdotes—edited to suit Victorian notions of propriety—were already in circulation. No high school history book is likely to ever include Lincoln's scandalous but hilarious story about Ethan Allen and the outhouse—though it appears, remarkably, in Kushner's screenplay for Spielberg's *Lincoln*.)

There's Lincoln the family man, the (supposedly) henpecked husband, the doting father who let his small son run wild through the White House, the brooding sufferer from depression, and (some say) the "first gay president." (More on that notion later.)

There's Lincoln the Byronic lifelong aspirant to power, whose ambition (according to his longtime law partner William Herndon) "was an engine that knew no rest," the debater and orator of unmatched wit and eloquence, the obsessively self-editing speechmaker and letter writer, and the master of public opinion and political timing.

And of course there is Lincoln the lifelong opponent of slavery, the single-minded Union man, the ruthless wielder of military power, the tenderhearted commuter of sentences, the grieving father of his people, the Great Emancipator, and, ultimately, the martyr and savior of the nation.

So many Lincolns, each one somebody's favorite—especially, perhaps, the Lincolns of myth and legend. For the incurable romantic, the Lincoln of choice may be the grief-stricken frontier lover at the grave of Ann Rutledge, reputedly the one true passion of his life. (The image derives from an old, unsubstantiated story popularized by Herndon, who never much liked Mary Lincoln, and by Carl Sandburg, Lincoln's sentimental, quasi-official historian for much of the twentieth century.) For the autodidact, there's Lincoln riding the rural legal circuit, his nag of a horse dwarfed by its giant rider and walking at a snail's pace as Lincoln neglects the spurs, eagerly devouring yet another volume of Blackstone's *Commentaries*. For the believer in genius through inspiration, there's the president hastily penning his immortal speech on a fragment of torn cardboard while riding the train to Gettysburg (another myth too good to be abandoned despite the evidence against it).

Of course, I have my favorite Lincolns, too. As a lifelong baseball fan, I have a soft spot for an old story that says that Lincoln was in the middle of a game when a delegation arrived in Springfield from the Republican National Convention to formally notify him that he'd been nominated for the presidency. According to legend, Lincoln demurred, "Tell the gentlemen they will have to wait a few minutes until I get my next turn at bat."

Did it really happen? It's certainly *possible*, but only in the sense that it's *possible* I myself might be nominated for the presidency by the next Republican convention. The Mills Commission, the baseball history committee that came up with this story in 1939, is the same group that declared Abner Doubleday the inventor of the sport, a finding that every serious historian considers a mere fairy tale. But we baseball aficionados cling to it because it validates the historical status of our favorite game by associating it with America's greatest president.

I haven't yet stumbled across any articles claiming that Lincoln was an avid golfer, but I don't doubt they exist.*

As George Orwell said about Charles Dickens, Lincoln is well worth stealing—so it's no wonder that practically everybody has tried to appropriate him in support of their particular cause. Advocates of civil rights and racial equality, of course, have always recognized Lincoln as a spiritual ancestor. Not for nothing did Martin Luther King Jr. give his greatest address under Lincoln's marble gaze. That hasn't stopped white supremacists from cherry-picking Lincoln quotes to declare him a racist, a staunch advocate of segregation, and an opponent of racial equality.

In similar fashion, Lincoln (who was in fact a teetotaler in life) has been claimed by antiliquor crusaders as a "dry" and by the opposition as a "wet." During the debate over prohibition, while temperance crusaders were quoting Lincoln's comments about the evils of drink, publicists for a liquor industry association had copies of a liquor license granted to Lincoln during his youthful days as a storekeeper printed and distributed for proud display on the walls of taverns around the country.

Lincoln has been cited as a pioneering anti-imperialist (based on his vocal opposition to the Mexican War) and enlisted as a jingoist advocate of America's Manifest Destiny to expand. As Christopher A. Thomas

---

* Unless you count Thomas Meehan's "Abraham Lincoln: Lawyer, Statesman, and Golf Nut," which appeared in the *New Yorker* in 1971 and reported that "Even during the Civil War, hardly a day went by that [Lincoln] wasn't up at dawn to play 18 holes before breakfast. He was also a top-notch bowler, a more than capable handball player, and an avid water skier." I have a sneaking suspicion that this article may be a spoof—the words "water skier" give it away, don't you think?

has explained, the Lincoln Memorial itself was designed and built as part of a program by Republican Party leaders to celebrate the "active presidency" they credited Lincoln with establishing and that they saw embodied in such later enterprises as the Spanish-American War and the global American empire it spawned.

Lincoln has been hailed as both a laissez-faire free marketer and a defender of the downtrodden working man. During the 1930s, financiers named savings banks and insurance companies after Lincoln even as the American Communist Party was staging "Lincoln-Lenin" marches in honor of his proletarian sympathies. And *Lincoln's Prophecy*, a bogus screed warning against capitalist tyranny and the enthronement of corporate power in America, still circulates over Lincoln's signature, more than a century after it was first forged for use in the 1896 presidential campaign—now appropriated, inevitably, in support of the Occupy movement.

Liberal New York governor Mario Cuomo has enlisted the spirit of Lincoln on behalf of a twenty-first-century campaign against poverty, while conservative columnist George Will has called him a forebear of the antiabortion movement. Lincoln has been depicted as a prototype of the management consultant, an erstwhile leadership coach, a glad-handing self-help guru in the mold of Dale Carnegie, and most recently (heaven help us) as a vampire hunter.

And of course the multifarious Lincoln legend has long transcended national boundaries. The Russian novelist and spiritual seeker Leo Tolstoy (who called Lincoln "a Christ in miniature") told of meeting a Muslim chieftain in the remote Caucasus who affirmed that, yes, he had heard of the great American Lincoln: "He was a hero. He spoke with a voice of thunder; he laughed like the sunrise and his deeds were as strong as the rock and as sweet as the fragrance of rose." Passed from place to place and from person to person, Lincoln's story had become transmuted into a larger-than-life tale from mythology. Years later, India's Jawaharlal Nehru kept two inspirational sculptures on his office desk—a statuette of Gandhi and a bronze cast of Lincoln's hand. The Republic of China issued postage stamps pairing Lincoln with Sun Yat-Sen, while Ghana issued a set of three depicting its prime minister Kwame Nkrumah paying homage at the Lincoln Memorial.

So many Lincolns—and who is to say that any of them is definitely wrong?

Even those who knew Lincoln personally confessed—often with bafflement—his many-sidedness and the essential elusiveness of his character. Frederick Douglass, the greatest African American leader of the nineteenth century, met with Lincoln on several occasions and was referred to by the president as "my friend Douglass." He visited Lincoln at the White House (sometimes having to argue with racist guards before gaining admittance), famously lauded the second inaugural address as "a sacred effort" and in his memoirs declared, "Mr. Lincoln was not only a great president, but a great man—too great to be small in anything. In his company I was never in any way reminded of my humble origin, or of my unpopular color." Yet in his 1876 speech at the unveiling of the Freedmen's Monument to Lincoln in Washington, Douglass also called him "preeminently the white man's President, entirely devoted to the welfare of white men," avowed that Lincoln "shared the prejudices common to his countrymen towards the colored race," and summed up Lincoln's antislavery efforts this way: "Viewed from the genuine abolition ground, Mr. Lincoln seemed tardy, cold, dull, and indifferent; but measuring him by the sentiment of his country, a sentiment he was bound as a statesman to consult, he was swift, zealous, radical, and determined." The description is paradoxical, as if, for Douglass, Lincoln's heroism, although undeniable, is festooned with caveats and limitations. (In his essay in this book, scholar Henry Louis Gates Jr. offers a much more detailed analysis of Lincoln's mixed meaning for Douglass and, indeed, for many African Americans.)

Some later interpreters of Lincoln have painted similarly mixed portraits. The great filmmaker D. W. Griffith somehow managed to treat Lincoln as a hero of unmatched nobility in the same film, *Birth of a Nation*, that depicted the terror-wielding Ku Klux Klan as representatives of Southern heroism, and, in his best-selling historical novel *Lincoln*, Gore Vidal portrayed him as a masterful politician, a would-be tyrant, and a calculating, devious egotist who even infected his family with syphilis.

Most Americans have a less ambivalent attitude toward Lincoln. Yet our emotional and intellectual ties to Lincoln tend to be far more

complicated and far more personal than our links to most other historical personages. Only Lincoln could have inspired perhaps the greatest
and most psychologically intimate elegy ever written about a public figure. Walt Whitman had never met Lincoln, though he often glimpsed
him in the streets of Washington during the war years when Whitman
worked as a nurse tending wounded soldiers. Yet Whitman's elegy reads
like a tribute from a lover to his beloved:

> *When lilacs last in the dooryard bloom'd,*
> *And the great star early droop'd in the western sky in the night,*
> *I mourn'd, and yet shall mourn with ever-returning spring.*
>
> *Ever-returning spring, trinity sure to me you bring,*
> *Lilac blooming perennial and drooping star in the west,*
> *And thought of him I love. . . .*
>
> *O how shall I warble myself for the dead one there I loved?*
> *And how shall I deck my song for the large sweet soul that has gone?*
> *And what shall my perfume be for the grave of him I love?*
>
> *Sea-winds blown from east and west,*
> *Blown from the Eastern sea and blown from the Western sea,*
> *   till there on the prairies meeting,*
> *These and with these and the breath of my chant,*
> *I'll perfume the grave of him I love.*

In his essay "Fern-Seed and Elephants," the literary critic, novelist,
and Christian apologist C. S. Lewis contrasts the ways we relate to historical figures and literary characters:

> There are characters whom we know to be historical but of whom we
> do not feel that we have any personal knowledge—knowledge by ac-
> quaintance; such are Alexander, Attila, or William of Orange. There
> are others who make no claim to historical reality but whom, none
> the less, we know as we know real people: Falstaff, Uncle Toby, Mr.
> Pickwick. But there are only three characters who, claiming the first

sort of reality, also actually have the second. And surely everyone knows who they are: Plato's Socrates, the Jesus of the Gospels, and Boswell's Johnson. . . . We are not in the least perturbed by the contrasts within each character: the union in Socrates of silly and scabrous titters about Greek pederasty with the highest mystical fervor and the homeliest good sense; in Johnson, of profound gravity and melancholy with that love of fun and nonsense which Boswell never understood though Fanny Burney did; in Jesus of peasant shrewdness, intolerable severity, and irresistible tenderness.

Of course, Lewis's list of complex, vibrantly *living* historical personages—Socrates, Jesus, and Johnson—is the list that a scholarly, Christian Englishman would propose. For Americans, Lincoln is the undeniable fourth. The more we learn about Lincoln, and in particular the more we read Lincoln's own writings—the great speeches, the transcripts of the Lincoln-Douglas debates, the letters and notes he drafted in response to personal queries and political controversies—the more deeply we feel the reality of his complicated and endlessly fascinating personality. Arch-cynic H. L. Mencken complained (in his third book of *Prejudices*, 1922) that "the varnishers and veneerers have been busily converting Abe into a plaster saint, thus making him fit for adoration in the Y.M.C.A.'s. . . . Worse, there is an obvious effort to pump all his human weaknesses out of him, and so leave him a mere moral apparition, a sort of amalgam of John Wesley and the Holy Ghost." Maybe so—but when it comes to Lincoln, the work of the varnishers and veneerers has been largely futile. Unlike George Washington, who *is* for most Americans a plaster saint, we feel we know Lincoln as we know a friend or a family member; we understand, accept, and even revel in the contrasts in his character.

Lincoln somehow belongs to each of us, with a special intimacy that marks our relationship to few other public figures—especially when we limit ourselves to public figures from before today's era of factitious hyperintimacy. Fueled by the Internet and by media phenomena ranging from *People* magazine and reality TV to continually streaming Twitter feeds, millions of ordinary citizens now apparently think of actors, athletes, and, yes, politicians as if they are close personal friends. It's an illusion, of course, but one that publicists, producers, and marketers are eager to feed and exploit. Lincoln is one of the few historical figures from the nineteenth century or earlier whom it's possible to imagine in this context, as Harold Holzer artfully explains in his essay in this book, "Lincoln—The Unlikely Celebrity."

And yet, despite the sense of intimacy we feel toward Lincoln (enhanced by the endless stream of biographies, histories, picture books, television shows, movies, and other bits of Lincolniana produced every year), it remains startlingly difficult to pigeonhole, dismiss, ignore, or patronize him. Lincoln still towers above us and our history, and the more we know about him the greater he seems to loom.

In this, our relationship to Lincoln mirrors that of his contemporaries. In Washington's lifetime, no one ever underestimated him; his physical stature, personal beauty, unblemished rectitude, and austere presence caused those around him to regard him with admiration bordering on awe. (On a bet, Gouverneur Morris once famously dared to greet Washington with a slap on the back; the blood-chilling glare he received in response made Morris vow never to repeat the gesture.)

By contrast, everyone underestimated Lincoln. Contemporary testimony makes it clear that most of the famous "team of rivals" who ended up as members of Lincoln's cabinet were initially baffled to find themselves politically outmaneuvered by someone they considered an uneducated frontiersman. But, the more they got to know him, the greater the depths of insight and wisdom they saw in him (one of the many nuances of the Lincoln story that is subtly and effectively captured in Tony Kushner's screenplay). By the time of his death, most had come to recognize in Lincoln a man of overpowering stature—not just politically but intellectually, spiritually, and morally.

Many have used the word "Shakespearean" to describe Lincoln and his story. It's apt in several senses. Lincoln himself loved the works of Shakespeare (especially *Macbeth*) and infused his own writings with Shakespearean echoes. More important, Shakespeare is the supreme literary depicter of genius. It's notoriously difficult for a writer to portray, in a novel or drama, a character who is more brilliant, more complex, or simply *bigger* than himself—but Shakespeare has done it. When we read *Hamlet* or *Lear*, *Henry IV* or *Othello*, we actually feel and believe that we are in the presence of personal greatness. And when we read Lincoln's life or his writings, we feel the same way.

Partly this is due to the circumstances of his life and death—the pre-eminent role he played, after being launched from obscurity, in the central drama of his day, which is still, a century and a half later, the central drama of American history. As many have noted, the Civil War is to the people of the United States what the Trojan War was to the ancient Greeks—the fount of our mythology, our literature, our complicated self-image, our enduring conflicts. The story of that war—its origin in the great national sin of slavery, its inexorable outbreak despite the efforts of generations of statesmen to avoid it, its horrific unfolding through a litany of Homeric clashes and grinding carnage, its remarkable cast of secondary characters, its shocking conclusion (including the martyrdom of its greatest hero—on Good Friday, no less) and, finally, its tragic, still-unfolding legacy—this story feels too vast and too mythic to be true.

Yet it is true. And the frontier lawyer Lincoln somehow rose in stature not simply to be worthy of that grand stage but to dominate it—even while remaining the husband of the troubled, often querulous Mary (fussing over dressmaker's bills), the shrewd politico (swapping postmasterships in little one-horse towns for the votes needed to free the slaves), the cackling teller of off-color stories, and all the rest. Somehow our Lincoln remains resolutely mortal and human while transcending mere mortality, mere humanity, as figures from mythology do.

The stature of Lincoln continues to amaze. He towers not only over his contemporaries but over us. And so, when we try to appropriate him to play a role in some modern controversy, we find (if we are honest) that he overwhelms us.

Take, for example, the issue of Lincoln's sexuality. For generations, some have wondered whether Lincoln was purely heterosexual in his orientation. Writing in 1926 about Lincoln's youthful friend Joshua Fry Speed, Sandburg described their friendship as having "a streak of lavender, and spots soft as May violets" (using common 1920s code for what we now call gay relations). In 1995, with the issues of gay rights

and even same-sex marriage having battled their way into the political
limelight, psychologist C. A. Tripp published a book that claimed Lincoln was fundamentally homosexual in orientation.

Most historians have dismissed Tripp's claim, saying he misinter-
preted such once-common practices as men sharing a bed while traveling. But for a time, the furor over Tripp's book catapulted Lincoln once
again to the center of the political stage. Emotions ran high. Conservative columnist (and gay rights advocate) Andrew Sullivan wrote an article in the *New Republic* in which he declared,

> The truth about Lincoln—his unusual sexuality, his comfort with
> male-male love and sex—is not a truth today's Republican leaders
> want to hear. They are well-advised to attack and suppress it. They
> are more closely related to the forces Lincoln defeated than those he
> championed; and his candor, honesty, and brave forging of a ho-
> mosocial and homoerotic life in plain sight would appall them. The
> real Lincoln is their greatest rebuke. Which is why they will do all
> they can to obscure the complicated, fascinating truth about the man
> whose legacy they are intent on betraying.

Sullivan's assumptions about Lincoln's erotic life may be questionable. But there's no doubt that the relationship between Lincoln—one
of the founders of the Republican Party—and the conservative religious
leaders who are among the chief supporters of today's Republican Party
is an uneasy one. (Historian Richard Carwardine analyzes the issue in
fascinating detail in his essay in this book "The Almighty Has His Own
Purposes": Abraham Lincoln and the Christian Right.) In that sense,
Sullivan's observation that Lincoln represents a "rebuke" to today's political leaders is an understandable one.

But the rebuke that Lincoln represents goes far beyond his sexuality,
as a careful reading of Lincoln's greatest utterance, the second inaugural
address, suggests.

Twenty-first century politicians, like their counterparts in Lincoln's
day, don't hesitate to invoke religion when they find it convenient.
Most citizens have learned to respond to such appeals with cynicism.
That makes it especially stunning to discover, in the second inaugural

address, the unmistakable voice of a politician who *actually believes in God*—who takes seriously the notion of divine justice and has wrestled in trembling and anguish with its implications for himself personally and for the nation he leads.

Everyone knows the fourth and final paragraph of the speech, which begins, "With malice toward none; with charity for all; . . . " It's a graceful, beautiful benediction. But its sweetness is deepened by the contrast with the two preceding paragraphs, which set forth a *moral* synopsis of the history and meaning of the Civil War.

It's noteworthy that Lincoln refuses to posture or congratulate his (Northern) audience about the justice of the Union cause in that war (though surely Lincoln believed that if any cause was ever just, that one was). Instead, he tartly observes:

> One eighth of the whole population were colored slaves, not distributed generally over the Union, but localized in the Southern part of it. These slaves constituted a peculiar and powerful interest. All knew that this interest was, somehow, the cause of the war.

That word "somehow" is a characteristically shrewd Lincoln touch. He meticulously refuses to be drawn into arguments about the precise relationship between slavery and the war. White Southerners would define that relationship one way; Northern abolitionists would define it another way; many others on both sides of the Mason-Dixon Line would define it in still other ways. Lincoln will not be drawn into a fruitless debate about how to apportion the blame for the war—but he wants to insist that, "somehow," it has been a war about slavery, because, as we will see, this is to be his central theme.

Lincoln presses on to describe how the Civil War, like many another war, has had unintended, far-reaching consequences:

> Neither party expected for the war, the magnitude, or the duration, which it has already attained. Neither anticipated that the cause of the conflict [i.e., slavery] might cease with, or even before, the conflict itself should cease. Each looked for an easier triumph, and a result less fundamental and astounding.

What *moral* sense does Lincoln make of these facts—of the appalling length and destructiveness of the war? He spends the rest of the long third paragraph offering his interpretation, which is deeply rooted in biblical notions of justice, retribution, and the inevitable consequence of sin. He quotes Matthew 18:7: "Woe unto the world because of offences! for it must needs be that offences come; but woe to that man by whom the offence cometh!" And from Lincoln's unflinchingly honest contemplation of the meaning of this text for Americans emerges this syllogism:

> If we shall suppose that American Slavery is one of those offences which, in the providence of God, must needs come, but which, having continued through His appointed time, He now wills to remove, and that He gives to both North and South, this terrible war, as the woe due to those by whom the offence came, shall we discern therein any departure from those divine attributes which the believers in a Living God always ascribe to Him?

For a modern reader, steeped in twenty-first century styles of political discourse, it's difficult at first to realize that Lincoln is saying exactly what he appears to be saying: "this terrible war" has been visited upon Americans *because we deserve it.* And, yes, "both North and South" deserve it, for both North and South countenanced the offence of "American Slavery." Note that last phrase. Unlike most writers of textbook histories and modern politicians, Lincoln refuses to pretend that the crime of slavery was some sort of aberration, irrelevant to the true "character" of our people. No, he brands it as what it was: "*American Slavery,*" our nation's uniquely tragic contribution to the register of historic evils.

Every schoolchild knows that the adjective "honest" is permanently affixed to Lincoln. That has been true since Lincoln's own time; as we've noted, the phrase "Honest Abe" originated as a campaign slogan. But the moniker is too cute, suggesting a president we might even be able to patronize. It conjures up the legend of the teenaged store clerk who walked three miles to return six cents in change mistakenly left behind by a customer—honest almost to excess. That's one kind of honesty, admirable in its own way.

But the really remarkable thing about Lincoln's honesty is its *ruthlessness* (akin to the "coldness" of which Herndon spoke). The Lincoln who speaks in this address is profoundly aware of the suffering of hundreds of thousands of mothers and fathers, wives and sweethearts, brothers and sisters who had lost loved ones to death, disease, or dismemberment in the war that Lincoln had insisted on prosecuting despite criticism from all sides, including some of his most fervent and moralistic supporters. He has spoken to many of those bereaved ones, held their hands, looked them in the eye. One need only reread Lincoln's famous letter to Mrs. Bixby to recall the tender sympathy of which he was capable:

> I have been shown in the files of the War Department a statement of the Adjutant General of Massachusetts that you are the mother of five sons who have died gloriously on the field of battle. I feel how weak and fruitless must be any word of mine which should attempt to beguile you from the grief of a loss so overwhelming. But I cannot refrain from tendering you the consolation that may be found in the thanks of the Republic they died to save. I pray that our Heavenly Father may assuage the anguish of your bereavement, and leave you only the cherished memory of the loved and lost, and the solemn pride that must be yours to have laid so costly a sacrifice upon the altar of freedom.

Yet this same man has the honesty—and the temerity—to address Mrs. Bixby and her fellow mourners (along with the rest of the nation that re-elected him) and say, in effect, *We deserve this war, and all the suffering it has brought.*

This is honesty almost beyond human bearing: fierce, fiery, implacable.

Thankfully, although Lincoln finds this harsh conclusion unavoidable, he refuses to take any pleasure in it. (In that, he is unlike, for example, some preachers of Lincoln's own time as well as today, who seem to *relish* the vision of apocalypse that sin is surely bringing to America.) Instead, Lincoln offers a plea that surely echoes the content of his private meditations in the White House: "Fondly do we hope—fervently do we pray—that this mighty scourge of war may speedily pass away."

But he still won't let us, his auditors and his fellow countrymen, off the hook:

> Yet, if God wills that it continue, until all the wealth piled by the bond-man's two hundred and fifty years of unrequited toil shall be sunk, and until every drop of blood drawn with the lash, shall be paid by another drawn with the sword, as was said three thousand years ago, so still it must be said "the judgments of the Lord, are true and righteous altogether."

Most politicians of Lincoln's era—and our own—who choose to speak about God do it purely to flatter themselves and their audience; to reassure their listeners that God is on their side. But Lincoln refuses to flatter himself or us. He respects us too much for that. Instead he models what may be the highest degree of spiritual maturity—the readiness to see and judge oneself through God's eyes, with unflinching honesty, not wallowing in one's sins (or those of one's people) but acknowledging them as the first essential step toward repentance, reform, and reconciliation.

Andrew Sullivan was right—but I would go farther than Sullivan did. The "real Lincoln" *is* the "greatest rebuke"—but not just for Republicans or Democrats, conservatives or liberals, Northerners or Southerners, but for all of us.

Lincoln is us—the "First American," in Merrill D. Peterson's words. But he is us at the peak of our greatness, continually reminding us of how far we fall short and urging us on to the heights of integrity and honesty, compassion and mutual forgiveness that he knows we are capable of achieving. This, for me, is the deepest message we read when we gaze yet again upon that face we've found so mesmerizing for the past century and a half—the face of the greatest American, the face of our Abraham Lincoln.

LINCOLN'S WORDS

To the People of Sangamo County (1832)

Lincoln's first political pronouncement

Fellow Citizens:

Having become a candidate for the honorable office of one of your representatives in the next General Assembly of this state, in accordance with an established custom, and the principles of true republicanism, it becomes my duty to make known to you—the people whom I propose to represent—my sentiments with regard to local affairs.

Time and experience have verified to a demonstration, the public utility of internal improvements. That the poorest and most thinly populated countries would be greatly benefitted by the opening of good roads, and in the clearing of navigable streams within their limits, is what no person will deny. But yet it is folly to undertake works of this or any other kind, without first knowing that we are able to finish them—as half finished work generally proves to be labor lost. There cannot justly be any objection to having rail roads and canals, any more than to other good things, provided they cost nothing.

The only objection is to paying for them; and the objection to paying arises from the want of ability to pay.

With respect to the County of Sangamo, some more easy means of communication than we now possess, for the purpose of facilitating the task of exporting the surplus products of its fertile soil, and importing necessary articles from abroad, are indispensably necessary. A meeting has been held of the citizens of Jacksonville, and the adjacent country, for the purpose of deliberating and enquiring into the expediency of constructing a railroad from some eligible point on the Illinois river, through the town of Jacksonville, in Sangamo county. This is, indeed, a very desirable object. No other improvement that reason will justify us in hoping for, can equal in utility the rail road. It is a never failing source of communication, between places of business remotely situated from each other. Upon the rail road the regular progress of commercial intercourse is not interrupted by either high or low water, or freezing weather, which are the principal difficulties that render our future hopes of water communication precarious and uncertain. Yet, however desirable an object the construction of a rail road through our country may be; however high our imaginations may be heated at thoughts of it—there is always a heart appalling shock accompanying the account of its cost, which forces us to shrink from our pleasing anticipations. The probable cost of this contemplated rail road is estimated at $290,000;—the bare statement of which, in my opinion, is sufficient to justify the belief, that the improvement of the Sangamo river is an object much better suited to our infant resources.

Respecting this view, I think I may say, without the fear of being contradicted, that its navigation may be rendered completely practicable, as high as the mouth of the South Fork, or probably higher, to vessels of from 25 to 30 tons burthen, for at least one half of all common years, and to vessels of much greater burthen a part of that time. From my peculiar circumstances, it is probable that for the last twelve months I have given as particular attention to the stage of the water in this river as any other person in the country. In the month of March, 1831, in company of others, I commenced the building of a flat boat on the Sangamo, and finished and took her out in the course of the spring. Since that time, I have been concerned in the mill at New Salem. These circumstances are sufficient evidence, that I have not been very inattentive to the stages of the water.—The time at which we crossed the mill dam, being in the last days of April, the water was lower than it had been since the breaking of winter in February, or than it was for several weeks after. The principal difficulties we encountered in descending the river, were from the drifted timber, which obstructions all know is not difficult to be removed. Knowing almost precisely the height of water at that time, I believe I am safe in saying that it has often been higher as lower since.

From this view of the subject, it appears that my calculations with regard to the navigation of the Sangamo cannot be unfounded in reason; but whatever may be its natural advantages, certain it is, that it never can be practically useful to any great extent, without being greatly improved by art. The drifted timber, as I have before mentioned, is the most formidable barrier to this object. Of all parts of this river, none will require so much labor in proportion, to make it navigable, as the last thirty or thirty-five miles; and going with the meanderings of the channel, when we are this distance above its mouth, we are only between twelve and eighteen miles above Beardstown, in something near a straight direction; and this route is upon such low ground as to retain water in many places during the season, and in all parts such as to draw two-thirds or three-fourths of the river water at all high stages.

This route is upon prairie land the whole distance;—so that it appears to me, by removing the turf, a sufficient width and damming up the old channel, the whole river in a short time would wash its way through, thereby curtailing the distance, and increasing the velocity of the current very considerably, while there would be no timber upon the banks to obstruct its navigation in future; and being nearly straight, the timber which might float in at the head, would be apt to go clear through. There are also many places above this where the river, in its zig zag course, forms such complete peninsulas, as to be easier cut through at the necks than to remove the obstructions from the bends—which, if done, would also lessen the distance.

What the cost of this work would be, I am unable to say. It is probable, however, it would not be greater than is common to streams of the same length. Finally, I believe the improvement of the Sangamo river, to be vastly important and highly desirable to the people of this county; and if elected, any measure in the legislature having this for its object, which may appear judicious, will meet my approbation, and shall receive my support.

It appears that the practice of loaning money at exorbitant rates of interest, has already been opened as a field for discussion; so I suppose I may enter upon it without claiming the honor, or risking the danger, which may await its first explorer. It seems as though we are never to have an end to this baneful and corroding system, acting almost as prejudiced to the general interests of the community as a direct tax of several thousand dollars annually laid on each county, for the benefit of a few individuals only, unless there be a law made setting a limit to the rates of usury. A law for this purpose, I am of opinion, may be made without materially injuring any class of people. In cases of extreme necessity there could always be means found to cheat the law, while in all other cases it would have its intended effect. I would not favor the passage of a law upon this subject, which might be very easily evaded. Let it be such that the labor and difficulty of evading it, could only be justified in cases of the greatest necessity.

Upon the subject of education, not presuming to dictate any plan or system respecting it, I can only say that I view it as the most important subject which we as a people can be engaged in. That every man may receive at least, a moderate education, and thereby be enabled to read the histories of his own and other countries, by which he may duly appreciate the value of our free institutions, appears to be an object of vital importance, even on this account alone, to say nothing of the advantages and satisfaction to be derived from all being able to read the scriptures and other works, both of a religious and moral nature, for themselves. For my part, I desire to see the time when education, and by its means, morality, sobriety, enterprise and industry, shall become much more general than at present, and should be gratified to have it in my power to contribute something to the advancement of any measure which might have a tendency to accelerate the happy period.

With regard to existing laws, some alterations are thought to be necessary. Many respectable men have suggested that our estray laws—the law respecting the issuing of executions, the road law, and some others, are deficient in their present forms, and require alterations. But considering the great probability that the framers of those laws were wiser than myself, I should prefer [not?] meddling with them, unless they were first attacked by others, in which case I should feel it both a privilege and a duty to take that stand, which in my view, might tend most to the advancement of justice.

But, Fellow-Citizens, I shall conclude.—Considering the great degree of modesty which should always attend youth, it is probable I have already been more presuming than becomes me. However, upon the subjects of which I have treated, I have spoken as I thought. I may be wrong in regard to any or all of them; but holding it a sound maxim, that it is better to be only sometimes right, than at all times wrong, so soon as I discover my opinions to be erroneous, I shall be ready to renounce them.

Every man is said to have his peculiar ambition. Whether it be true or not, I can say for one that I have no other so great as that of being truly esteemed of my fellow men, by rendering myself worthy of their esteem. How far I shall succeed in gratifying this ambition, is yet to be developed. I am young and unknown to many of you. I was born and have ever remained in the most humble walks of life. I have no wealthy or popular relations to recommend me. My case is thrown exclusively upon the independent voters of this county, and if elected they will have conferred a favor upon me, for which I shall be unremitting in my labors to compensate. But if the good people in their wisdom shall see fit to keep me in the back ground, I have been too familiar with disappointments to be very much chagrined.

Your friend and fellow-citizen,
A. Lincoln

New Salem, March 9, 1832.

The so-called tousled hair photo,
taken by Alexander Hesler in Chicago
(February 28, 1857). *Library of Congress*

2

ELIZABETH KECKLEY

Bringing an Extraordinary Woman
to the Screen

GLORIA REUBEN

Gloria Reuben is an actress, singer, and social activist. One of her most memorable roles was the HIV-positive health-care professional "Jeanie Boulet" on the hit NBC series ER, *which garnered her two Emmy nominations and a Golden Globe nomination. Since then, Reuben has had multiple regular starring roles in a variety of television series.*

Her film credits include Timecop, Nick of Time, *and* Shaft. *In addition to portraying Elizabeth Keckley in Steven Spielberg's* Lincoln, *she will costar with Tina Fey in the film* Admission, *to be released in the spring of 2013.*

Reuben's portrayal of Condoleezza Rice in David Hare's play Stuff Happens *garnered her a Lucille Lortel Best Actress Award.*

Reuben's musical career includes singing backup for Tina Turner in 2000, recording the solo album Just For You, *and enjoying a blossoming jazz and cabaret career.*

Reuben is also a committed social activist. Her priority is raising awareness of the global climate crisis. She actively participates with many organizations including Al Gore's

Climate Reality Project, the National Wildlife Federation, Waterkeeper Alliance, and the RFK Center for Justice and Human Rights.

It was the grace and dignity in her face that caught my attention when I first gazed at her photograph. I couldn't help but stare.

Her eyes were deep. Dark. Certain. Yet also a little melancholic.

Her chin was held high. Not in a conceited fashion, but in a way that suggested she was a warrior—a woman who had seen and experienced a great many things that challenged the soul. Yet she persevered. She had always kept moving forward.

In that first glance, I felt as if I knew Elizabeth Keckley.

I am in no way suggesting that I can even remotely imagine what life was like during those conflicted and challenging times in America, particularly for a mixed-race woman. Yet somehow my heart understands.

What a life she led. A hardworking wage earner and a successful entrepreneur, she was often caught between two worlds—black and white; slave and freedwoman. And it is how she deftly wove a path through those worlds that I intuitively connect to.

The more I discovered about Elizabeth Keckley, the more my life experience seemed to mesh with hers. Her experiences of loss, grief, and survival were somehow familiar; they resonated instantly with my own memories of the tragic parts of life. Keckley and I have carved out our lives in very different circumstances, of course, but the fabric is woven from a similar thread. Here is her story:

She is born into slavery in 1818 in Dinwiddie, Virginia. Her mother, Agnes, is deeply in love with George Hobbs, a literate slave who lives on a nearby farm. Agnes names her baby daughter Elizabeth Hobbs.

Elizabeth assumes that George Hobbs is her biological father. But in reality her father is her owner and master, Colonel Armistead Burwell—a fact she will not learn until she is a full-grown woman at her mother's deathbed.

When Elizabeth is a little girl, at the age of four, she is put in charge of tending to the newest infant born into the Burwell family. Just a child herself, she doesn't know how to soothe the baby when it cries. In her efforts to cease the crying, she rocks the cradle too hard and the little infant falls onto the floor. The parents and other family members rush into the room. Although the child isn't seriously injured, Elizabeth pays dearly for her inexperience. She is beaten with a fire shovel.

At the age of fourteen, Elizabeth is given as a wedding gift to the eldest legitimate son, Robert Burwell. (This was a common practice employed by slaveholders, a way of keeping the unacknowledged slave family united with the white family.) Robert's new wife Anna is a severe and harsh mistress, demanding from Elizabeth enough work to exhaust three slaves.

The Burwells move to Hillsborough, North Carolina, where Robert becomes a minister and teacher at the Anna Burwell School for Girls. Between the ages of fourteen and twenty-one, Elizabeth takes care of the Burwells' children as well as many of the young girls attending the school.

Elizabeth grows into a lovely young woman, with a strong yet feminine personality, and that strength and beauty are too much for Anna Burwell to bear. So she sends Elizabeth on loan to one of the neighbors, a man named William J. Bingham, who is well known in the community not only as a faithful member of the parish where Robert Burwell is minister but also as a man who quickly and gleefully crushes the spirit of slaves. He flogs Elizabeth repeatedly. Each time, Elizabeth does not utter a sound. She will not allow him to see her pain. Finally, unable to break Elizabeth's will and wracked with guilt, Bingham ceases the beatings and begs for her forgiveness.

During this time, Alexander Kirkland, a wealthy plantation owner who lives a mile away, has sex with Elizabeth against her will. This goes on for four years. She bears him a son whom she names after George Hobbs, the love of her mother's life and the only father she ever knew.

In her early twenties, Elizabeth and George are sent back to Virginia, where Elizabeth works as a slave in the family of Robert Burwell's younger sister Ann—and therefore Elizabeth's own half sister—who is now married to a man named Hugh Garland. Elizabeth moves with the Garland family to various cities and towns in Virginia and North Carolina, finally settling in St. Louis, Missouri.

All the while, Elizabeth is mastering the household skills that a smart and gifted young woman is capable of developing. One of these skills is dressmaking. She has a deft hand, an eye for color and style, and a creative flair with the scissors and the needle. By her late thirties, Elizabeth is a talented dress designer. She enjoys a growing reputation among relatives and friends of the Garland family, and over time she becomes a well-respected seamstress in St. Louis, known for her extraordinary and unique gowns.

Even as Elizabeth is developing a successful business career, she remains a slave. Eventually she goes to Ann Burwell, shortly after her husband, Hugh, dies, and reminds Ann of a promise he had made—that one day Elizabeth would be free. Ann tells Elizabeth that, yes, she and her son will be free—but only if Elizabeth can raise $1,200.

Elizabeth's clients decide to help. One woman in particular, a Mrs. Elizabeth LeBourgeois, makes it her personal mission to raise the funds needed to purchase Elizabeth's and George's freedom. Finally, in 1855, Elizabeth and George are freed.

George enrolls in Wilberforce University in Ohio, and Elizabeth continues to live and work in St. Louis until she has repaid every penny to Mrs. LeBourgeois and her other benefactors.

In 1860, on the eve of the Civil War, Elizabeth moves to Washington, DC, and opens a dressmaking shop. Immediately she garners a bevy of new clients, including Varina Howell Davis, the wife of US senator and future Confederate president Jefferson Davis. She hires a team of seamstresses to assist her.

Four months after arriving in Washington, on the morning of the inauguration of Abraham Lincoln, Elizabeth meets Mary Todd Lincoln, the president's wife. She becomes the First Lady's modiste, best friend, and confidante. Their friendship lasts through the Lincolns' four years in the White House and beyond, surviving the untimely death of the president.

An extraordinary life. A brave and adventurous soul. A wise and clever businesswoman. Yet the matters of the heart present her greatest challenge.

James Keckley, a man Elizabeth marries while in St. Louis, claims that he is a freedman, but this is a lie. When James turns out to be a drunkard as well as a slave, Elizabeth leaves him. She never marries again, and there is no record of her ever having another romance.

Elizabeth's son George, eager to battle the forces of oppression, joins the Union army at the beginning of the Civil War. At that time, black men are ineligible to fight, but George passes as white. In his very first battle, the Battle of Lexington at Wilson's Creek, Missouri, George is killed and buried in an unmarked shallow grave. Elizabeth never has another child.

Meanwhile, she witnesses the intense emotional ups and downs of her highly intelligent but incredibly volatile friend, Mary Todd Lincoln. As Mary's stylist and personal dresser, she shares many of the First Lady's most intimate moments, including the death of her son Willie. She comforts Mary after her husband's murder and accompanies her when she leaves Washington for Chicago and New York, distraught, deeply in debt, and widely scorned by the press and public.

But, though the friendship between the two women is a solid and steadfast one, it cannot survive misunderstanding and miscommunication. In 1868, Elizabeth publishes her autobiography, *Behind the Scenes, Or, Thirty Years a Slave and Four Years in the White House.* The book is intended to garner support for Mrs. Lincoln in the midst of her personal and financial woes. But the boldness of a black woman in daring to write about her relationship with a white woman—and the First Lady, at that—produces outrage, anger, and responses that include a racist parody that makes a mockery of Elizabeth's life.

Mary Lincoln herself feels betrayed by the disclosure of private confidences, and she permanently severs their friendship. Elizabeth outlives Mrs. Lincoln by twenty-five years, and one of the few items she has in her possession at the time of her death is a photograph of her beloved "Mrs. L."

* * *

Elizabeth Keckley's story is filled with strange and tragic twists and turns—yet it's a story that so many of us can identify with, physically, psychologically, and emotionally.

Like Elizabeth, I, too, grew up as part of a "second family." My father was married once before marrying my mother. He had five children with his first wife, then five more with my mother. My father was white and my mother mulatto, so we are a mixed-race family. Some of my siblings can pass as white. As best I can recall, my brothers and sisters were never embraced by our half siblings.

My parents separated when I was five, and my childhood was over. Forced to learn how to stand on my own emotionally, I grew up quickly. My mother is extremely intelligent but psychologically troubled, and so I became her emotional caretaker at an early age. My father died when I was twelve, and soon thereafter my family moved from our home in Toronto.

By the age of fourteen I was already in the workplace, with a job as a waitress. I enjoyed the freedom and independence of the job, and I especially loved the interaction with people.

When I was just shy of sixteen, I was raped. I told no one for almost twenty-three years. The emotional scar left me struggling to be truly intimate with anyone. I moved out on my own when I was seventeen.

Through it all, my creative endeavors kept me sane. Playing the piano, singing in bands, and writing daily in my journal were the only forms of self-expression that I could fully own—that were and are mine—in a life where everything else seemed out of control.

My brother Denis, fourteen years my senior, was my rock. When I was twenty-one, I returned to Toronto and moved in with him. The next three years were the happiest of my young life. I finally learned about and experienced the joys of life—friendship, dinner parties, music, dance, just plain fun—all for the first time.

But fate took a tragic turn. Five days before his twenty-second birthday, my sweet little brother David took his own life. Though I was just two years older, I had always thought of David as "mine"—the one I was supposed to look after and protect. To this day I feel as though I failed him.

I fled Toronto after David's death and moved to Los Angeles where I knew just one person, a friend of my brother Denis.

Like Elizabeth, I had nothing handed to me. I invented and built a life and a career one step at a time. For me, as for most aspiring performers, finding a place in the entertainment industry was a struggle . . .

one that I am still trying to master. I leaned on Denis's strength until I could no longer do so. He died suddenly in the fall of 2010.

The look in Elizabeth Keckley's eyes, so dark, deep, and mysterious . . . I relate to all that I see there.

* * *

When I received the fantastic news that I was going to portray Elizabeth under the direction of the one and only Steven Spielberg, my first reaction was a wide-eyed shout of glee. My second was to immediately go online and order many books. I first read Elizabeth's autobiography and found it an incredible read. Other very helpful books that allowed me to travel deeply into Elizabeth's life and world included *An Unlikely Friendship: A Novel of Mary Todd Lincoln and Elizabeth Keckley*, by Ann Rinaldi; *Mary Lincoln's Dressmaker: Elizabeth Keckley's Remarkable Rise from Slave to White House Confidante*, by Becky Rutberg; and *Mrs. Lincoln and Mrs. Keckly: The Remarkable Story of a Friendship Between a First Lady and a Former Slave*, by Jennifer Fleischner. (Elizabeth's last name is sometimes spelled "Keckly," as in this last title.) These books, along with articles and sections of other books, offered a plethora of information about the historical and emotional details that defined Elizabeth. They also offered great insight into her relationships with Mary Todd Lincoln and President Lincoln.

In the late summer of 2011, it was time to begin the process of preparing the look of Mrs. Keckley for the film.

Joanna Johnston is the incredibly talented costume designer for the film. I just love her—so smart, creative, sassy, and British! We met on the day of my first fitting in Richmond, Virginia, and we sensed an immediate kinship. I could feel the electricity in the air: the anticipation of a great thing to come . . . the making of this powerful and important film.

In the costume room, seamstresses were everywhere. No surprise, as there are over a hundred actors in the film (and that's counting only those with lines of dialogue—countless others were "background"), and each and every one of them had to be fitted and costumed. I was in awe of the tenacity and focus of Joanna's seamstresses, and I made sure that I had ample time to spend with them.

I remember sitting with them a couple of weeks prior to filming, with a little bag that held some small sewing tasks for me to do on set in between scenes. It was important for me to stay focused on my role by doing the kinds of little things that Elizabeth would have done—beadwork and sewing seams with small, steady, and perfectly aligned stitches. There I was, sewing my little satchel, while Joanna Johnston's team worked on their masterpieces! Never did they make me feel inferior. We were all working together. It was wonderful.

On that first day in Richmond, I could barely contain my excitement. Costumes, hair, and makeup transform a person, externally and internally. Remember the days of childhood when you would dress up for Halloween? Imagine that feeling times a thousand—that's what it's like to be prepared for a role by a creative mastermind like Joanna and the wonderful artists in the hair and makeup departments.

I entered the fitting room, and there was a photo of Elizabeth Keckley on the wall. It was a Mathew Brady photo, one of just a handful ever taken of Elizabeth. It's the photo that captured me from the beginning, showing her in her early forties, right around the time she became Mrs. Lincoln's modiste. (The other surviving photos of Elizabeth were taken much later in life, when she taught in the Department of Sewing and Domestic Science Arts at Wilberforce University in the 1890s. Still so dignified and beautiful.)

After Joanna and I talk with the assistant costumers about the movie and our excitement about it, it's time to try on the dress she has designed for me. It's almost identical to the one that Elizabeth is wearing in the photo. The color is a beautiful coppery bronze.

I have no makeup on, and my hair is pulled back, over my ears, into a low bun at the nape of my neck—a style similar to the one Elizabeth herself wore.

The dress is on. It fits me perfectly. The buttons are done up. The lace collar attached.

I turn to look in the mirror, and I gasp.

There stands Elizabeth Keckley.

I clasp Joanna's arm, my eyes wet with tears. "There she is. My God."

* * *

While working on the film, I would seize any available opportunity to walk around the set replicating the second floor of the White House when it was empty and quiet.

The exquisite commitment to detail and authenticity were everywhere. The furnishings, artwork, window dressings, light fixtures, books, papers strewn on a desk—all of them immediately transported me back in time.

I would always venture to the quiet set while in costume. It just didn't feel right to be there in my contemporary clothes. Every now and then, I would run into a fellow actor doing the same thing—soaking it all in. More often than not, he, too, would be in costume, his hair and beard styled perfectly to match the era, his gait slow and assured.

When we filmed in the state capitol in Richmond, I would sit in the balcony even when I wasn't scheduled to work. To be in that room and watch the men who were portraying the members of Congress in 1865 as they voted yea or nay for the Thirteenth Amendment to the Constitution—the amendment that freed the slaves—was a powerful and unforgettable experience.

But it was the set that embodied the Lincoln family's rooms that I adored and longed to be in.

I would take my little satchel, sit in the elaborate replica of Mary Lincoln's boudoir, and sew or just look around and imagine what life in the Lincoln White House must have felt like. The daily routines. The conversations in Mary's room between her and her husband. Between her and her sons. Between her and Elizabeth.

I would imagine the countless fittings they would have whenever Mary wanted a new dress—which was often. Mary's taste for beautiful clothes was very controversial in her day. The press and the public questioned how she could spend so much money on clothes, gloves, hats, and furnishings when wounded soldiers were dying and newly freed black people were living in squalor within yards of the White House. But Elizabeth understood. She knew that Mary was trying to use material things to fill the gaping hole of loss—loss of her two sons, loss of her husband's solicitous attention, loss of the many members of her own family who were fighting for the Confederacy.

I would imagine Elizabeth consoling Mary during her bouts of deep depression. And I often wondered about Elizabeth's own thoughts and feelings. Where did she go for comfort or solace? After her only son died, to whom did she turn?

History provides some of the answers. We know that she took great comfort in the teachings of the Bible and the church services she attended. And she drew enormous solace from helping others. Not only did she cofound the Home for Destitute Women and Children, she was also president of the Contraband Relief Organization, a group that raised funds to help ease the suffering of newly freed men and women and help them transition into the world of independent living. Elizabeth Keckley was an activist, driven by the need to help others.

Yes, I would imagine all of these things and more while sitting on a settee, with needle and thread in hand. Diving deeply into silence and my imagination.

* * *

During the summer of 2011, I planned and took a research road trip to visit and document the places where Elizabeth Keckley lived. I started in Washington, DC, where she spent the second half of her life.

After taking the train from New York, I rented a car at Union Station. I felt like a kid again, my eyes wide with the excitement and anticipation of a new adventure.

I knew I would go to the Library of Congress, where I would see letters written by Mary Todd Lincoln—two of them mentioning Elizabeth—and artifacts directly linked to the Lincoln White House. I would gaze close-up at a dress designed and made by Elizabeth for Mary, encased in glass at the Smithsonian Institution for their exhibit commemorating the one-hundred-fiftieth anniversary of the Civil War. And I would visit the places in the capital that were of great importance to Elizabeth—the Fifteenth Street Presbyterian Church; the site where the Home for Destitute Women and Children used to stand and where she spent her last years; and, of course, the Walker Lewis

Boardinghouse at 1017 Twelfth Street NW, where she lived and ran her successful dressmaking business.

But first I wanted to go where she went last. Where she was laid to rest.

I drove forty minutes to the National Harmony Memorial Park in Largo, Maryland. As I drove through the gates, my heartbeat started to quicken, as it always does when in a cemetery. (I've spent too much time in them.) I went straight to the office where I told the record keeper a little white lie, calling myself a "distant relative" of Elizabeth Keckley. Then, armed with the plot and grave number in hand, I set out to find my Elizabeth.

It took me a while to find her. When I finally saw the marker, my breath stopped. Installed in 2010 with the help of donations by history-minded organizations and individuals, the marker contains an image of her face and this inscription:

ELIZABETH KECKLY
1818 – 1907

Enslaved   Modiste   Confidante

Born into slavery, Elizabeth Keckly purchased her freedom using her exceptional skills as a seamstress. After establishing her own business, she was employed as a modiste (dressmaker) by Mary Lincoln, becoming her trusted friend and confidante. Mrs. Keckly's autobiography "Behind the Scenes" provides intimate details about life inside the Lincoln White House.

* * *

The magnitude of the journey that I was about to embark on hit me. The desire to portray Elizabeth in as truthful and as deep a way as possible was stronger than any desire I had had in a long while. I wanted to do her justice.

The responsibility of helping to tell the story of President Lincoln, at a time when our country is yet again cracked and on the brink of fracturing in a way that could have severe ramifications for decades, weighed more heavily on me than I had anticipated.

But as I stood at Elizabeth Keckley's grave, I knew that the time was right for all of this to happen. That our country and the world would benefit from the retelling of the story of a true leader who made the toughest decisions in the most critical of times with courage, compassion, and strength. That people from all cultures, countries, and religions would have the opportunity to rethink their politics and behavior through this magical mode called filmmaking.

And I hoped, too, that people around the globe might be curious to learn more about the remarkable woman named Elizabeth Keckley. That perhaps we all would embrace the lessons embodied in her courage. Her integrity. Her dignity. Her grace.

LINCOLN'S WORDS

Handbill Replying to Charges of Infidelity (1846)

Was Lincoln an atheist? His response to the accusation

To the Voters of the Seventh Congressional District.

FELLOW CITIZENS:

A charge having got into circulation in some of the neighborhoods of this District, in substance that I am an open scoffer at Christianity, I have by the advice of some friends concluded to notice the subject in this form. That I am not a member of any Christian Church, is true; but I have never denied the truth of the Scriptures; and I have never spoken with intentional disrespect of religion in general, or any denomination of Christians in particular. It is true that in early life I was inclined to believe in what I understand is called the "Doctrine of Necessity"—that is, that the human mind is impelled to action, or held in rest by some power, over which the mind itself has no control; and I have sometimes (with one, two or three, but never publicly) tried to maintain this opinion in argument. The habit of arguing thus however, I have, entirely left off for more than five years. And I add here, I have always understood this same opinion to be held by several of the Christian denominations. The foregoing, is the whole truth, briefly stated, in relation to myself, upon this subject.

I do not think I could myself, be brought to support a man for office, whom I knew to be an open enemy of, and scoffer at, religion. Leaving the higher matter of eternal consequences, between him and his Maker, I still do not think any man has the right thus to insult the feelings, and injure the morals, or the community in which he may live. If, then, I was guilty of such conduct, I should blame no man who should condemn me for it; but I do blame those, whoever they may be, who falsely put such a charge in circulation against me.

A. Lincoln, July 31, 1846

Photograph taken by William Marsh
in Springfield, Illinois (May 20, 1860).
Library of Congress

3

"A SACRED EFFORT"

Lincoln's Unfinished Journey from Slavery to Freedom

HENRY LOUIS GATES JR.

Henry Louis Gates Jr. is the Alphonse Fletcher University Professor at Harvard University, as well as director of the W. E. B. Du Bois Institute for African and African American Research. He is the author most recently of Black in Latin America *(New York University Press, 2011) and* Faces of America *(New York University Press, 2010), which expand on his critically acclaimed PBS documentaries, and* Tradition and the Black Atlantic: Criticism in the African Diaspora *(Basic Books, 2010). He is the coeditor of* Call and Response: Key Debates in African American Studies *(W. W. Norton, 2011).*

Professor Gates earned his MA and PhD in English Literature from Clare College at the University of Cambridge. He received a BA in English Language and Literature, summa cum laude, from Yale University in 1973. Before joining the faculty of Harvard in 1991, he taught at Yale, Cornell, and Duke Universities. Professor Gates has received fifty-one honorary degrees, as well as a 1981 MacArthur

Foundation Genius Award, the 1993 George Polk Award for Social Commentary, and the 2008 Ralph Lowell Award, the Corporation for Public Broadcasting's highest award. In addition, Professor Gates was named one of Time *magazine's 25 Most Influential Americans in 1997, and one of* Ebony *magazine's 100 Most Influential Black Americans in 2005, and he was selected for* Ebony's *Power 150 list for 2009 and its Power 100 list for 2010. He received a National Humanities Medal in 1998 and in 1999 was elected to the American Academy of Arts and Letters. In 2006, he was inducted into the Sons of the American Revolution after tracing his lineage back to John Redman, a free Negro who fought in the Revolutionary War.*

The essay below is adapted, in part, from the introduction to Professor Gates's book Lincoln on Race and Slavery *(Princeton, NJ: Princeton University Press, 2009).*

All throughout his debates with Stephen Douglas, Abraham Lincoln never allowed himself to be without a thin black leather notebook that he had converted into a scrapbook, preparation for the war of words in which he and his ardent foe were so passionately and desperately engaged. It served Lincoln almost as a cheat sheet, a ready-reference tool to which he could conveniently revert for facts and figures, opinions from editorials and letters to the editor, and clips from newspaper stories about all those pressing issues of the day over which he and Douglas so thoughtfully, if feverishly, were debating. The notebook, now housed in the Lincoln Papers at the Library of Congress—six inches high, three and three-quarters inches wide, an inch thick, its covers made of hardboard—was small enough to slip into his coat pocket, discreet enough for Lincoln to consult on the podium while preparing his rebuttals as Douglas redoubled his ferocious attacks. The notebook's metal clasp is broken; it is boxed closely for protection. What a wealth of information about slavery and the most important issues of his day does that slim volume contain! Lincoln knew what he needed to know, or didn't know, to hold his own with Douglas. And he consulted his commonplace book frequently, judging from the wear of the clasp and its well-thumbed, glue-stiff pages.

Among its many gems, two newspaper clippings—anonymous and undated—are especially arresting, because they offer diametrically opposed positions on three related but distinct issues: first, the institution of slavery as practiced in America, the right of whites to hold persons of African descent in bondage; second, race and the nature of the Negro (a complex subject often conflated with slavery in American historical discourse, but a very distinct thing, in fact, especially in Lincoln's mind); and, third, the colonization of former slaves in Africa, the Caribbean, or South America, an idea that Lincoln contemplated until late in his presidency.

One of the editorials that Lincoln clipped for his notebook is proslavery, vulgarly anti-Negro, yet anticolonization: slavery "is a thing that we cannot do without, that is righteously profitable and permanent and that belongs to southern society as inherently, intricately and durably as the white race itself. Yea, the white race will itself emigrate from the southern states to Africa, California or Polynesia, sooner than the African. Let us make up our minds, therefore to put up with and make the most of the institution. Let us not bother our brains about what Providence intends to do with our negroes in the distant future but glory in and profit to the utmost by what He has done for him in transplanting him here, and setting him to work on our plantations. . . . keep . . . slaves at hard work, under strict discipline, out of idleness and mischief, while they live . . . instead of sending them off to Africa, or manumitting them to a life of freedom, licentiousness and nuisance."

The other editorial, curiously enough, argues the opposite case: it is antislavery and pro-Negro: "We were brought up in a State where blacks were voters, and we do not know of any inconvenience resulting from it. . . . We have seen many a 'nigger' that we thought much more of than some white man." Yet the editorial writer is also procolonization: "Our opinion is that it would be best for all concerned to have the colored population in a State by themselves," either their own country or even a state within the United States. One can imagine Lincoln mulling over these two opinions while Stephen Douglas droned on, trying to decide where the voluntary colonization of the Negro figured into his firm opposition to the institution of slavery.

In preparation for writing, hosting, and narrating *Looking for Lincoln*, a television documentary about Abraham Lincoln to be aired in celebration of the bicentennial of his birth, since I am not a Lincoln scholar, I began to read for the first time in a systematic way Lincoln's collected speeches and writings, as well as the major biographies and studies of Lincoln's private and public life both before and during his presidency. One of the most striking conclusions that a close reading of Lincoln's speeches and writings yielded to me was that "slavery," "race," and "colonization," were quite often three separate issues for him. Sometimes these issues were intertwined in Lincoln's thinking, but far more often they seem to have remained quite distinct, even if we have difficulty understanding or explaining how this could have been so. And this difficulty has led far too many scholars, I believe, when writing about Lincoln's views on slavery, for example, to blur distinctions that were important to him and to his contemporaries as they reflected upon the institution of slavery, the status of African Americans both as human beings and as potential citizens in the United States, and whether or not voluntary colonization was an inseparable aspect of abolition.

In Lincoln's case, we can trace these three strands of thought clearly within three distinct discourses that braid their way through his speeches and writings: in his early and consistent abhorrence of slavery as a violation of natural rights, as an economic institution that created an uneven playing field for white men, and that dehumanized and brutalized black human beings; in the fascinating manner in which he wrestled with the deep-seated, conventional ambivalence about the status of Negroes vis-à-vis white people on the scale of civilization, his penchant for blackface minstrelsy and darky jokes, his initially strong skepticism about the native intellectual potential of people of color and the capacity of black men to serve with valor in a war against white men; and, finally, his long flirtation with the voluntary colonization of the freed slaves either in the West Indies, in Latin America, or back in Africa.

Interspersed, as it were, among these three separate but sometimes overlapping discourses is the manner in which he seems to have wrestled with his own use of the "n-word," which he used publicly at least until 1862, and which most Lincoln scholars today find so surprising and embarrassing that they consistently avoid discussing it, since for a politician to do so today would be quite scandalous, and since this is not in accord with the image most of us share of Lincoln as the Great Emancipator, the champion of black slaves. And for that reason alone, it deserves to be discussed, if only briefly, to help us to begin to understand how complex the issue of "race" actually was in Lincoln's era, and how very different it was from our discussions of race today.

It is worth noting that although Lincoln used the "n-word" far less than did Stephen Douglas (next to Douglas, who used it as much as possible, Lincoln, in his relatively rare usages, more closely resembles John Brown than a recovering racist), he did indeed use that word in prominent public contexts. Most of us would be surprised to learn that Lincoln used it twice in his first debate with Douglas, once in the Freeport debate, once in the debate at Jonesboro, seven times in a speech in 1860 in Hartford, and once in a letter to Newton Deming and George P. Strong in 1857. Even as late as April 1862, James Redpath recorded Lincoln's saying of President Geffrard of Haiti (who had offered to send a white man as his ambassador to the United States), "You can tell the President of Haiti that I shan't tear my shirt if he does send a nigger here."[1]

Today, we often tend to think of the nineteenth-century rhetoric of antiblack and proslavery racist discourse as hyperbolic or melodramatic, and that when the Founders argued that "all men were created equal," they, of course, recognized that the sons and daughters of Africa were, indeed, human beings, even if they were systematically deprived of their rights. At its most extreme, however, the discourse of antiblack racism sought to exclude black women and men from the human community. To take just two of hundreds of examples, when the *Richmond Examiner*, as Frederick Douglass reported in a speech in 1854, declared in all capital letters that "[The Negro] is not a man," and when Alexander H. Stephens, vice president of the Confederacy, maintained in 1861 that the South represented "the highest type of civilization ever exhibited by man," because "its cornerstone rests upon the great truth that the Negro is not equal to the white man, that slavery—subordination to the superior

race—is his natural and normal condition," neither was referring to a socially constructed difference between blacks and whites, a gap in condition that reflected the results of environmental variables.[2]

No, they were attempting to define black people as an "other species
of men," as David Hume had put it in 1754, an opinion shared even as
late as 1850 by the Harvard scholar Louis Agassiz, one of the most influential ethnologists of his day. "It was in Philadelphia," Agassiz wrote,
"that I first found myself in prolonged contact with negroes; all the do-
mestics in my hotel were men of color. I can scarcely express to you the
painful impression that I received, especially since the feeling that they
inspired in me is contrary to all our ideas about the confraternity of the
human type [genre] and the unique origin of our species. But truth before all. . . . It is impossible for me to [ignore] the feeling that they are
not of the same blood as us. In seeing their black faces with their thick
lips and grimacing teeth, the wool on their head, their bent knees, their
elongated hands, their large curved nails, and especially the livid color
of the palm of their hands, I could not take my eyes off their face in order to tell them to stay far away. And when they advanced that hideous
hand towards my plate in order to serve me, I wished I were able to de-
part in order to eat a piece of bread elsewhere, rather than dine with
such service."[3]

Thomas Jefferson may or may not have understood, through his
personal relations with Sally Hemings, for example, that black people
were human beings, just like white people; but he never stated this in
his writings, and he most certainly did not include black people within
his definition of "men" when he wrote the Declaration of Independence. In fact, as Jefferson put it in *Notes on the State of Virginia*, "It
is not their condition then, but nature, which has produced this
distinction"[4]—a distinction between those of African descent, meant
forever to be subordinate, and those of European descent, meant forever to be dominant. And distinctions in kind or type created by Nature
itself could never be altered. All men may have been created equal; the
real question was who was a man, and what being "a man," in fact,
meant. Thomas Jefferson most certainly was not thinking of black men
and women when he wrote the Declaration of Independence, and no
amount of romantic historical wishful thinking can alter that fact.

However, Abraham Lincoln most certainly and most impressively did hold, as he stated privately in 1858 and publicly throughout his career, a belief that boldly challenged the Dred Scott decision of 1857; but even this rather radical belief did not translate, in Lincoln's mind, into an embrace or advocacy of "social and political equality" between blacks and whites, as he put it in the same letter to James N. Brown. It is important for us to understand that Lincoln did not find these positions contradictory or inconsistent, even if we might today. How did his thinking about these issues evolve during his presidency, during the course of the deadly Civil War?

The Abraham Lincoln of the popular American imagination— Father Abraham, the Great Emancipator—is often represented almost as an island of pure reason in a sea of mid-nineteenth-century racist madness, a beacon of tolerance blessed with a certain cosmopolitan sensibility above or beyond race, a man whose attitudes about race and slavery transcended his time and place. It is this Abraham Lincoln that many writers have conjured, somewhat romantically—for example, as Ralph Ellison often did—to claim for him and those who fought to abolish slavery a privileged, noble status in the history of American race relations from which subsequent, lesser mortals disgracefully fell away. This is one reason that blacks such as Marian Anderson in 1939 and Martin Luther King Jr. in 1963 used the Lincoln Memorial as the most ideal symbolic site through which to make a larger, implicit statement about race prejudice in their times, and why Barack Obama launched his campaign for president in Springfield, Illinois, Lincoln's home. Black people, to an extent that would no doubt have surprised Frederick Douglass, have done more perhaps than even white Americans have to confect an image of Lincoln as the American philosopher-king and patron saint of race relations, an image strenuously embraced and enthusiastically reproduced in lithographs by Booker T. Washington at the turn of the century to sanctify the authority of his leadership in a direct line of descent from both Frederick Douglass and Father Abraham himself.

However, contemporary views of Lincoln, and of the abolitionists, as the sources of the modern civil rights movement have sometimes been naïve and have almost always been ahistorical. Black abolitionists, keenly aware of the vast difference between finding the economic institution of slavery a harmful and repugnant force of inequity in the marketplace, on the one hand, and embracing black people as equal human beings, on the other, were fond of saying that the only thing some of the white abolitionists hated more than slavery was the slave. While this was meant to criticize their white associates for unconscious forms of racism, it is certainly true that many white abolitionists treated black people paternalistically. But at least they advocated emancipation, both immediate and gradual, and in theory called for racial equality, even if they often had a difficult time realizing it in their personal relations with actual former slaves. What's more, many of the abolitionists came to define themselves against colonizationists, those who would free the slaves only to remove them outside of the country.

It should not surprise us that Lincoln was no exception to his times; what is exceptional about Abraham Lincoln is that, perhaps because of temperament or because of the shape-shifting contingencies of command during an agonizingly costly war, he wrestled with his often contradictory feelings and ambivalences and vacillations about slavery, race, and colonization, and did so quite publicly and often quite eloquently. It is the progress of his fraught journey through the thickets of slavery and race that Lincoln's own words enable us to chart, beginning in 1837 and ending in his final speech, delivered just before his assassination in April 1865, in which he said that he intended to secure the right to vote for "very intelligent negroes" and the 200,000 black Civil War veterans. It was this speech, overheard by John Wilkes Booth, by Booth's own admission, that led to his decision to assassinate the president.

It is fascinating to trace how these three strands of Lincoln's thought about the status of black people in America manifested themselves in his attitudes about voluntary colonization, for example. Lincoln favored colonization initially because of a genuine concern that blacks and whites could not live in social harmony. He continued to contemplate colonization for much of his term as president because of an equally genuine concern that the huge number of slaves who would ultimately be freed by the Thirteenth Amendment would never be accepted by the former Confederates and white people in the North, whither at least some of the former slaves would sooner or later migrate. There were

3.9 million slaves in 1860, and it is quite surprising to most people that, according to the historians David Blight and Allen Guelzo, only about 500,000 of these slaves were actually freed between 1863 and the end of the war by the Emancipation Proclamation;[5] the remainder would not be freed until passage of the Thirteenth Amendment.[6] It was certainly not unreasonable for Lincoln, and anyone else who took a moment to think about it, that it would be extraordinarily difficult to assimilate this mass of former slaves into an integrated American society without extended social, political, and economic conflict. But he was willing to accommodate those "very intelligent negroes," whom he never defined, but whom, at the maximum, we can define as the 488,000 Negroes who were free in 1860, and more realistically as those free Negroes who were literate, plus those 200,000 soldiers to whom he proudly referred as his "black warriors," whose right to vote he was determined to effect, and to whom he remained doggedly loyal.

Given the vexed history of race relations in America between the end of the Civil War and the election of President Barack Obama, 143 years after the final abolition of slavery, Lincoln would have been politically naïve not to have these concerns, and he was not, by and large, a naïve leader. In the end, however, both because the scheme of voluntary repatriation would have been too costly (not to mention too unpopular among blacks) ever to have succeeded, and because of the evolution in his own thinking about who blacks were as human beings in relation to whites and the capacity of at least some of them eventually to become fully vested American citizens, Lincoln seems to have lost confidence in his commitment to colonization as a possible solution to postwar race conflict. Lincoln's words enable us to chart the evolution of his thinking about this tangled mass of issues concerning slavery and race, so that we can, as it were, overhear the conversation that he was having with himself and with other Americans about these vexed issues. Some Lincoln scholars seem to examine his thoughts and feelings about slavery and race through the mediation of a certain rose-colored filter, apparently embarrassed by Lincoln's inconsistencies and his complexity, and determined to reinvent Lincoln as a race-relations patron saint, outside of his time and place, a man less complicated, flawed, contradictory, and interesting than he, in fact, actually was.

* * *

On March 4, 1865, just about a month before he died, Lincoln delivered what for Frederick Douglass, and many other African Americans, was his most resonant speech, a speech more about them and for them than any of Lincoln's other speeches or writings, not excluding the Emancipation Proclamation. As Ted Widmer notes, "His oration consisted of 703 words, 505 of which were words of one syllable, neatly distributed across 25 sentences tucked into four paragraphs. . . . In all of American expression, it would be difficult to imagine a higher ratio of thought-per-word."[7] It lasted all of six minutes. But in three distinct sections of his third paragraph, Lincoln pronounced, more powerfully than he ever had, the institution of slavery to be the inextricable cause of the war that would soon grind to an end, a war that had left 623,000 Americans dead.

"These slaves," he wrote ("one eighth of the whole population"), "constituted a peculiar and powerful interest. All knew that this interest was, somehow, the cause of the war." This would seem to be the most direct statement that Lincoln made about slavery as the origin of the war, since his meeting with the black delegation at the White House in August 1862. While he had referred to slavery in relation to the war on several occasions by now, he had never before stated the matter so clearly. For instance, in his first inaugural address, Lincoln said that "the only substantial dispute" between the North and the South was, in fact, over the extension of slavery, even though "one section of our country believes slavery is right . . . while the other believes it is wrong." During the first year of the war, he declared flatly, "We didn't go into the war to put down slavery, but to put the flag back, and to act differently at this moment, would, I have no doubt, not only weaken our cause but smack of bad faith; for I never should have had votes enough to send me here if the people had supposed I should try to use my power to upset slavery." If for no other reason, he continued, "the first thing you'd see, would be a mutiny in the army." No, for this reason among others, "we must wait until every other means has been exhausted. This thunderbolt will keep."

Even more important, in his first annual message to Congress, Lincoln declared that "the insurrection is largely, if not exclusively, a war upon the first principle of popular government—the rights of our people." And Lincoln made the direct connection between slavery and the origins of the war again just a week before issuing the Proclamation—during his conversation with the delegation of antislavery ministers, when he said "I admit that slavery is the root of the rebellion," then qualifying it somewhat by adding "or at least its sine qua non." But by the time he wrote the second inaugural, all qualifications had disappeared. There, before the most integrated audience that a president had ever addressed, Lincoln, curiously, seemed to have accepted the mantle of "Father Abraham" to the newly freed slaves.

According to the *Times* of London, "at least half the multitude were colored," newly freed slaves and free Negroes, among them Frederick Douglass, and this speech seemed tailor-made for them.[8] Following his often cited comment that "Both [the North and the South] read the same Bible and pray to the same God; and each invokes His aid against the other," Lincoln slyly implies that it is slavery that makes all the difference: "It may seem strange that any men should dare to ask a just God's assistance in wringing their bread from the sweat of other men's faces; but let us judge not that we be not judged." Then, most astonishingly and boldly, Lincoln dares to suggest that perhaps—just perhaps—the reason why 623,000 Americans would lie dead, Americans North and South who "both read the same Bible, and pray to the same God," is that this is the price God is extracting for the history of slavery: "Fondly do we hope—fervently do we pray—that this mighty scourge of war may speedily pass away. Yet, if God wills that it continue, until all the wealth piled by the bond-man's two hundred fifty years of unrequited toil shall be sunk, and until every drop of blood drawn with the lash, shall be paid by another drawn with the sword, . . . so still it must be said 'the judgments of the Lord, are true and righteous altogether.'" It is safe to say that never before in the history of the American presidency had the political economy of suffering, the rhetoric of a white eye for a black eye, been applied to the condition of the black enslaved. No wonder the reporter of the *Times* of London was struck by the call-and-response of

Lincoln's black audience, the shouts and murmurs of "bless the Lord" and similar phrases still familiar in the black church, which must have reached a crescendo as he hit his stride in that remarkable third paragraph of his speech.

Frederick Douglass would later note "a leaden stillness" about the white half of the crowd. For black folks in attendance that day, Abraham Lincoln had come home, and blacks had every reason to believe that, at long last, they had found a permanent home in America as freedmen at last. On that day, within that third paragraph, Abraham Lincoln became the president of black men and women, far more so than he had before, even through the Emancipation. No wonder Douglass, who had to fight his way past two racist guards to gain entrance to the White House immediately following the speech, told the president in response to his questioning, "Mr. Lincoln, that was a sacred effort." Never before had anyone but the most rabid abolitionist—the sentiment calls to mind any number of pronouncements by John Brown—ever dared to argue that the God of the white man was punishing him for his treatment of blacks.

Forty-one days later, Lincoln would be killed by John Wilkes Booth, who was in the audience that day, as he was on the day of Lincoln's final speech, an informal address from the second floor of the White House in which he favored giving the vote to "very intelligent" blacks, and to those black men who had fought to save the Union. That speech, as Booth himself confessed in a letter, led to his decision to assassinate Lincoln. A year before the second inaugural, Lincoln had floated this idea to Michael Hahn, the governor of Louisiana, in almost the identical words he would use in his final speech, suggesting that the state of Louisiana might consider enfranchising "very intelligent . . . colored people" and those black warriors who had served "gallantly in our ranks," who "would probably help, in some trying time to come, to keep the jewel of liberty within the family of freedom." This idea, however, he was quick to add, "is only a suggestion, not to the public, but to you alone." Bear in mind that all Lincoln had the authority to do was to suggest a course of action to the governor of a state; enfranchisement, we often forget, remained a state prerogative until passage of the Fifteenth Amendment. In his last public address, on April 11, 1865, it was these few words about black enfranchisement that so infuriated Booth, and, one must imagine, his fellow Confederate sympathizers: "It is also unsatisfactory to some that the elective franchise is not given to the colored man. I would myself prefer that it were now conferred on the very intelligent, and on those who serve our cause as soldiers." If we do not take this course, Lincoln maintains, it would be as if "to the blacks we say 'This cup of liberty which these, your old masters, hold to your lips, we will dash from you, and leave you to the chances of gathering the spilled and scattered contents in some vague and undefined when, where, and how.'" Nowhere had Lincoln been stronger on the case for the enfranchisement of these two segments of the soon-to-be-born black citizenry; universal black male suffrage was not, of course, even secured by the Thirteenth Amendment. That right was still two constitutional amendments away.

If the second inaugural was Lincoln's black speech, then why would Frederick Douglass, just eleven years later, after Lincoln had been transformed into the American Christ, remember him at the dedication of the Freedmen's Monument, in the presence of President U. S. Grant, his cabinet, the Chief Justice and all of the associate justices of the Supreme Court, and just about anyone who was anyone in Washington on April 14, 1876, as "preeminently the white man's President, entirely devoted to the welfare of white men"? Douglass said that "truth compels me to admit even here in the presence of the monument we have erected to his memory, Abraham Lincoln was not, in the fullest sense of the word, either our man or our model. . . . The race to which we belong were not the special objects of his consideration. . . . First, midst and last you and yours were the object of his deepest affection and his most earnest solicitude. You are the children of Abraham Lincoln. We are at best only his step-children, children by adoption, children by force of circumstances and necessity."

Douglass—himself once a fugitive slave—was keenly aware that Lincoln had supported the Fugitive Slave Act of 1850, an act that was anathema to Douglass and his fellow abolitionists, and most certainly to any fugitive slave. As John Stauffer puts it, "unlike many of his antislavery colleagues," Lincoln "never questioned the validity of the Fugitive Slave Act of 1850, either politically or constitutionally. . . . Lincoln believed that the Constitution called for 'an efficient fugitive slave law.'" Douglass, once a slave in Maryland, also recalled that the very day on which Lincoln "revoked General Hunter's emancipation proclamation," in 1862; as Stauffer puts it, "he publicly told Maryland's slaveholders that he would rigorously defend the Fugitive Slave Act."[9] For Douglass, these were twin offenses, of the gravest consequences. In addition, a large measure of Douglass's frustration with Lincoln stemmed from his decision at the end of the war to endorse a lenient view of Reconstruction that would allow the seceded states back into the Union based on pledges of loyalty from 10 percent of the prewar population, but without enfranchising the most loyal part of the South: the former slaves and free blacks. But most of all, Douglass reminded his audience of the meeting with the black delegation in 1862, when Lincoln "strangely told us that we were the cause of the war . . . [and] were to leave the land in which we were born."[10] It was Lincoln's determined advocacy of colonization that most deeply disturbed Douglass, even eleven years after he had been assassinated.

In spite of these surprisingly critical remarks, Douglass's assessment of Lincoln was quite nuanced. In fact, he defended Lincoln's priority of union over abolition: "Had he put the abolition of slavery before the salvation of the Union," he would have alienated large numbers of people and "rendered resistance to rebellion impossible. Viewed from the genuine abolition ground, Mr. Lincoln seemed tardy, cold, dull, and indifferent; but measuring him by the sentiment of his country, a sentiment he was bound as a statesman to consult, he was swift, zealous, radical, and determined." Curiously, here Douglass is reversing himself; Douglass consistently argued during the war that abolishing slavery immediately (just after war broke out) would bring a swift end to the conflict.

Douglass confessed a second reason for his unease with Lincoln: to what must have been a shocked audience, he said that Lincoln "came into the Presidential chair upon one principle alone, namely, opposition to the extension of slavery. His arguments in furtherance of this policy had their motive and mainspring in his patriotic devotion to the interest of his own race." Like most African Americans of my generation, I was raised to believe that Lincoln hated slavery because he loved the slaves. Anyone who has given Lincoln's writings even a cursory glance comes quickly to understand that Lincoln did indeed hate slavery, but he hated it because he thought that human bondage was evil and because he thought that it created unfair competition in the marketplace, first and foremost for other white men. Some historians believe that it is not clear that Lincoln had completely abandoned at least a theoretical interest in voluntary colonization for the bulk of the freed slaves. Even if he had abandoned it, he had done so only a year or two before his death. It is noteworthy that Douglass referred to Lincoln's views on colonization, as well as his curious twists and turns about slavery, abolition, and Negro rights. No doubt, all these things informed Douglass's surprisingly critical assessment of Lincoln's legacy rendered at such a solemn and august occasion, but none more than his enthusiasm for voluntary colonization, which Douglass abhorred.

* * *

Historians have sought to sweep Douglass's 1876 assessment of Lincoln under the carpet of revision by portraying Douglass as a fervent admirer of the president, citing brief but deeply respectful remarks about Lincoln that Douglass made both before and after 1876. And, indeed, at several ceremonial occasions, Douglass praised Lincoln for being the Great Emancipator, as he most certainly was, especially through his advocacy of the (second) Thirteenth Amendment, which in fact freed all of the slaves. In December 1865, for instance, Douglass eulogized Lincoln by contrasting him to other presidents: "As compared with the long line of his predecessors, many of whom were merely the facile and servile instruments of the slave power, Abraham Lincoln, while unsurpassed in his devotion to the white race, was also in a sense hitherto without example, emphatically the black man's president."[11] After meeting Lincoln, he wrote that "I have never seen a more transparent countenance. There was not the slightest shadow of embarrassment after the first moment. . . . I was never in any way reminded of my humble origin, or of my unpopular color."[12] After Lincoln's death, Douglass frequently referred to him as "the king of self-made men," "the greatest statesman that ever presided over the destinies of this Republic" and the man most responsible for "American liberty."[13] We can see in Frederick

Douglass's attitudes toward Lincoln's legacy the roots of the very dual-
ity in assessment that continues to manifest itself among black politicians and scholars, ranging from the untroubled adoration expressed by
Booker T. Washington (who clearly sought to position Lincoln as his
long-lost white metaphorical father figure) through the bitter denuncia-
tions of Malcolm X and the searching critiques of Lerone Bennett,[14] to
the more nuanced yet strongly favorable assessment of Barack Obama.[15]

For his part, however, Douglass never intended his polite, sometimes quite sentimental, and genuinely heartfelt remarks about Lincoln's considerable strengths to deconstruct his considered assessment
of Lincoln overall. In fact, he endeavored to avoid any confusion about
his feelings, seeking to ensure that the force and impact of his 1876
speech would not be lost by appending the entire Freedmen's Monument speech to the last two editions of his third and final book, his autobiography, *The Life and Times of Frederick Douglass*, published in
1881, and revised in a final edition published just three years before his
death, in 1892. Douglass knew Lincoln, and he came to like and admire
him as a man and as his president, but he refused to whitewash what he
considered Lincoln's flaws when it came to slavery and race, perhaps
most important among them the president's refusal to embrace full
emancipation as early as July 1861, which Douglass believed would
have led to a swift Union victory, saving hundreds of thousands of lives,
despite the fact that Lincoln believed that he did not have the power to
do this, and that such an attempt would have been unconstitutional.
Douglass also consistently abhorred Lincoln's attempts to encourage
voluntary colonization, and continued to stand firm about emigration
after Lincoln's death, even when it experienced an upsurge of support
among both black and white leaders in the mid-1870s, as Reconstruction was being systematically and often violently dismantled.

W. E. B. Du Bois, Frederick Douglass's most legitimate heir within
the black political tradition, shared Douglass's measured assessment of
Lincoln on slavery and race. In 1922, Du Bois wrote that "As sinners,
we like to imagine righteousness in our heroes. As a result, when a great
man dies, we begin to whitewash him. We seek to forget all that was
small and mean and unpleasant, and remember only the fine and brave
and good. We slur over and explain away his inconsistencies until there

appears before us, not the real man but the myth—immense, perfect, cold, and dead." Du Bois loved Lincoln but refused to deify him. "I love him not because he was perfect but because he was not and yet triumphed," he said. Lincoln was among those white folks "whose taste was educated in the gutter. The world is full of people born hating and despising their fellows. To these I love to say: See this man. He was one of you and yet he became Abraham Lincoln." For Du Bois, Lincoln was "big enough to be inconsistent," the phrase that proved so resonant for George M. Fredrickson in his last reflections on Lincoln's views on race, by which both Du Bois and Fredrickson meant that Lincoln grew and evolved, he faced and confronted his own prejudices, and, to a remarkable extent, overcame them.[16] Lincoln remade himself as a proponent of black freedom, fully aware of how far he had come in doing so.

We can do Lincoln no greater service than to walk that path with him, and we can do him no greater disservice than to whitewash it, seeking to give ourselves an odd form of comfort by pretending that he was even one whit less complicated than he actually was.

* * *

This, then, is what the historical record tells us about Lincoln's attitudes on race and slavery. It's clear that those attitudes evolved over time, though it's difficult to say with certainty exactly what he felt and believed about African Americans and their role in society by the moment when an assassin's bullet cut his life short. And of course it's impossible to say how his thinking and behavior might have further evolved if he'd lived to serve out his second term as president and, perhaps, to observe and comment on events as an elder statesman in the 1870s, 1880s, and even beyond. (Lincoln would have celebrated his eightieth birthday on February 12, 1889.)

As Martin Luther King Jr. so wonderfully said, "The arc of the moral universe is long, but it bends toward justice." Many people—especially mainstream historians and biographers of Lincoln—would like to apply this dictum to the Great Emancipator. They see him as having traced an arc of moral reversal from his youth, when he evidently accepted unthinkingly some of the antiblack racism of his time, through his hatred of slavery and his advocacy of colonization, until the end of his life when he came to recognize the full humanity of the slaves, their right to the benefits of their labor, and the right of at least some black men to vote. They'd like to assume that, had he lived on, Lincoln's personal moral arc would have bent even further toward justice and that he would eventually have become a staunch supporter of full citizenship as well as social and economic equality for all black Americans. It's a convenient, compelling narrative. And it is wonderfully touching. But I'm not so sure it's true.

We must remember that Lincoln was not just a moral leader. He was also—and above all—a practical politician. For President Lincoln, the end of the war and the abolition of slavery would have led to an enormous national crisis in terms of the labor supply. What happens when, all of a sudden, 3.9 million newly freed people enter the marketplace? What happens to wages and workers' rights? What kinds of social friction are likely to arise when millions of white laborers suddenly find themselves facing a vast new source of competition for jobs? Under these circumstances, it's hard to imagine whites welcoming their new black brother and sister citizens into the labor force with open arms.

Experience shows us that transitions of this kind can be extremely difficult to manage well. Look at the economic and political problems that erupted when the Berlin Wall fell and two German economies with dramatically different market structures suddenly had to be integrated. In that instance, there were no major cultural, ethnic, or racial differences to complicate the situation. For a comparison closer to home, consider the toxic stew of economic, political, cultural, and ethnic tensions currently bubbling in our own border states of Texas, Arizona, New Mexico, and California over the issue of Mexican immigration and its impact on white workers. There's no way any president could wave a magic wand and make the integration of almost four million new workers into an existing economy trouble free.

In these conditions, it's hard to believe that the notion of colonization would *not* have been put back on the table—and that's true whether or not we believe that Lincoln was still toying with the concept as late as the spring of 1865, as Benjamin Butler insists he was.

Of course, one problem with colonization—aside from its inhumanity—was its sheer impracticality. There was no country in

Africa or the Caribbean with the land or economic capacity to easily absorb millions of new immigrants—to say nothing of the political will. While governments in Haiti issued open calls for African Americans to emigrate there (and even the stalwart patriot Frederick Douglass toyed with this idea as late as the eve of the Civil War), and while Liberia has had a long history of relations with African American émigrés, black African kingdoms weren't exactly clamoring to be taken over and "civilized" by their long-lost African American kinsmen. And even if a place had been found for this most unlikely of outcomes, how would the logistics of arranging transportation and resettlement for four million black Americans have been organized and paid for? Where would the trains, ships, food, housing, and other necessities come from? The more one considers the realities behind the scheme, the more absurd it appears.

What's more, the vast majority of black Americans understandably had no interest in leaving the country of their birth—the country they and their recent ancestors since 1619 had spent their lives helping to build and the culture which they had fundamentally helped to shape. The relative handful who did find the notion of emigrating attractive did so. The rest shared the attitude of James Forten, an early abolitionist leader. Forten flirted with the colonization movement in his youth, supporting the work of his friend Paul Cuffe, who helped transport thirty-eight American blacks to Sierra Leone in 1815. But, by 1817, Forten was helping to organization the first Convention of Color, a Philadelphia gathering of over three thousand black men who adamantly opposed the concept of colonization. Writing to his friend, Cuffe, on January 25, Forten related that "there was not one soul that was in favor of going to Africa. They think the slaveholders want to get rid of them so as to make their property more secure." And just a month before Cuffe's death on September 9, Forten coauthored an address, the salient line of which said "The plan of colonization is not asked for by us. We renounce and disclaim any connection with it."

So the prospect of removing American blacks to Africa, the Caribbean, or South America was essentially impractical as well as unjust, and no serious plan for carrying it out was ever formulated. The same is true of the even less substantial schemes occasionally suggested for relocating blacks to designated areas within North America. Little came of these ideas, other than such fleeting movements as the Exo-duster migration of blacks from the South to Kansas—which as it happens my own great-grandparents participated in. (They moved to Leavenworth for a year or two, then returned home to their farm in Patterson Creek, Maryland.)

For all these reasons, it's tempting to think that Lincoln would have quickly realized that the notion of colonization was ridiculous, but of course there's no way to be certain about a purely speculative matter like this.

So, given the impracticality of colonization, what program could Lincoln have proposed for the integration of freed blacks into the US economy and society? It seems most likely to me that he would have clung to the concept of a class-based integration of a segment of the black population, just as he proposed in his last speech. As we've seen, in that address—which so enraged John Wilkes Booth that it helped trigger the assassination—Lincoln did not support extending voting rights to all black men. Instead, he specifically proposed giving the franchise to "the very intelligent" and to "those who serve our cause as soldiers." In effect, Lincoln was offering a special political and social status for an elite slice of African American society, much like those whom W. E. B. Du Bois would later dub "the Talented Tenth."

Would the granting of voting rights to blacks have stopped there? Who can say for sure? Looking at the gradual extension of the franchise throughout American history—first to white males who owned property, then to non–property owners, and ultimately to women and to all citizens aged eighteen or older—it's plausible to imagine a scenario in which, over decades, the vote would gradually have been extended to the vast majority of black Americans, if not to all. This is certainly what the so-called Radical Republicans in Congress would have been pushing for, and a President Lincoln who survived 1865 would have been pressed to balance their demands against the resistance of many other white Americans—a balancing act much like the one he performed over slavery itself throughout his lifetime.

But the challenge of economic integration would have remained a daunting one. A program of land confiscation and redistribution like the short-lived policy established by William Tecumseh Sherman under the rubric of "Forty Acres and a Mule" would have represented a radical solution that might have had a hope of beginning to achieve a measure of economic equality for the property-less former slaves. But it's highly unlikely that President Lincoln would have succeeded in implementing such a controversial program—even had he tried to do so. Instead, the economic and social system that in fact evolved in the South over the second half of the nineteenth century, especially after the collapse of Reconstruction, might well have grown up in a roughly similar form. In combination, the sharecropping system of agriculture and the harsh, often violent program of disenfranchisement, segregation, and repression known as Jim Crow came to constitute what has been aptly called "slavery by a different name." What forces in post–Civil War America could have combined to stop it?

Americans are still living with the tragic consequences of that period: a profound class division between the races as well as within the African American community, persistent widespread poverty among black Americans, and a lingering racial divide breeding resentment and tension—even in a country that elected its first black president in 2008.

Given the challenges of rebuilding the former Confederate states, the problems of the postwar economy, and the inherent difficulties in integrating 3.9 million former slaves into a free-market economy, would the national response have been fundamentally altered had Lincoln lived? That's the crucial, unanswerable question. Perhaps if Lincoln had lived, there wouldn't have been the kind of desperate reaction to Reconstruction that the United States actually experienced. The conservative, racially biased Andrew Johnson would not have been handed the national reins of power. Perhaps the dismantling of Reconstruction would have been prevented or slowed; perhaps at least some former slaves would have had access to land. Perhaps the worst crimes of the postwar period, including the creation of Jim Crow, might have been avoided or mitigated. But these are merely suppositions, impossible to prove or disprove.

If Lincoln had outlived the Civil War and been required to wrestle with the practical political problems of Reconstruction, how would his historical legacy have been changed? Would the stature of Lincoln—his popular image as Savior of the Nation and Great Emancipator—have been dramatically reduced?

Again, the answer depends on some unknowable factors. Clearly Lincoln's status as the political leader who saved the Union and freed the slaves would have been firmly established, and rightly so. But how effectively would he have dealt with the challenges of the postwar world? How long might he have pursued the illusory vision of colonization? How forcefully would he have defended the economic and social rights of the freed slaves, beyond citizenship and his advocacy of the vote for a limited segment of the black community? We'll never know the answers to these questions.

If I can risk a speculation, however, it seems to me that even if Lincoln had continued to support the idea that colonization was a way "to erase the original sin by returning blacks to their homeland," as Adam Gopnik so brilliantly put it to me[17] (and as Grant would do after Lincoln's death, after all), this would not sully his reputation in any meaningful way, if we judge him by nineteenth-century standards, and when we recall how very far Lincoln had come in his thinking about race and the abolition of slavery, from the debates with Stephen Douglas through the signing of the Emancipation Proclamation and finally to the passage of the Thirteenth Amendment, which he insisted upon signing and which he clearly supported, understood, and championed as it made its way through congressional debate, and which, ultimately, was responsible for abolishing slavery. Moreover, I believe that the most radical thing that Abraham Lincoln did, as Adam Gopnik argues, given what we know about Thomas Jefferson's views of the "nature" of blacks and his limited definition of "men" in the Declaration, was his invocation of its opening line unequivocally on behalf of African Americans in a public debate well before the Civil War, and his insistence upon the inclusion of blacks in that definition consistently through his presidency.[18] Against his flirtation with colonization—and, indeed, trumping this—is the fact that he worked his way to declaring his support for limited black suffrage in the final speech of his life, which, as David Donald tells us, made him the very first president to do so, and which turned out to be the final speech of his life, in fact, precisely because of this declaration of support.[19] Perhaps this, in the end, was Abraham Lincoln's most "sacred effort" of all.

LINCOLN'S WORDS

Notes on the Practice of Law (1850)

"If you cannot be an honest lawyer,
resolve to be honest without being a lawyer"

I am not an accomplished lawyer. I find quite as much material for a lecture in those points wherein I have failed as in those wherein I have been moderately successful.

The leading rule for the lawyer, as for the man, of every calling, is diligence. Leave nothing for tomorrow which can be done today. Never let your correspondence fall behind. Whatever piece of business you have in hand, before stopping, do all the labor pertaining to it which can then be done. When you bring a common law suit, if you have the facts for doing so, write the declaration at once. If a point of law be involved, examine the books, and note the authority you rely on, upon the declaration itself, where you are sure to find it when wanted. The same of defences and pleas. In business not likely to be litigated—ordinary collection cases, foreclosures, partitions, and the like—make all examinations of titles, and note them, and even draft orders and decrees in advance. This course has a triple advantage; it avoids omissions and neglect, saves your labor, when once done; performs the labor out of court when you have leisure rather than in court when you have not.

Extemporaneous speaking should be practiced and cultivated. It is the lawyer's avenue to the public. However able and faithful he may be in other respects, people are slow to bring him business if he cannot make a speech. And yet there is no more fatal error to young lawyers than relying too much on speech-making. If anyone, upon his rare powers of speaking, shall claim exemption from the drudgery of the law, his case is a failure in advance.

Discourage litigation. Persuade your neighbours to compromise when you can. Point out to them how the nominal winner is often a real loser—in fees, and expenses, and waste of time. As a peace maker, the lawyer has a superior opportunity of being a good man. There will still be business enough. Never stir up litigation. A worse man can scarcely be found than one who does this. Who can be more nearly a fiend than he who habitually overhauls the Register of deeds, in search of defects in titles, whereupon to stir up strife, and put money in his pocket? A moral tone ought to be infused into the profession, which should drive such men out of it.

The matter of fees is important far beyond the mere question of bread and butter involved. Properly attended to fuller justice is done to both lawyer and client. An exorbitant fee should never be claimed. As a general rule, never take your whole fee in advance, nor any more than a small retainer. When fully paid beforehand, you are more than a common mortal if you can feel the same interest in the case, as if something was still in prospect for you, as well as for your client. And when you lack interest in the case, the job will very likely lack skill and diligence in the performance. Settle the amount of fee, and take a note in advance. Then you will feel that you are working for something, and you are sure to do your work faithfully and well. Never sell a feenote–at least, not before the consideration service is performed. It leads to negligence and dishonesty–negligence, by losing interest in the case, and dishonesty in refusing to refund, when you have allowed the consideration to fail.

There is a vague popular belief that lawyers are necessarily dishonest. I say vague, because when we consider to what extent confidence, and honors are reposed in, and conferred upon lawyers by the people, it appears improbable that the impression of dishonesty is very distinct and vivid. Yet the impression, is common–almost universal. Let no young man, choosing the law for a calling, for a moment yield to this popular belief. Resolve to be honest at all events; and if, in your own judgement, you cannot be an honest lawyer, resolve to be honest without being a lawyer. Choose some other occupation, rather than one in the choosing of which you do, in advance, consent to be a knave.

Life mask made by sculptor Leonard Volk
in Chicago in the spring of 1860 and used as the basis for
later busts and statues. *Library of Congress*

"BY NO MEANS EXCLUDING FEMALES"

Abraham Lincoln and Women's Suffrage

JEAN BAKER

Jean Harvey Baker is the Bennett-Harwood Professor of History at Goucher College, where she teaches courses in the Civil War and women's history. She is the author of nine books, including Mary Todd Lincoln: A Biography; The Stevensons: Biography of an American Family; *and* James Buchanan. *She has also published studies of the leaders of the suffrage movement, and her most recent book,* Margaret Sanger: A Life of Passion, *is a biography of the birth control pioneer. She has both lectured and appeared on radio and television shows about the Lincoln family.*

I n the summer of 1836, Sangamon County voters prepared to elect representatives to their state legislature. Some had already signed a letter, published in a Springfield newspaper, demanding that the seventeen announced candidates, with seven to be elected, "show their hand"—that is, publicly declare their positions on the issues of the day. The twenty-seven-year-old Abraham Lincoln, seeking the second of his four terms in the Illinois state assembly, promptly responded in the *Sangamon Journal.* He went, he wrote, "for all sharing the privileges of the government who assist in bearing its burthens. Consequently I go for all whites to the right of suffrage, who pay taxes or bear arms, (by no means excluding females.)"[1]

At the time, the enfranchisement of unnaturalized male immigrants was a controversial matter in Illinois and other western states, with Democrats in favor and Whigs like Lincoln usually taking a more restrictive view. Some foreign-born residents did not meet Lincoln's requirements, though; no nativist, he later opposed a bill that would have required new citizens to wait two years before they voted. But it was this issue to which Lincoln, with tongue in cheek about the matter of "females," was responding. No one, even among those advanced bluestockings in New England, was promoting the idea of women as voters in 1836. Certainly Abraham Lincoln was not.

For nearly two decades, ever since the ratification of its first constitution of 1818, white males over twenty-one who had resided in Illinois for six months or more had enjoyed the franchise. This reflected a democratizing process occurring throughout the United States. No longer was it necessary to demonstrate electoral worthiness by owning property and paying taxes. Despite Lincoln's reservations, tying voting to "bearing the burthens of society" was becoming outdated, as democracy in America, measured by the electoral voice of the people, took hold. Yet during the 1840s and 1850s only a portion of those people could vote: in fact, only about one in five Illinoisans enjoyed the privilege. Large segments of the population—African Americans, youths under twenty-one, recent newcomers to the state, immigrant noncitizens, and all women—were disenfranchised.

Although the voting status of the unnaturalized had not been resolved, that of women was clear. Political scientist Carole Pateman calls this arrangement a "sex contract" in which men enjoyed rights in the political realm and held authority over women, who were subordinated within the private domain. Inherited from the English legal tradition, the common law of coverture ruled not just domestic relations but property and public rights. A married woman was removed from civic life, rendered one with her husband, submerged into his identity, and consigned to domesticity and the family roles of wife and mother. The male members of a household—fathers, brothers, and husbands—represented women in all legal, political, and economic affairs. By extension, unmarried and widowed *femme sole* (women alone) could neither vote nor hold office nor become members of the popular political parties that engaged Abraham Lincoln throughout his life.

Certainly the gendering of politics did not escape the attention of the great protagonist of women's suffrage, Elizabeth Cady Stanton. "All men," she informed a woman's convention in Worcester, Massachusetts, in the 1840s, "had the same rights, however, they may differ in mind, body or estate . . . to have the rights of drunkards, idiots, horseracing rum-selling rowdies, ignorant foreigners and silly boys fully recognized when we ourselves are thrust out from the rights belonging to citizens, it is too grossly insulting to the dignity of woman to be longer quietly submitted to."[2] It was from such outrage that the women's suffrage movement grew during the nineteenth century, culminating in 1920 with the ratification of the Nineteenth Amendment, which mandated that the right to vote could not be denied on the basis of sex.

Stanton's commonsense articulation of justice and natural rights might be expected to appeal to Lincoln, the Great Emancipator. However, Abraham Lincoln was a prudent lawyer and, later, a cautious leader of the republic. William Blackstone's *Commentaries on the Laws of England* had been essential reading for him, and in his habitual fashion he had not just memorized its common law precepts but had also rendered them into his own words and thereby fixed them in his mind. As this essay later suggests, Lincoln found them useful, though inhibiting for women, during his career as a lawyer in Springfield.

In the election that took place in September 1836, the incumbent Lincoln ran at the head of the ticket. As far as we can tell, no one had paid any attention to his throwaway parenthesis "by no means excluding females," which, as he no doubt recognized, would have enfranchised only widows and unmarried women who paid taxes. There were no women shouldering the burdens of society in the ragtag local militia units that intermittently paraded outside of Springfield. As all Americans knew, husbands represented wives in public matters; they paid the taxes and carried what Lincoln called "the burthens" of society. Those men who met the qualifications were admitted to the essential lever of democracy—voting.[3] And so Lincoln's only statement on women's suffrage, delivered twelve years before the Seneca Falls convention of 1848 and the emergence of the women's movement, holds relevance only for those who would quote it out of context. Lincoln left no further statements about women's suffrage, but he did leave clues in both his public and private life as to what he might have thought—or more important, done—as the notion of women's suffrage moved from the ridiculous in 1836 to the unacceptable in the 1870s and finally, seventy-two years after the Seneca Falls convention, to actuality.

These clues are the subject of this essay, but not from the perspective of what is popularly called counterfactual history. Lincoln had no opportunity to support—or reject—women's suffrage. The matter had no relevance in the world of practical politics that Lincoln inhabited. There is no alternative history—no "what if" here. Instead, this essay is an exercise in extrapolation based on conjecture about a hypothetical intersection of Lincoln and the suffrage movement. Yet to investigate what Lincoln might have thought about a future issue offers a novel opportunity to say something new about our much-studied sixteenth president—about whom so much has been written, spoken, and often, repeated.

For example, Lincoln had plenty to say about democracy and the importance of elections. In remarks to the Illinois legislature in January of 1837, he had already developed his belief in the importance of public opinion as measured by elections: "the people," he asserted, "know their rights and are never slow to assert and maintain them, when they are invaded."[4] But were women part of the people? Lincoln wrote often of the Declaration of Independence with its pledge that "all men are created equal" and "endowed by their Creator with certain unalienable rights." He compared the founding document of the American Revolution to "an electric chord linking patriots and the liberty loving." But would he interpret Jefferson's use of the term "men" as a generic expression about humankind—and thereby include women?

After his re-election to the presidency in 1864, Lincoln noted that elections were a necessity in a democracy. There could be no free government without the kind of electoral process that measured the people's voice, even during wartime. But to what extent should women participate? And is it possible to extrapolate from Lincoln's well-known antislavery views to make the case, as this first generation of feminists did, that women were also enslaved, their freedom controlled by men, their bodies the legal possession of their husbands?

In his law practice, Lincoln occasionally encountered public women, especially in conjunction with the temperance movement, which Lincoln supported. In 1854, he represented nine women from nearby DeWitt County who had entered a saloon, opened several whiskey barrels, and dumped the contents, in unladylike fashion, on the ground. In his defense of the women, Lincoln, who acknowledged he hated "the stuff," compared their actions to those of Boston's Tea Party patriots. He lost the case but may have learned a lesson about these kinds of transgressive, but increasingly popular, female behaviors outside the home.

Of course, in his companionate marriage to Mary Todd, he also revealed his attitudes toward the unequal half of the population who had few legal protections and almost no civic presence during his lifetime. What does Lincoln's private life reveal about his possible attitudes toward women's suffrage? In 1842, Abraham Lincoln married the tempestuous Mary Todd and set up a household with her, first in a boarding house in Springfield, Illinois, and then later in a house, soon to be improved with money from his father-in-law, Robert Smith Todd, on Eighth and Jackson Streets. Then, in the winter of 1861, as all the world knows, the Lincoln family moved from Illinois to the White House. Throughout the twenty-three-year duration of this marriage, a powerful source of congeniality was the couple's shared interest in politics, with Mary displaying a lively concern with the great game of partisan competition. As a committed Whig and later Republican, she followed the elections and knew the parties, platforms, and leaders. She wrote patronage letters for her husband in 1850. She advised him not to accept the governorship of faraway Oregon, a choice that would have doomed any opportunity for the presidency. She entertained and courted the politicians of Springfield at her famous "strawberry parties." She studied the allegiances of Illinois legislators and, as her husband prepared to run for the US Senate in the 1850s, she gave him the unlikely gift, wrapped in red ribbon, of a list of the Illinois state senators who might—or might not, as it turned out—vote for her husband. She even watched from the galleries of the Illinois State Capitol when the legislature twice rejected Lincoln for the US Senate in 1855 and 1859.

Once on a train returning from one of his circuit court trials, Lincoln, guffawing at the outlandish prospect, told a friend that his wife thought he would become president one day. With her interest in politics, Mary Lincoln was rehearsing the new roles sought by women who, by the 1850s, were moving from their status as benevolent activists working in moral reform societies to demand full membership in the body politic. Lincoln surely learned lessons about female activism from his wife, though, as the father of four sons, he had no daughters to acquaint him with a younger generation's attitudes toward women's rights. When in 1860 the election returns came in from Pennsylvania, Lincoln hurried home from the telegraph office, saying there was a little lady at home who would want to hear the news. And as he turned the corner onto Eighth Street, he called out in loving recognition, "Mary, Mary we are elected." How could such a man not endorse women's suffrage?

In 1848, the year Lincoln represented the voters of Illinois' Seventh Congressional District in Washington, a small group of women organized a convention to assert their claim to the same rights that Lincoln and most other Americans of the time would grant to white men only. Led by Elizabeth Cady Stanton, these activists resolved at the famous Seneca Falls, New York, convention that, in a government that denied women the vote, "all laws which place [women] in a position inferior to that of man are contrary to the great precept of nature and are of no force and authority." Such were Stanton's additions to the convictions of the founders: liberty was the natural condition of all humans, and the US Constitution's powerful introductory phrase "We the People" included women.

Stanton based her call for women's liberation on the Declaration of Independence, the very document that undergirded Lincoln's democratic values. "The principles of Jefferson," he wrote in 1859, "are the definitions and axioms of free society."[5] Stanton extended those principles to women, arguing that suffrage was inseparable from freedom and that taxation without representation (as experienced by *femmes sole* who paid taxes) violated the principles of the nation. At the end of their Declaration of Sentiments, the women of Seneca Falls committed themselves to "use every instrumentality in our power to effect our object." They would lobby, seek to educate the public through propaganda, and "endeavor to enlist the pulpit and the press in our behalf."

And so began the women's rights movement. At first, the movement proclaimed a full agenda of reforms, including control of property and entrance to colleges; after the Civil War, its focus narrowed to suffrage. Enfranchising women was the most audacious of their demands, for the vote would establish the autonomy and personhood of all women in ways that other claims would not. If they could vote, women would be independent practitioners in the civic community, not simply members of a family unit controlled by a male relative. Yet, throughout Lincoln's life, votes for women remained one of those moral questions unattended to by politicians who rarely take sides in any such transformative, marginal issue not yet in the political domain.

As a politician, Lincoln also met a new type of woman—the partisan enabler who attended political speeches, when, as Stanton acidly noted, there was spare room for the ladies and political parties wanted to fill the seats. Women participated as spectators in the rallies and marches that were fixtures of nineteenth-century electioneering. Some waved handkerchiefs as their preferred candidates marched by; others stayed indoors, illuminating their windows when their favorites came by and darkening their kerosene lamps and candles when the opposition appeared. Women could not vote, acknowledged one New Hampshire woman, but they could speak and write, thereby demonstrating their interest in the great game of politics. (Later in the century, the argument that women were not interested in politics surfaced as a powerful, if incorrect, reason to deny women the vote.) Lincoln's Whig Party was especially well known for courting women during the 1840s, inviting them to rallies where their presence testified to the party's commitment to the American family.

While female activists began the tedious work of changing the opinion of the public on what most considered the settled matter of the legal status of women, Abraham Lincoln was impressing some of his friends with his liberal views on the subject. William Herndon, his law partner from 1844 to 1861 and one of his earliest biographers, wrote after Lincoln's assassination that the president believed in women's rights—had in fact always "advocated " for them. Lincoln, according to Herndon, believed "that Woman was denied in *free* America her right to the franchise, being the equal but the other side—but the other better half of man."[6] Of course, Herndon, who once called Lincoln "the most shut-mouthed man" he knew, is not always the most accurate informant about the president. Himself a supporter of the Married Women's Property Acts passed in 1861 by the Illinois legislature and later of women's suffrage, Herndon no doubt wanted his hero to be on the right side of history. Other associates of Lincoln noted his compassionate nature toward women, along with children and animals. But compassion is often a Trojan horse for paternalism, whereby male dominance remains in place but is supposedly mitigated by mutual obligations and reciprocal rights. In any case, paternalism denied any tendency toward the kind of civic equality that Stanton and Susan B. Anthony were demanding with their growing concentration on women's suffrage.

In the public realm, Lincoln also revealed his attitudes toward women and their legal rights through his law practice. Recent studies of Lincoln's cases reveal that nearly one-fifth of Lincoln's clients (of more than five thousand) were women, who employed him primarily to make their claims in inheritance, estate, divorce, and foreclosure litigation. Lincoln certainly saw married women as vulnerable to the rigidities of coverture. And as an increasingly respected lawyer in the courts of the Eighth Illinois Judicial Circuit, Lincoln offered women judicial opportunities to take advantage of the few protections offered, especially through chancery law. Mostly the remuneration he received for such services was limited. Nor were the cases prestigious for an ambitious man who had corporate clients. Yet the fact that he took some of these cases suggests a benevolent attitude toward women.

Of course, in his handling of these cases, Lincoln necessarily followed the dictates of precedent in a male-ordered system where actions involving women as petitioners, plaintiffs, and occasionally defendants were dictated by common law. For example, married women needed the permission of their husbands even to orchestrate any legal actions, and women's inheritance claims were bound by rigid applications of the dower rights of widows. Lincoln surely noted the disparity between the sexes in the ways that his chosen profession dealt with gender.

In the Dorman case, in which Nancy Robinson Dorman waged a fifteen-year legal battle against her stepfather to recover the property of her deceased father, Lincoln took the appeal and successfully argued that earlier courts had neglected their obligation to appoint a legal guardian for the underage, then unmarried, Nancy Robinson. When Lincoln's appeal was successful, the grateful Dormans promised that if they had another son, they would name him Abraham Lincoln. In the divorce cases he took to court, Lincoln showed obvious concern for wives who had been deserted by husbands as well as for impoverished widows and jilted brides. Students of Lincoln and the legal system have described the judicial operation of this period as "a jurisprudence of the heart" in which the severity of common law was moderated by the paternalistic sentiments of lawyers like Lincoln.[7] Yet such "tender considerations," as they have been called, were far removed from support of women's suffrage and in fact suggest that Lincoln might have opposed votes for women for the very reason that they were already protected by common law.

As president, Lincoln retained his protective instincts, taking time—too much time, according to his secretaries—evaluating the pleas of women for jobs, of mothers for sons accused of desertion from the army, and of female abolitionists for slave emancipation. Lincoln approved the appointment of a "lady" as chaplain of a Wisconsin regiment, though Secretary of War Edwin M. Stanton objected.[8] He also heard from women whose letters displayed their interest in politics. "May I a wife, mother, taxpayer and hardworking woman of America be heard when I ask from you, a man in power, a juster recognition of woman's individuality than has been shown in the distribution of such offices as she is well-fitted for?" wrote one New Yorker.[9] But such appeals were balanced by letters attacking Stanton and Anthony for their wild ideas about women's equality.

Other women wrote the president asserting their right to take an interest in public affairs, and Lincoln was well aware of the rising star of the lecture circuit young Anna Dickinson, who became an important advocate for the Republican Party. The president was in attendance when Dickinson spoke in January 1864 in the House of Representatives on the "Perils of the Hour." Reportedly, both Mary and Abraham Lincoln met with Dickinson, in the office of the Speaker of the House. And Lincoln applauded "the industry, enterprise and intelligence" of women who raised money at Sanitary Fairs for private relief efforts to benefit sick and wounded soldiers during the Civil War—thereby fulfilling his earlier requirement that those who would vote must share "the burthens of society."

Lincoln also supported the concept of fair pay for women. When the female textile workers in Philadelphia protested that they could not survive on their declining wages and appealed to Secretary of War Stanton for redress, Lincoln commented that, in fairness, they should at least be paid as much as they had at the beginning of the war. And he met with their leaders in February 1865 and promised to run at full capacity the government factories where the women sewed uniforms that, as the war ended, would no longer be needed.

Perhaps the most fertile ground for discovering Lincoln's views on women's suffrage rests with his attitude toward another minority group—enslaved black Americans. "If slavery is not wrong," he wrote the editor of a Kentucky paper in 1864, "nothing is wrong." In his habitual use of reverse logic and analogy, Lincoln noted that he knew of no man who wished to be a slave and wondered whether anyone knew any "good thing, that no man desires for himself."[10] For Lincoln the institution of slavery violated the basic entitlement in the Declaration of Independence to equality. The issue, he said in his famous Peoria speech in 1854, revolved around whether "a negro is not or is a man. If he is not a man slavery could be justified." On the other hand, "if the negro is a man," then it was a total affront to the concept of self-government to say that he shall not govern himself. "When the white man governs himself that is self-government, but when he governs another man, that is more than self-government—that is despotism." Employing similar logic, the small band of midcentury feminists demanded self-government delivered through the vote—though, as we've seen, Lincoln was under no pressure to apply his logic about slavery to women. In mainstream political circles, the issue did not yet exist.

Convictions about equality underwrote Lincoln's policy that slavery must not be extended into the new territories of the West, although he agreed the institution was constitutionally protected in the southern states. To nationalize slavery, as southerners were demanding in the 1850s, would be to deny the principle of equality established in the promises of the Declaration of Independence. Yet—and here was a possible application to women's suffrage—a government organized under the principles of democracy demanded citizens of intelligence, morality, and respect for the law. Later in the century, suffragists would make the claim that the addition to the body politic of women, the more ethical, right-acting gender, would clean up America's dirty politics of stolen elections, rowdy election days, and rampant corruption.

Yet for Lincoln, in his comments on the *Dred Scott* decision, the brutality of slavery destroyed such attributes. As a result, enslaved blacks were not equal to whites in matters of intellect or what he called "social capacity." There was no social equality: he wanted no black woman for a wife, but that did not mean that he wanted her for a slave. Yet, "in her natural right to eat the bread she earns with her own hands without asking leave of anyone else, she is my equal, and the equal of all others."[11] Clearly, then, Lincoln would have supported the Married Woman's Property Acts that gave married women the control of their wages and inheritance. But would he have extended his understanding that slavery's restrictions had handicapped blacks to women who knew little of politics? Certainly the assertion that all *men* were created equal and that equality presumed the right to suffrage remained a promissory note from the Declaration of Independence for possible future application in the thinking of a man who fervently believed in the possibility of human improvement.

As Lincoln developed his positions on the great moral question of his day, so the progressive women of his time began learning public roles beyond domesticity through their activities in antislavery societies. Many began strategically comparing themselves to slaves. Reshaping public opinion, as Lincoln had long understood as a politician, became their task. Using slavery as their reference point, the women of the early suffrage movement decried the destruction of family ties caused by an institution that severed the relationships of parents and children, husbands and wives. Many women were already aware of the discrimination against them as autonomous human beings and saw the parallels to slavery: as blacks were oppressed, so women, their enslaved sisters, must fight the tyranny of sex. In the schoolhouse of antislavery, women absorbed the American principles of human rights—of justice, liberty, and equality. They would make their claim unsuccessfully in 1868 and 1869 during the national discussion of what became the Fifteenth Amendment, which granted voting rights regardless of race.

But Lincoln was three years dead by that time. Had he been alive, would his exposure to women's rights through his wife, through the women's rights movement, and through the workings of his own conscience have led him to champion women's suffrage? And, if not, at what point during the seventy-two-year-long crusade that culminated in the ratification of the suffrage amendment in 1920 would he have supported votes for women?

During the Civil War, Lincoln's views on the status of blacks in American society shifted. For a time he believed in the "colonization" of blacks (the nineteenth century's euphemism for deportation). He worked unsuccessfully to persuade the congressmen of the Union border states to accept a policy of compensated emancipation. And then, under his powers as a commander in chief, he committed the federal government to a wartime policy of liberation for the enslaved, underscoring that commitment with his support of what became the Thirteenth Amendment, abolishing slavery. But emancipation was not enfranchisement, and only at the end of his life did Lincoln confront the issue of black male voting. In a letter to Michael Hahn, the governor of newly freed Louisiana in 1864, the president endorsed the vote for those who had shouldered what he had earlier called "the burthens of society." These African American men included, he noted with classic Lincolnian restraint, "the very intelligent and those who have fought gallantly in our ranks. They would probably help, in some trying time to come, to keep the jewel of liberty within the family of freedom."[12]

Meanwhile, the cause of female emancipation languished. As is often the case with women's wartime activism, the leaders of the movement had buried their own claims for equal rights during the Civil War in patriotic efforts such as the Women's Loyal Patriotic League. Privately Stanton and Anthony castigated the president for his dilatory emancipation policy and opposed his re-election in 1864. By the end of the war, they were ready to begin again. Wrote Stanton in 1865, "as the question of Suffrage is now agitating the public mind, it is the hour for woman to make her demand." Both women hurried to Washington when Congress began its deliberations, where they argued that the female case for the vote was unassailable in a republic based on the people's will. Disenfranchisement was an anomaly as cruel as slavery had been. Women needed the vote for their protection; they had earned it through their wartime contributions, and besides they shared with men the natural right to suffrage in a democracy. "The representative women of the nation feel they have an interest and duty equal with men in the struggle and triumphs of this hour. Has not the time come to bury the black man and the woman in the citizen?" wrote Stanton.[13]

Most public officials saw the issue differently: one reform at a time, they cautioned. After all, said the great African American leader Frederick Douglass, women were not being strung up from lampposts and lynched the way black men were (though certainly both black and white women were still the victims of rape and had few protections under common law from violence in their homes). The time for women's suffrage hadn't yet come. Instead, the Fourteenth Amendment gave citizenship to all persons born or naturalized in the United States—including women and blacks—but in its second article it introduced, for the first time in American history the exclusionary classification "male" into the US Constitution.

Despite the Republican Party's supermajorities in Congress during the 1870s, only a few senators, among them Henry Wilson and Benjamin Butler of Massachusetts, and Thaddeus Stevens of Pennsylvania, spoke for the addition of the three-letter word "sex" to the Fifteenth Amendment. Their hopes ruined after their exclusion from that amendment, women introduced the Susan B. Anthony Amendment, believing that it would grant women the vote when it became the sixteenth addition to the US Constitution. But for years the judiciary committees of the House and the Senate either tabled or rejected the measure. Only a handful of states accepted women's suffrage before

1900, and only in 1917 did the women's suffrage amendment pass both houses of Congress.

It seems likely that none of Lincoln's liberating encounters with women would have led him to differ from his Republican colleagues in Congress as they delivered the vote to black males, but not women, during Reconstruction. After all, he had lagged behind many of his Radical Republican colleagues on matters relating to enslaved black Americans. There is no reason to believe that he would have led the way for women, however attracted he might have been to their natural rights argument of common humanity and the consent of the governed. As president in the 1870s—perhaps enjoying a precedent-defying third term—it's hard to imagine Lincoln speaking out for the enfranchisement of women.

Lincoln would likely have endorsed some feminist goals. Holding fast to his aspirational philosophy of self-improvement through hard work, he would have accepted the right of women to control their inheritance and their wages, to attend male colleges, and to seek jobs currently closed to them. He would have noted, and decried, Susan B. Anthony's arrest and felony prosecution by the federal government for voting in the presidential election of 1872. But to deliver the vote to all women was too controversial. Lincoln might well have agreed with the Supreme Court's decision in the 1875 case of *Minor v. Happersett* that federal citizenship did not include the vote. That privilege must be earned, as black men had earned it through their wartime service.

Nor would Lincoln have accepted Stanton's argument that women were enslaved. He would have focused on the question of whether they shared "the burthens" of society with men. Pondering and probing in his habitual temperate manner, Lincoln would only gradually have come to accept the importance of enfranchising women. His wife would have encouraged him, his encounters with the suffragists of the late nineteenth century would have expedited his understanding, and his egalitarian instincts would have further hastened the process. By 1917—and surely before—Abraham Lincoln would have supported the Nineteenth Amendment. He might even have urged a hesitant President Woodrow Wilson to grant to half the population a natural right and responsibility.

It was, reprising Lincoln's powerful words of the past, time to think and act anew and to rise with the occasion. Rejecting any state-by-state strategy for the achievement of women's suffrage, he would have noted that the government had the right to redress national wrongs so that women could be "henceforth and forever free."

LINCOLN'S WORDS

Two Unpublished Fragments (1854)

Fragment on Government:

The legitimate object of government, is to do for a community of people, whatever they need to have done, but can not do, at all, or can not, so well do, for themselves—in their separate, and individual capacities.

In all that the people can individually do as well for themselves, government ought not to interfere.

The desirable things which the individuals of a people can not do, or can not well do, for themselves, fall into two classes: those which have relation to wrongs, and those which have not. Each of these branch off into an infinite variety of subdivisions.

The first—that in relation to wrongs—embraces all crimes, misdemeanors, and nonperformance of contracts. The other embraces all which, in its nature, and without wrong, requires combined action, as public roads and highways, public schools, charities, pauperism, orphanage, estates of the deceased, and the machinery of government itself.

From this it appears that if all men were just, there still would be some, though not so much, need for government.

Fragment on Slavery:

If A. can prove, however conclusively, that he may, of right, enslave B.—why may not B. snatch the same argument, and prove equally, that he may enslave A?—

You say A. is white, and B. is black. It is *color*, then; the lighter, having the right to enslave the darker? Take care. By this rule, you are to be slave to the first man you meet, with a fairer skin than your own.

You do not mean *color* exactly? You mean the whites are *intellectually* the superiors of the blacks, and, therefore have the right to enslave them? Take care again. By this rule, you are to be slave to the first man you meet, with an intellect superior to your own.

But, say you, it is a question of *interest*; and, if you can make it your *interest*, you have the right to enslave another. Very well. And if he can make it his interest, he has the right to enslave you.

Ambrotype of Lincoln as presidential candidate,
taken by Preston Butler in Springfield, Illinois (August 13, 1860).
Library of Congress

LINCOLN, FDR, AND
THE GROWTH OF FEDERAL POWER

DANIEL FARBER

Daniel Farber teaches constitutional law at the University of California, Berkeley. He is a graduate of the University of Illinois Law School. After law school, he clerked for Justice John Paul Stevens on the United States Supreme Court. Prior to joining the Berkeley faculty, he practiced law in Washington, DC, and taught at the University of Illinois and the University of Minnesota.

Although Abraham Lincoln and Franklin D. Roosevelt lived in very different times, their presidencies have more in common than most people realize. Both presidencies featured major legislative accomplishments as well as wartime challenges. Lincoln did not just fight the Civil War and free the slaves. Like FDR, he presided over a huge expansion in the federal government's role in the economy.

Like Lincoln, FDR took office in a time of crisis—but this time the crisis was the deepest recession in US history rather than the threat of secession. Like Lincoln, he responded boldly. Within the first hundred days of his presidency, he had addressed the collapsing financial system by immediately closing the banks, getting authority from Congress to reopen the sound ones and supply them with Federal Reserve notes as currency, and pushed Congress into passing the first federal law regulating securities. On top of those actions, his first three months in office included the creation of the National Recovery Authority, with wide authority over industry, and the launch of a massive public works program.

Before it was done, FDR's New Deal had remade American government. It created government agencies like the Securities and Exchange Commission and the National Labor Relations Board, established the Social Security system, put millions of Americans to work building highways and dams, and initiated government regulation of everything from stock trading to union organizing. Then, as now, there were those who felt that FDR had created a dangerous Leviathan, a federal government with far too much power.

We cannot be sure what Lincoln would have thought of the specifics of the New Deal. His basic economic philosophy, focusing on equal opportunity and the initiative of individual entrepreneurs, was probably more like Herbert Hoover's than FDR's. But, then, even Hoover, by the end of his presidency, had begun to recognize the need for more activist governmental responses to the Depression. Lincoln's willingness to rethink ideas in a time of crisis is shown by his views of presidential power and of abolition, both of which changed in the heat of the Civil War from his earlier views. In an unprecedented emergency like that of the 1930s, it seems likely that Lincoln (like so many others) would have been led to question the traditional assumptions of laissez-faire capitalism.

Regardless of how Lincoln would have viewed specific measures, however, we can be confident of his willingness to use government power to strengthen the economy. Lincoln was never in doubt about the active role of government in promoting the public good. And the fact is that Lincoln himself presided over the largest expansion of federal power up to that time.

We naturally focus on the Civil War when we think of Lincoln, but his presidency would have been notable just for its other legislative accomplishments. During the Lincoln years, the federal government adopted its first income tax, created national banks, subsidized the creation of railroads, and founded the modern system of state universities. States-rights advocates had blocked many of these measures for decades. Lincoln's attention was largely focused on the war, but his administration backed all of these efforts. And that is not even to mention the aggressive use of the federal government's constitutional powers in the Civil War struggle itself.

The Origins of the Debate over Federal Power

To understand Lincoln's views about government, we need first to put them into historical context. How big a role should the federal government play in running the economy? That is a question that still divides Americans today, but many people would be surprised to learn that it first arose while the ink was barely dry on the Constitution. The echoes of that early debate still reverberated in Lincoln's time.

After the Constitution was ratified, Alexander Hamilton became the first secretary of the treasury. He hatched a plan to jump-start the American economy by creating a new financial system and using tariffs (taxes on imports) to support the government. Hamilton's plan was a daring effort to try to rescue a foundering national economy saddled with debt from the Revolutionary War and hampered by the absence of any national financial institutions.

The heart of Hamilton's plan was an ambitious scheme for the federal government to raise revenue through tariffs and then to refinance both the federal government's war debt and that of the states. Establishing a national bank was a key part of this scheme. Banking was in an early stage of development in the United States, and the new federal bank would immediately become a dominant player. Hamilton planned to use the bank's notes to expand the national money supply. He also planned for the bank to be the government's chief fiscal agent, making it easier to collect taxes, make payments, and obtain short-term loans. Its notes would provide a national currency, and it would provide a source of capital for financing businesses. This plan was modeled closely on the Bank of England, which had helped bring Britain back from the verge of bankruptcy.

The plan ignited a fierce controversy. In Congress, James Madison led the opposition to the bank. He and Hamilton had been among the primary advocates for adopting the Constitution, and they had teamed to write the *Federalist Papers*. But now they decisively parted course.

Madison argued that the bank proposal was dubious as a policy matter. More important, he contended that it was unconstitutional. Congress had only limited enumerated powers. At most, the bank would be convenient rather than necessary to carrying out those powers, so its creation couldn't be upheld under the "necessary and proper" clause of the Constitution. All in all, Madison viewed the bank as an infringement of states' rights.

Madison had several discussions about the bank with President Washington, who was sufficiently concerned to tell Madison to prepare a veto message for possible use. Washington then asked Attorney General and Secretary of State Thomas Jefferson to advise him about the constitutionality of the bill. Jefferson had been out of the country when the Constitution was written, but he was quickly emerging as the leader of an important faction within the new political system.

Hamilton's economic schemes were anathema to Jefferson. Jefferson's vision of the American future was agrarian, and he was suspicious of manufacturing, commerce; and finance. Like most Southern planters, he was deeply hostile to banks of all kinds—the planters were always borrowing money and had trouble repaying their debts. (Jefferson himself was to die deeply in debt.) Jefferson also feared that Hamilton's plan would create a privileged class of financiers who would have too much influence on politics. It was clear from the start that he would side with Madison against the national bank—in fact, from that time forward, the two of them were an inseparable political duo.

Jefferson responded to Washington's request for advice with a vigorous attack on the constitutionality of the bank. He began by cataloguing the ways in which the federal bank statute might conflict with state laws, which it would override. In his view, the foundation of the Constitution was the Tenth Amendment's reservation of power to the states: "To take a single step beyond the boundaries thus specially drawn around the powers of Congress," Jefferson said, "is to take possession of a boundless field of power, no longer susceptible of any definition."[1] Jefferson also pointed out that the Constitutional Convention had voted down a proposal to give the federal government the power to charter corporations, in part because of fears that Congress would establish a bank.

Washington wanted to hear both sides before deciding. After receiving Jefferson's views, Washington asked Hamilton to respond. Hamilton's response was cogent and powerful, anticipating in many ways the US Supreme Court's opinion more than three decades later upholding the constitutionality of the bank.

Hamilton argued that constitutional powers, especially those relating to finance, trade, and defense, should be construed liberally. Because the means for promoting the national interest "are of such infinite variety, extent and complexity," Congress needed "great latitude of discretion in the selection & application of those means." Lincoln and FDR would both have wholeheartedly agreed. Hamilton also argued that the need for the bank was dire enough to justify it under the Constitution's "necessary and proper" clause. In contrast, Jefferson had argued that this clause did not apply because the bank wasn't indispensable to the use of other federal powers.

The decision on whether to sign or veto the law rested with George Washington as president. He apparently found Hamilton more persuasive than Jefferson. Two days after receiving Hamilton's opinion, Washington signed the bank bill. This decision carried great weight: Washington had presided at the Constitutional Convention and was of course a revered national figure. For the time, at least, Hamilton had prevailed in the constitutional debate.

Ultimately, the Supreme Court would side with Washington and Hamilton, not with Jefferson. Chief Justice John Marshall's opinion in *McCulloch v. Maryland* (1819) emphasized the paramount importance of federal power and the need for broad construction. He argued that a constitution written in narrow, specific terms would be unmanageable: it would have to be so detailed and complicated that it would "partake of the complexity of a legal code, and could scarcely be embraced by the human mind." Instead, constitutional powers need to be broad to cope with unforeseen circumstances. In considering the scope of federal powers, Marshall wrote, "we must never forget that it is a Constitution we are expounding." And, given the broad powers entrusted to the federal government—the "sword and the purse, all the external relations, and no inconsiderable portion of the industry of the nation"—it must be entrusted with equally ample means to utilize those powers.

Marshall argued that it was in the interest of the nation to facilitate the exercise of these crucial federal powers. It could not have been the intention of the Framers to "clog and embarrass" the use of federal power to solve national problems. The power to create a corporation was just a means, like any other means, to be used where appropriate. The bottom line was that the court upheld the constitutionality of the bank, for very much the same reasons as Hamilton had argued earlier.

Hamilton was successful in part of this scheme. By establishing a dependable method of financing a public debt, he put the country's credit on a firm footing for the first time. But the Bank of the United States ultimately died an inglorious death at the hands of Andrew Jackson, who first vetoed a renewal of its charter and then brought it down by withdrawing all federal deposits. Perhaps confirming the views of its supporters about the genuine need for the bank, the economy promptly went into a tailspin. The Bank of the United States never rose again, but the process of replacing it began during the Lincoln administration.

Lincoln's View of the Role of Government

Before we examine how federal power fared under Lincoln, however, we need to look at how his views were rooted in the philosophy of a now-forgotten political party, the Whigs. The Whigs had emerged in reaction to Jackson and his populist movement. Lincoln began as a Whig and never lost his attachment to their philosophy.

For most of the nineteenth century, the Democrats were the "small government" party. Their opponents—first the Federalists, then the Whigs, and then the Republicans—favored a more vigorous government that would take an active role in promoting national prosperity.

The administration of John Adams was more or less the last hurrah for the Federalists. Beginning with Jefferson's election in 1800, the Democrats took control of the White House. They dominated the federal government basically uncontested throughout the "Era of Good Feelings" until a new party developed to challenge them, the Whigs. The catalyst for developing the party was Andrew Jackson's autocratic style of governance, which he combined with populist rhetoric. The Whig Party crystalized in opposition to Jackson.

Lincoln began his career as a Whig. Of the Whigs, the one best known today and most admired by Lincoln was Henry Clay, still remembered as the Great Compromiser. Lincoln revered Clay and delivered a moving eulogy after Clay's death. After commenting on Clay's long career, Lincoln said Clay had "constantly been the most loved, and most implicitly followed by friends, and the most dreaded by opponents, of all living American politicians." Clay, said Lincoln, "loved his country partly because it was his country, but mostly because it was a free country, and he burned with zeal for its advancement, prosperity and glory, because he saw in such, the advancement, prosperity and glory, of human liberty, human right, and human nature."

Lincoln firmly believed in Clay's program, whose heart was what he called the "American System." Clay viewed economic strength as necessary for national security. His program included a high tariff, designed as a form of industrial policy to protect growing industries and to provide government revenue. According to Clay, protective tariffs would help the country become economically independent of Britain. Thus, protective tariffs involved both a tax policy (higher revenues) and an industrial policy (government protection of growing industries).

Clay also supported the Bank of the United States, unlike Andrew Jackson. The War of 1812 persuaded him that a national bank was needed to stabilize the country's money supply and credit. And he promoted a system of "internal improvements," meaning roads and canals, to hold the country together and to strengthen the country militarily as well as economically. In the age of the federal interstate system, this position may seem uncontroversial, but many considered it to be an unconstitutional intrusion by the federal government into local affairs. A Jeffersonian accused him of "out-Hamiltoning Hamilton."

There was a strong intellectual continuity from Hamilton to Clay to Lincoln. Although Lincoln revered Jefferson's Declaration of Independence, his views about the role of the federal government were closer to Hamilton's as refashioned by Clay. From the start of his career, Lincoln supported a vigorous program of public works. In his 1832 communiqué to the people of Sangamon County, he emphasized that "time and experience have verified . . . the public utility of internal improvements," and he proclaimed that "no other improvement could equal the rail road" as a "never failing source of communication" between places of business. Government support for railroad building, then, would be ideal, but, given limited state resources, he thought improving river navigation was a better first step. Lincoln said he also hoped to see a time when education was more widespread among the population.

Once elected to the state legislature, Lincoln worked hard in favor of these causes. Early in his legislative career, he supported legislation to create a canal connecting Lake Michigan to the Mississippi River and provided the decisive vote to authorize a $500,000 loan for the project. In the next session, he strongly supported a measure providing up to $10 million in state loans to construct railroads and another $400,000 for canals. This was a lot of money for a frontier state at the time. In response to arguments that internal improvements would cause spiraling debts and deficits, he compared the opposition to an eccentric bachelor who was "very famous for seeing big bugaboos in every thing" but turned out merely to have a louse on one of his eyelashes.

Despite the financial panic of 1837, Lincoln continued to support internal improvements. He said that the state was "now so far advanced in a general system of internal improvements, we cannot retreat from it, without disgrace and great loss." He favored plans to support the projects by raising taxes or by getting land from the federal government that the state could resell at a profit.

Lincoln was also a strong backer of the state-chartered Bank of Illinois. As a Whig, he had preferred a strong national bank. But after Jackson destroyed the Bank of the United States, the state banks were the best alternative. In an 1839 public debate, however, he defended the concept of a national bank as a bulwark of economic stability.

Lincoln Versus State Sovereignty

Economic issues were sidelined in Lincoln's thinking as the Civil War approached and as slavery and secession loomed larger. But slavery itself raised other questions about federal power. Republicans like Lincoln wanted the federal government to ban slavery in the territories, but Democrats—and ultimately the Supreme Court—held that doing so fell outside of Congress's enumerated powers. Lincoln gave deep thought to issues of federalism in the context of slavery, and then even more so as states claimed the sovereign right to secede.

In Lincoln's time, like today, state sovereignty was often raised as an argument against federal power. It was the rallying cry of the secessionists and their Northern sympathizers. But state sovereignty had little appeal for Lincoln.

In a speech shortly after the Confederate attack on Fort Sumter, Jefferson Davis defended the constitutionality of secession. During the American Revolution, Davis said, the British threat to American liberty led to a close alliance among the states—something like NATO today—under which each state expressly retained its sovereignty. The war was won by this "contract of alliance." In 1787, the states then appointed delegates to the Constitutional Convention, and those delegates negotiated what Davis called "a compact between independent States." State sovereignty, Davis said, was then explicitly reaffirmed in the Tenth Amendment. But a heresy soon arose in the North, according to Davis—a heresy that held that that Constitution created a national government rather than a compact among the states. Despite the Constitution's support for slavery, Davis claimed, the Republicans were seeking to stamp it out in violation of the original compact, and the Southern states were forced to secede.

From our perspective today, Davis's view was the heresy, not the North's. But the "compact theory" was a heresy with a long history. North Carolina's John Calhoun was perhaps its most articulate spokesman. He claimed that the states had separately become sovereign when they declared independence from England. This sovereignty remained intact through the Articles of Confederation, he believed, and in the Constitution all the states had done was to appoint the federal government as their agent to perform certain functions. Calhoun drew a distinction between a "national" government and a "government formed by the States; ordained and established by the States, and for the States—without any participation . . . on the part of the people, regarded in the aggregate as forming a nation."

There was, Calhoun said, "no such community, politically speaking, as the people of the United States" in the sense of "constituting one people or nation." In short, Davis said, the Constitution created "the government of a community of States, and not the government of a single State or nation."

Lincoln's views were starkly different. Where Calhoun spoke of a government "by the states . . . and for the states," Lincoln would refer in the Gettysburg Address to a government "of the people, by the people, and for the people." Lincoln insisted that the "Union is older than any of the States; and, in fact, it created them as States." Before that, they were only colonies. It was only as a collective body that they threw off allegiance to England in the Declaration of Independence. Indeed, Lincoln said, despite all the talk about the "sovereignty" of the states, the word itself doesn't even occur in the Constitution. He added, "The states have their *status* IN the Union, and they have no other *legal status*. If they break from this, they can only do so against law, and by revolution."

Lincoln may be best remembered, in legal terms, for how he exercised the power of the presidency. After Fort Sumter, he summoned the militia, imposed a naval blockade, and suspended the writ of habeas corpus. Later, he would institute military trials for suspected Confederate agents, begin Reconstruction in the South, and free the slaves—all without congressional authorization. He justified these actions in terms of the president's war powers as chief executive and commander in chief. But that did not mean that he was skeptical of Congressional power. He continued to support congressional legislation on economic issues, though it was not his focal point.

National Power in the Civil War Era

While Lincoln was focused on fighting the war, however, his cabinet members and fellow Republicans in Congress began to enact the old Whig vision into federal law. Thus, during the Lincoln administration, part of the vigorous government program that he had endorsed as a young man began to take hold.

Lincoln's administration saw the passage of more important government legislation than the entire previous half century. That legislation would have made Lincoln's presidency historic by itself, though it was overshadowed by the drama and urgency of the Civil War.

To begin with, the Republicans reasserted the federal role in the financial system, taking the side of Washington and Hamilton rather than Jefferson and Jackson. One of the achievements of the Lincoln years was the passage of the National Banking Acts of 1863 and 1864. Until then, the national currency supply was a mess, a hodgepodge of bank notes issued by state-chartered banks, whose value depended on the varying creditworthiness of the banks involved. The country needed a unified monetary system. The new national banks were authorized to issue national bank notes backed by US government bonds. The old state bank notes were wiped out a couple of years later when Congress imposed a tax on them.

Previously, the Legal Tender Act of 1862 had already authorized the issuance of paper money, so-called greenbacks. Over $400 million in greenbacks were issued to help finance the war. The constitutional-ity of paper money was hotly disputed, and in 1870 the Supreme Court briefly held it unconstitutional in a decision that was written, ironically enough, by Chief Justice Salmon Chase, who had helped create the greenbacks as Lincoln's secretary of treasury. This decision, in turn, was reversed in 1871 thanks largely to the votes of two newly appointed members of the court. Paper money, as it turned out, was here to stay. Thus, the contents of wallets today are a historical prod-uct of the Lincoln years.

Congress also took steps to support the economic growth of the West. It opened the region to public settlement with the 1862 Home-stead Act. Settlers could receive 160 acres of federal land by investing five years in farming and building a house on the land. By the end of the decade, tens of thousands of new farms would be created. The year 1862 also saw the creation of the Department of Agriculture, which distributed new types of seeds and circulated scientific informa-tion to farmers.

The government also finally made a move, after years of debate and discussion, to connect the West and East by railroad. Lincoln signed the authorizing legislation on July 1, 1862. The builders of the transcontinental railway were awarded more than twenty-five acres of public land for every mile of track they laid. Government bonds were also issued to these companies to help finance their con-struction. In short, the transcontinental railroad was built with mas-sive federal subsidies.

In 1862, Congress also stepped into the area of education with the passage of the Morrill Act, which financed a new string of land-grant universities with gifts of land—thirty thousand acres of federal land to each state for each representative in Congress (making the grants roughly proportional to population). The land could then be sold to pay for creating the universities. The main purpose of the universities was to promote practical education in agriculture and industry. More than seventeen million acres of land were distributed, a total of more than $7 million in value. A previous version of the law had been ve-toed by President James Buchanan, a Democrat who argued that the

law exceeded Congress's enumerated powers and invaded the constitutional prerogatives of the states. Institutions such as Cornell and
Rutgers as well as the Universities of Illinois, Michigan, Minnesota,
and California, among others, were supported by this initiative.

Another innovation was the creation of the federal income tax as
one provision of an 1862 law that was the longest, most detailed
statute passed by Congress till that point. The tax applied to all in-
comes over $300 per year, later raised to $600. The latter figure was
about the average income of urban workers, so most people did not
have to pay the 3 percent tax. More money was actually raised from a
massive excise tax that applied to the manufacturers and sellers of a
huge range of goods and services, from agriculture to the professions.

The railroad system was crucial to the war effort, because it allowed troops and supplies to be quickly moved around the country.
Lincoln obtained legislation authorizing him to take control of the
railroads. The law gave Lincoln so much bargaining leverage that he
never actually had to take formal control. When he and other officials
met with railroad executives to discuss the need to standardize operations and keep rates low, a casual chat about the government's power
was enough to make sure that the railroads got the message.

The creation of the Civil War pension system was another notable
accomplishment of the Lincoln administration. Pensions were originally granted to disabled veterans and the widows and children of war
casualties, but the system gradually expanded over the next forty years
until it provided retirement and survivor's benefits as well. At its peak,
the Civil War pension system was the largest department of government, accounting for nearly half the federal budget. (The last Union
veteran receiving a pension died in 1956, and, as late as April of 2012,
there were still two children of Civil War veterans who were receiving
pensions, according to press reports.) Modern historians see the Civil
War pensions system as providing an important precedent for FDR's
Social Security system.

This is a remarkable list of presidential achievements: a national
banking system, paper currency, the Homestead Act, the Department
of Agriculture, land-grant universities, the transcontinental railroad,

improved railroad operations, and a massive pension system. The early years of Lincoln's presidency were equaled only by the first years of the republic and the New Deal era in terms of important new legislation passed. That Lincoln-era legislation set the stage for further expansion of federal powers under Teddy Roosevelt, Woodrow Wilson, FDR, and later presidents. Clearly, during the Lincoln administration, the government turned decisively away from the small-government vision that Jefferson and his followers had embraced.

Lincoln and FDR could not have been more different in personality. No one would be likely to call FDR "brooding" or Lincoln "jaunty." They lived in very different times, in Americas with very different needs. Their personal philosophies were shaped by their own lives and eras. But they both stood for a strong federal government that would act decisively to strengthen the national economy.

LINCOLN'S WORDS

From a Speech on the Dred Scott Decision at Springfield, Illinois (1857)

Lincoln explains how All Men Are Created Equal"

Chief Justice Taney, in his opinion in the Dred Scott case, admits that the language of the Declaration is broad enough to include the whole human family, but he and Judge Douglas argue that the authors of that instrument did not intend to include negroes, by the fact that they did not at once, actually place them on an equality with the whites. Now this grave argument comes to just nothing at all, by the other fact, that they did not at once, or ever afterwards, actually place all white people on an equality with one or another. And this is the staple argument of both the Chief Justice and the Senator, for doing this obvious violence to the plain unmistakable language of the Declaration. I think the authors of that notable instrument intended to include all men, but they did not intend to declare all men equal in all respects. They did not mean to say all were equal in color, size, intellect, moral developments, or social capacity. They defined with tolerable distinctness, in what respects they did consider all men created equal—equal in "certain inalienable rights, among which are life, liberty, and the pursuit of happiness." This they said, and this meant. They did not mean to assert the obvious untruth, that all were then actually enjoying that equality, nor yet, that they were about to confer it immediately upon them. In fact they had no power to confer such a boon. They meant simply to declare the right, so that the enforcement of it might follow as fast as circumstances should permit. They meant to set up a standard maxim for free society, which should be familiar to all, and revered by all; constantly looked to, constantly labored for, and even though never perfectly attained, constantly approximated, and thereby constantly spreading and deepening its influence, and augmenting the happiness and value of life to all people of all colors everywhere. The assertion that "all men are created equal" was of no practical use in effecting our separation from Great Britain; and it was placed in the Declaration, nor for that, but for future use. Its authors meant it to be, thank God, it is now proving itself, a stumbling block to those who in after times might seek to turn a free people back into the hateful paths of despotism. They knew the proneness of prosperity to breed tyrants, and they meant when such should re-appear in this fair land and commence their vocation they should find left for them at least one hard nut to crack.

June 26, 1857

THE LINCOLN FAMILY.

Currier and Ives print of Lincoln with his wife, Mary, and their sons, Robert and Tad (1867). *Library of Congress*

"THAT THIS MIGHTY SCOURGE OF WAR MAY SPEEDILY PASS AWAY"

Lincoln and the Hiroshima Decision

JAMES TACKACH

James Tackach, a professor of English at Roger Williams University in Bristol, Rhode Island, is the author of Lincoln's Moral Vision: The Second Inaugural Address *(University Press of Mississippi, 2002) and, for young readers,* The Emancipation Proclamation: Abolishing Slavery in the South *(Lucent Books, 1999). He serves as president of the Lincoln Group of Boston.*

My favorite photograph of my father, George Tackach, is a wartime black-and-white snapshot taken on the Pacific island of Okinawa. He is arm in arm with his best army buddy, a man I came to know as "Uncle" Norman. The two young men are shirtless, and their slender bodies suggest that wartime rations constituted a diet that rarely resulted in significant weight gain. George—who was not yet my father—and Norman are smiling, and a sense of relief is visibly etched in their young bodies. There's no need to

101

wonder whether the photo was taken during the Battle of Okinawa, shortly after the battle, or after the armistice ending World War II had been signed. The two soldiers' faces and body language clearly convey the sense that the war was over. Norman wears an almost cocky facial expression; George is grinning widely. They were alive; they were going home; they had won the war.

But just a few weeks earlier, in late July of 1945, a US victory and a safe return home for soldiers like George Tackach and Norman Majesky were far from certain. They had survived the horrendous Battle of Okinawa, during which more than seventy-five hundred US soldiers, sailors, and marines gave their lives, with another forty thousand wounded. And more bloodshed seemed to lie ahead. George and Norman were two of hundreds of thousands of US servicemen awaiting orders for an invasion of Japan planned for the fall of 1945. These war-weary men preparing for the invasion had survived bloody battles in the Pacific Theater—Iwo Jima, Guadalcanal, the Solomon Islands, Okinawa. Men who had survived the fighting in Europe—on Normandy Beach, at Salerno, in the Battle of the Bulge—were being expeditiously shipped to the Pacific after Germany's surrender, in May 1945, to join the attack planned on the Japanese mainland. All in all, a million US soldiers, sailors, marines, and airmen were supposed to carry out the assault. General George C. Marshall was predicting 250,000 American casualties in this invasion, which was to commence on the island of Kyushu in November 1945, with a landing on Honshu—the largest Japanese island, which holds Tokyo—planned for the following March. Some casualty estimates ran much higher than General Marshall's. My father George and "Uncle" Norman had themselves fought in Okinawa in flame-throwing tanks—heavy artillery pieces that could play a vital role in an invasion of Japan.

Some eighty years earlier, in late 1864 and early 1865, President Abraham Lincoln was dealing with a similar endgame to a bloody war that had engulfed his nation. Lincoln had won re-election in November 1864—to a large extent because the tide of the Civil War had turned in favor of the North during the late summer and fall before the election. But Union armies pushing through the South were still incurring heavy casualties as they encountered stubborn Confederate resistance. In his second inaugural address, delivered on March 4, 1865, Lincoln noted that the "progress of our arms" was "reasonably satisfactory and encouraging to all"; he held "high hope for the future" yet offered no prediction when the terrible war would end.[1]

In 1945, eight decades later, President Harry Truman was in a similar situation, sensing victory over the Japanese and an end to a devastating four-year war, yet hardly certain when it would end and how many more lives it would claim. But President Truman had an option for ending his war that President Lincoln lacked eighty years earlier: a powerful new kind of bomb that would revolutionize warfare and ultimately cast its long shadow over world history for generations to come.

Truman, of course, used that weapon. Would Lincoln have done the same had he been in the White House in 1945? To answer that question, we need to examine how both Truman and Lincoln managed the endings of their respective wars.

* * *

In late July 1945, President Truman, having taken office less than four months earlier after the death of Franklin D. Roosevelt, met with Winston Churchill of Great Britain and Joseph Stalin of the USSR in Potsdam, Germany, near Berlin, to discuss war and postwar strategy. On July 26, these three leaders issued a demand for the unconditional surrender of Japan, which meant that, unless Japan capitulated, the plans for the invasion would move forward. For several months, US planes had been firebombing the Japanese mainland, hoping that the devastation might bring the Japanese emperor, Hirohito, to the peace table, negating the need for the invasion. One air attack on Tokyo, in March 1945, killed one hundred thousand Japanese civilians; another in May completely leveled a five-square-mile section of that city. Still Emperor Hirohito and his war cabinet remained unwilling to surrender, and the Japanese army continued to fight.

By the summer of 1945, however, President Truman knew that he had at his disposal history's most devastating weapon—the atomic bomb. German scientists had discovered uranium fission in December 1938. By the time the United States entered World War II in December 1941, scientists had learned that the energy released by atomic fission could be harnessed in a weapon. Allied leaders believed that German scientists were working on such a weapon, which could bring Germany a swift victory in the European Theater. In 1942, American scientists, including Albert Einstein, convinced President Franklin Roosevelt to establish a team of American researchers to work on creating an atomic bomb. Their effort was named the Manhattan Project. In 1943, a research laboratory, under the direction of Julius Robert Oppenheimer, was established in Los Alamos, New Mexico, to facilitate this work. By early 1945, the weapon was ready. It was successfully tested at Alamogordo, New Mexico, on July 15, 1945, a few weeks after the Japanese surrender of Okinawa.

Two months earlier, in May 1945, having been briefed about the Manhattan Project upon his succession to the presidency, Truman established a committee to discuss the use of the atomic bomb. This committee, headed by Secretary of War Henry Stimson, concluded that the atomic bomb should be used against Japan as soon as possible. Secretary Stimson carried the committee's findings to President Truman. Stimson himself had grave misgivings about using such a destructive weapon, especially if it were to be deployed upon a civilian population center. In his diary entry of May 31, 1945, Stimson wrote that this new atomic weapon might bring about "a revolutionary change in the relations of man to the universe" and might even spell "the doom of civilization," like some Frankenstein monster created in a lab that could wreak havoc when released upon humankind. Nonetheless, in advising President Truman, Stimson asserted that the atomic weapon might provide a needed "shock value" that would force Japan to surrender, thus ending the war. The bomb, in Stimson's view, would actually save thousands of both American and Japanese lives by obviating the need for an invasion of the Japanese homeland.

Stimson's concern for Japanese citizens was legitimate. Civilian populations already had suffered greatly in this war. When the conflict began in Europe in 1939, before US involvement, President Roosevelt had urged the warring nations to avoid civilian deaths as much as possible. But as German armies marched across Europe, they imprisoned millions of conquered people in concentration and death camps. The German Luftwaffe blitzed London, inflicting extensive carnage on civilian population centers. In turn, Allied planes bombed Dresden, Berlin, and other German cities. The firebombing of Dresden, which burned most of the city to the ground, resulted in 135,000 civilian deaths. In the summer of 1945, American pilots were bombing Japanese cities, inflicting heavy civilian casualties. In the invasion of Okinawa, 150,000 civilians perished while the battle raged. An invasion of Japan would likely result in hundreds of thousands of Japanese military and civilian deaths.

Japan was preparing for a fight to the death. In the summer of 1945, the country was already mobilizing for an American invasion, urging citizens—young and old, men and women—to prepare to fight to save the homeland with any weapon at hand: garden and carpentry tools, bamboo sticks sharpened as spears, handguns. The kamikaze tradition conveyed to the Japanese people the idea that death was far superior to surrender, which would bring dishonor to the individual and to the nation. One kamikaze pilot stated, "I see the war situation becoming more desperate. All Japanese must become soldiers and die for the Emperor."

Truman never hesitated in his decision to use the atomic bomb when it became available. He had fought during World War I as captain of an artillery battery in the brutal fighting in the Argonne Forest; thus, he'd experienced and understood firsthand the horrors of combat. He was also painfully aware of the horrific casualty counts in the battles to secure Iwo Jima, Okinawa, and other Pacific islands; an attack on the main islands of Japan could be catastrophic. "I'll say that we'll end the war a year sooner now," Truman wrote in a letter to his wife, Bess, on July 18, 1945, three days after the atom bomb was successfully tested, "and think of the kids who won't be killed! That's the important thing."

According to Truman biographer David McCullough, those kids fighting the battle were "always the important thing" in President Truman's view. In his memoirs, Truman later stated, "The final decision of where and when to use the atomic bomb was up to me. Let there be no mistake about it. I regarded the bomb as a military weapon and never had any doubt that it should be used."

And so it was used. On August 6, 1945, an American B-29 bomber, the *Enola Gay*, dropped an atomic bomb on the Japanese city of Hiroshima. The result was devastating. Eighty thousand Japanese civilians and military personnel were killed instantly; another fifty to sixty thousand would die during the next few months. John Hersey's *Hiroshima*, first published in the *New Yorker* in 1946 and later in book form, vividly depicts what happened on the ground after the *Enola Gay* dropped its payload: first, a noiseless flash; next, a fast-spreading fire. Hersey describes a German missionary priest, Father Wilhelm Kleinsorge, coming upon twenty Japanese soldiers shortly after the bomb fell, "all in exactly the same nightmarish state: their faces were wholly burned, their eyesockets were hollow, the fluid from their melted eyes had run down their cheeks. . . . Their mouths were swollen, pus-covered wounds, which they could not bear to stretch enough to admit the spout of the teapot."

Despite the carnage at Hiroshima, however, the Japanese refused to surrender.

Three days later, another American bomber released a second atomic bomb over the city of Nagasaki with similarly gruesome results. About seventy thousand Nagasaki residents died instantly. As McCullough reports in his biography of Truman, when the bomb hit Nagasaki, the Japanese military command was meeting in a bomb shelter in Tokyo to discuss war plans in light of the Hiroshima bombing three days earlier. Two high-ranking generals and an admiral were arguing against surrender. Japanese war minister General Korechika Anami advocated waiting and preparing for the American invasion of Japan that they knew was coming soon.

But the Japanese had no idea whether the United States had more of these terrible bombs that had just been dropped. (According to McCullough, Truman had only one more immediately ready for use—perhaps on Tokyo.) When the news of the second bomb, on Nagasaki, reached this war council, Emperor Hirohito decided to end the war. Japan's official surrender came on August 14.

US soldiers around the globe were elated. On the island of Okinawa, George Tackach and Norman Majesky, dizzy with joy, headed to a beach for a swim. Perhaps as he plunged into the refreshing water, George, the American-born son of Hungarian immigrants who came to the United States around the turn of the twentieth century, thought about Loretta Rys, a pretty brunette whom he had met in early 1943 at a church dance during his two-week furlough after basic training, before he was sent overseas for tank training and combat. Loretta had graduated from high school in 1942 and had seen many high school classmates go off to war; some would not return. One friend died in the water before reaching Normandy Beach on D-Day. Fulfilling a patriotic duty, Loretta had written letters to George during his service stint; perhaps he could see her when he returned home in a few months. Loretta had just turned twenty-one years old. With the surrender of Japan, George reckoned that he would surely reach his milestone twenty-fifth birthday in October. By then he might be back home, ringing the bell at Loretta's front door. . . .

In the postwar euphoria, few Americans criticized President Truman's decision to drop the bombs. Newspaper editorials did warn of the tremendous power that the Americans had unleashed over Hiroshima and Nagasaki—power that could be used for good or evil purposes. Many sensed that a new, more dangerous kind of warfare had come upon the earth. But the overwhelming sentiment among Americans was relief that the war was over and jubilation over the fact that the United States, and not one of the Axis powers, had been the first to develop the bomb.

In the decades that followed, however, a serious debate over Truman's decision ensued. Particularly troubling for many was the huge number of civilian deaths caused by the assaults on Hiroshima and Nagasaki. The economist John Kenneth Galbraith—who worked in the Office of Price Administration in Washington during the war, and after the war as director of the US Strategic Bombing Survey—visited Hiroshima and other sites where extensive bombing had taken place, claimed that an invasion of Japan would not have been militarily necessary: that a Japanese surrender would have come in a matter of a few weeks if the bombs were not dropped, sparing the lives of thousands of Japanese civilians. To this day, millions of people in the United States and around the world are troubled by the reflection that the United States is the only nation in history to have employed the ultimate weapon of mass destruction.

On the other hand, Paul Fussell, who has written eloquently about war in *The Great War and Modern Memory* and other books, offers this rebuttal to Galbraith and other critics of Truman's decision in his essay "Thank God for the Atom Bomb": "'Two or three weeks,' says Galbraith. Two weeks means 14,000 more [Americans] killed and wounded, three weeks more, 21,000." Later in his essay, Fussell, who had been wounded in action in Europe and was on his way to the Pacific when the atom bombs fell, asks, "Why delay and allow one more American high school kid to see his own intestines blown out of his body and spread before him in the dirt while he screams and screams when with the new bomb we can end the whole thing just like that?"

In the same vein, McCullough rhetorically asks, "And how could a President, or the others charged with the responsibility for the decision, answer to the American people if when the war was over, after the bloodbath of an invasion of Japan, it became known that a weapon sufficient to end the war had been available by midsummer and was not used?" McCullough points out that, had the atomic bomb been ready for use in March 1945, fifty thousand American lives lost in Pacific battles would have been saved, "not to say a vastly larger number of Japanese lives."

Truman himself never second-guessed his decision to use the atom bombs. Writing to Senator Richard B. Russell of Georgia after the second bomb was dropped, Truman stated, "My object is to save as many American lives as possible but I also have a human feeling for the women and children of Japan." A few months after the war ended, he remarked that "a quarter of a million of the flower of our young manhood were worth a couple of Japanese cities, and I still think they were and are."

* * *

Harry Truman and Abraham Lincoln had much in common. Both were midwesterners who had risen from humble beginnings to high office despite their lack of formal education. Both favored plain speech over high rhetoric. Both entered political life in times of national crisis—Lincoln with the "house divided" and Truman during the Great Depression. Both had presidencies marked by devastating wars. Lincoln was born in Kentucky, a slave state, and Truman in Missouri, a former slave state, yet both, as presidents, pushed civil rights initiatives: Lincoln was largely responsible for freeing American slaves, and he opened the United States Army and Navy to African American recruits, while Truman desegregated the American armed forces after World War II.

Had he been president during the early 1940s, Lincoln would surely have supported scientific research on atomic fission. Originally a member of the Whig Party, Lincoln shared the Whigs' strong advocacy of federal government support for so-called internal improvements—the building of canals, bridges, railroads, highways, telegraph networks, and other infrastructure—that might augment American trade and facilitate communication and connection throughout a rapidly expanding country. Lincoln also had a keen interest in new inventions and scientific discoveries. In February 1859, he delivered the Lecture on Discoveries and Inventions in Jacksonville, Illinois. In that speech, Lincoln highlighted the significance of key inventions of his lifetime—the steamboat, the passenger railroad, and the telegraph. "All nature—the whole world, material, oral, and intellectual,—is a mine; and, in Adam's day, it was a wholly unexplored mine," he stated. "Now, it was the destined work of Adam's race to develope, by discoveries, inventions, and improvements, the hidden treasures of this mine." Lincoln himself remains the only US president to secure a patent. Everything we know about his personality, interests, and attitudes suggests that Lincoln would certainly have lobbied Congress to fund the Office of Scientific Research and Development, established in 1941, the umbrella organization that oversaw the work of the Manhattan Project.

Lincoln also had a keen interest in new weaponry. During his presidency, he often received visits from gun and munitions makers who claimed to have developed more powerful and more efficient weapons. *The Collected Works of Abraham Lincoln* includes several letters written by Lincoln addressed to his secretary of war or military commanders urging them to review and test this or that new weapon that had come to his attention—cannons, breach-loading rifles, balls and shells, powder, even a submarine. He reportedly tested some of these weapons himself before sending them along to military commanders for more rigorous evaluation. So it's easy to picture Lincoln reading the periodic reports coming from the scientists involved with the Manhattan Project with keen personal interest.

As president, Lincoln waged a war even more devastating than the one later waged by Presidents Roosevelt and Truman. In his second inaugural address, he referred to it as "this mighty scourge of war," explicitly likening it to an instrument of torture, and before it was over the Civil War would claim the lives of more than six hundred thousand Americans, North and South. As Lincoln stated in the second inaugural, "Neither party expected for the war, the magnitude, or the duration, which it has already attained." But the war came, and Lincoln executed it to its bloody conclusion, repeatedly and unwaveringly rejecting the option of ending the killing by recognizing the Confederacy as an independent nation. He was willing to shed vast quantities of blood so that his nation—and its fragile democratic form of government—would remain intact.

So Lincoln was no pacifist. He waged war when he felt it was unavoidable and that the cause was just. But would Lincoln, sitting in President Truman's White House, have ordered the implementation of a devastating new weapon that would kill not only enemy soldiers but large numbers of civilians? Would Lincoln have made the same military and moral choice that Truman made?

Certainly we consider Lincoln a great humanitarian and a man of great moral vision. His sensitivity to human suffering exceeded that of many of his contemporaries. Early in life, for example, Lincoln developed a genuine sympathy for Americans held in bondage—an attitude that many of his white compatriots did not share. One of the most quoted passages from the Lincoln canon is a description, in an 1841 letter to a friend, of slaves whom he had seen while traveling aboard a Mississippi River steamboat:

> A gentleman had purchased twelve negroes in different parts of Kentucky and was taking them to a farm in the South. They were chained six and six together. A small iron clevis was around the left wrist of each, and this fastened to the main chain by a shorter one at a convenient distance from, the others; so that the negroes were strung together precisely like so many fish upon a trot-line. In this condition

they were being separated forever from the scenes of their childhood, their friends, their fathers and mothers, and brothers and sisters, from their wives and children, and going into perpetual slavery where the lash of the master is proverbially more ruthless and unrelenting than any other where.

As president, Lincoln acted on this strongly felt moral attitude. Acting very deliberately, he freed most American slaves when he issued the Emancipation Proclamation on January 1, 1863, and (as dramatized in Steven Spielberg's 2012 film *Lincoln*) he used his political skills and personal power to promote passage of the Thirteenth Amendment to the United States Constitution, which eventually freed all American slaves.

President Lincoln also showed an unusual degree of sympathy and sense of justice in his dealings with Native Americans. In October and November of 1862, a Sioux uprising took place in the Minnesota Territory that claimed the lives of more than three hundred white settlers. The uprising was eventually put down by federal troops, and three hundred members of the Sioux tribe were held in captivity, about to be executed for their actions. At a time when few white Americans considered the plight of Native Americans and most would have applauded the Sioux' sentence, Lincoln ordered a halt to the executions. He reviewed the case of each individual Sioux warrior and identified only thirty-nine for capital punishment. Later explaining his actions to a questioning US Senate, Lincoln reserved the death sentence for those "who were proven to have participated in *massacres*, as distinguished from participation in *battles*." Lincoln reasoned that Sioux warriors who fought federal troops were engaged in war, not in a crime worthy of execution; these warriors could be held as prisoners of war but could not be put to death. In April 1862, receiving a report from a missionary to the Sioux that the members of the tribe serving time in a federal penitentiary for their actions during this uprising would be peaceful if released, Lincoln pardoned twenty-five Sioux prisoners and ordered them "to be sent to their families or relatives."

Of course, Lincoln was especially sympathetic to the Union soldiers fighting the war and to their parents, wives, and children. Throughout

the course of the war, dozens of appeals on behalf of Union soldiers sentenced to die for desertion came across his desk. In almost every case,
Lincoln issued a stay of execution or a pardon. After reviewing the cases
of several fifteen-, sixteen-, and seventeen-year-old boys who had deserted the Union ranks and were marked for execution, Lincoln issued
an executive order in the form of a letter to General George Meade,
commander of the Army of the Potomac: "I am appealed to in behalf of
August Blittersdorf, at Mitchells Station, Va. to be shot to-morrow as a
deserter. I am unwilling for any boy under eighteen to be shot; and his
father affirms that he is yet under sixteen." Lincoln did not consider it a
capital crime for a teenage drummer boy who became scared during an
engagement to flee the battlefield.

   One of Lincoln's most striking humanitarian gestures toward Union
soldiers concerned African American troops. After the battle of Fort Pillow in May 1864, during which two hundred African Americans were
killed in combat or executed after the battle, Mrs. Lionel Booth, widow
of the slain white Union commander at Fort Pillow, appealed to Lincoln on behalf of the widows of the soldiers who were killed. At the
time, Congress was debating a widows' pension bill that would provide
funds for the families of Union soldiers who died during the war. Mrs.
Booth was concerned about the wives of those "colored" troops who
might not be able to produce a valid marriage license or other proof of
marriage that would be required for them to receive a pension. Some of
the African American soldiers who fell at Fort Pillow were former slaves
who had lived on plantations with wives and escaped from slavery with
their families, but they never went through any formal marriage ceremony or registered their marriages with state or local government. Lincoln at once understood and sympathized with the circumstances of
these widows. In a letter to Senator Charles Sumner of Massachusetts,
then perhaps the leading advocate of civil rights in the US Senate, on
May 19, 1864, Lincoln wrote:

> The bearer of this is the widow of Major Booth, who fell at Fort-
> Pillow. She makes a point, which I think very worthy of consideration
> which is, widows and children *in fact*, of colored soldiers, who fall in
> our service, be placed in law, that same as if their marriages were legal,

so that they can have the benefit of the provisions made the widows &
orphans of white soldiers. Please see & hear Mrs. Booth.

When Congress passed a widows' pension bill in July 1864, it contained
provisions for the widows of African American soldiers.

By 1864, the war was making thousands of widows every month.
The tide had turned in favor of the Union during the summer of 1863,
with Union victories at Vicksburg and Gettysburg, but the Confederates fought hard as Union troops penetrated the South. In several weeks
of bitter fighting in the late spring and early summer of 1864, the
Union army suffered nearly one hundred thousand casualties; in one
bloody morning of fighting in early June at Cold Harbor, Virginia, almost seven thousand Union soldiers fell. By the summer of 1864, Generals William T. Sherman and Ulysses S. Grant were hitting
Confederate armies hard, inflicting massive casualties, but the Union
armies were also losing men by the thousands. Army hospitals in Washington and elsewhere were filling up, and public support for the war
was waning.

The bloodshed took a personal toll on Lincoln. In his book *Lincoln's
Last Months*, William C. Harris presents Lincoln as "care worn and haggard" as the Union casualties pile up. Biographers depict Lincoln at this
time as being depressed, often sleepless, brooding, wondering whether
all of the killing was worth it and when it might cease. In his prize-
winning *Lincoln*, David Herbert Donald re-creates a scene between Lincoln and Representative Daniel Voorhees of Indiana. "Doesn't it strike
you as queer that I, who couldn't cut the head off a chicken, and who
was sick at the sight of blood, should be cast into the middle of a great
war, with blood flowing all about me?" Lincoln asks.

Lincoln himself had lost two young sons to illness, one while he
served as president, so he sympathized in a very direct way with families
who had lost sons during the war. In a sense, they were all his sons. The
fiction writer Adam Braver, in his collection *Mr. Lincoln's Wars*, realistically depicts Lincoln during this time period as an insomniac shocked
by the tragedy surrounding him. In the novella titled "The Necropsy,"
Braver creates a conversation between Lincoln and his old Illinois friend
Orville Browning. "I lay awake all night, Orville," says Lincoln. "And

all these disjointed fragments of my past start weaving in and out. . . . I swear to God, Orville, my life is unraveling before me in a very purposeful manner."

Had Lincoln occupied the White House in the spring and early summer of 1945, the astounding number of deaths in the Pacific would likely have haunted him. Certainly, like Truman, Lincoln would have wanted to accomplish his war goals and end the slaughter of American soldiers as soon as possible. Lincoln's second inaugural address, delivered a month before the Civil War ended, offers a poetic prayer for peace: "Fondly do we hope—fervently do we pray—that this mighty scourge of war may speedily pass away." If Lincoln's secretary of war had reported to him that a weapon was available that might provide a "shock value" that would prompt a speedy Japanese surrender, saving the lives of thousands of American soldiers, Lincoln surely would have listened.

But we have also painted a picture of Lincoln as a humanitarian with great moral vision. Would the potential for scores of thousands of civilian deaths have made Lincoln pause and morally reflect before ordering bombs to be dropped on Hiroshima and Nagasaki? The answer to that question might hinge on how Lincoln came to understand, during the last two years of the Civil War, how modern wars can be won.

In his biography of General Sherman, Lee Kennett notes Winston Churchill's claim that the American Civil War was the last "gentlemen's war." Indeed, in his short book *The American Civil War*, Churchill contrasts the relative civility of the American Civil War with the brutality of the First and Second World Wars. Churchill comments on a truce called between Generals Ulysses S. Grant and Robert E. Lee during the bloody battle of Cold Harbor to permit both sides to bury their dead and care for the wounded. "During the World Wars through which we have lived," writes Churchill, "no such indulgences were allowed." During these so-called gentlemen's wars, the battle was essentially confined to the battlefield, and the combatants strove to avoid civilian casualties and wholesale destruction of population centers.

Perhaps the American Civil War began that way. At the First Battle of Bull Run, civilian spectators in horse and buggy, sporting the latest Victorian-era clothing styles, came out to see the action. But, early in the Civil War, it became obvious that the battles in this conflict would not resemble some summer picnic or outdoor sporting event; this conflict would turn into a total war that would produce civilian casualties and cause great damage to population centers and infrastructure.

One of the first military commanders to sense that the Civil War was no gentlemen's war was Union general William Tecumseh Sherman. When the war began, in the early battles in which he participated, Sherman, an 1840 graduate of West Point, ordered his men to restrain themselves from damaging Southern property and harming civilians; indeed, he punished soldiers accused of looting, pillaging, or setting fires to civilian buildings. But, as the war progressed, Sherman began to see it differently. As his armies moved across the Southern landscape, eastward from Mississippi, he realized the difficulty of keeping his supply lines intact; hence, his soldiers began to live off the land, consuming produce and confiscating and killing livestock; he once boasted that his men were eating large sections of Tennessee. On the march, Sherman's troops were constantly harassed by what he called guerrilla fighters—Southern civilians who organized themselves into paramilitary groups to attack the Union invaders. For Sherman, the distinction between civilian and soldier began to blur as the war continued. On August 11, 1862, Sherman, a very direct speaker and writer, penned a letter to Salmon P. Chase, secretary of the treasury, explaining his newly formed theory of war:

> I will write plainly and slowly, because I know you have no time to listen to trifles. This is no trifle; when one nation is at war with another, all the people of the one are enemies of the other; then the rules are plain and easy of understanding. Most unfortunately, the war in which we are now engaged has been complicated with the belief on the one hand that all on the other side are *not* enemies. It would have been better if, at the outset, this mistake had not been made, and it is wrong longer to be misled by it. The Government of the United States may now safely proceed on the proper rule that all in the South *are* enemies of all in the North; and not only are they unfriendly, but all who can now procure arms now bear them as organized regiments, or as guerrillas.

As Sherman's army moved eastward through the South after the Union victory at Vicksburg, his troops tore up railroad lines, destroyed mills and warehouses, and cut telegraph lines; he made the local populations suffer "this mighty scourge of war." Writing to Union general Henry Halleck in 1864 as his army approached Atlanta, Sherman stated, "If the people raise a howl against my barbarity and cruelty, I will answer that war is war, and not popularity-seeking. If they want peace, they and their relatives must stop the war."

Sherman's army marched into Atlanta on September 2, 1864. In short order, Sherman ordered every civilian out of the city. When the mayor of Atlanta, James M. Calhoun, protested in a letter to Sherman, the general curtly replied, "You cannot qualify war in harsher terms than I will. War is cruelty, and you cannot refine it; and those who brought war into our country deserve all the curses and maledictions a people can pour out." When the civilians evacuated Atlanta, Sherman's troops burned large sections of the city. After subduing Atlanta, he wrote to his superior officer, General Ulysses S. Grant, proposing to "march across Georgia to Savannah or Charleston, breaking roads and doing irreparable damage." In another message to Grant, Sherman stated that "the utter destruction of its [Georgia's] roads, houses, and people, will cripple their military resources. I can make this march [across Georgia], and make Georgia howl!" He made good on his promise as he engineered his now famous March to the Sea. When Sherman's men captured Columbia, South Carolina, in February 1865, they also burned that city.

Writing to General Halleck in December 1864, Sherman stated that "this war differs from European wars in this particular: we are not only fighting hostile armies, but a hostile people, and must make old and young, rich and poor, feel the hard hand of war, as well as their organized armies." Southern newspapers likened Sherman to Attila the Hun and the barbarians who invaded ancient Rome. But the Confederates, too, did extensive damage to population centers and did not always spare civilians. On August 25, 1863, Captain William Clarke Quantrill invaded Lawrence, Kansas, with his cavalry and burned the town, then ordered the killing of every male resident. Men and boys of all ages were summarily executed.

Lincoln condemned the Lawrence invaders as murderers, and he took measures to make certain that Union soldiers not, in turn, retaliate against Southern civilians. Still, he clearly began to understand and accept Sherman's strategy of total war: not merely defeating Confederate armies but making the entire South suffer during the conflict. According to Lincoln biographer Ronald C. White, "Lincoln understood this aggressive military destruction as necessary to end the Confederacy's resistance." Documents in Lincoln's *Collected Works* indicate that he approved of Sherman's tactics. When Sherman captured Atlanta, Lincoln ordered hundred-gun salutes in Washington, New York, Boston, Philadelphia, and other major cities. In his annual message to Congress, delivered on December 6, 1864, Lincoln stated, "The most remarkable feature in the military operations of the year is General Sherman's attempted march of three hundred miles directly through the insurgent region." On December 26, 1864, Lincoln wrote to Sherman, "Many, many thanks for your Christmas-gift—the capture of Savannah."

One of the tragedies of modern warfare is that wars can rarely be won by merely defeating opposing armies on the battlefield. Modern wars are often won by inflicting heavy damage on the enemy's infrastructure and civilian population. No nation, no matter how determined its armies, can continue the fight if its cities are being leveled and its civilians slaughtered. Sherman, and probably Lincoln, grasped this horrific truth about modern war. In his memoirs after the war, Sherman asserted, "My aim then was, to whip the rebels, to humble their pride, to follow them to their inmost recesses, and make them fear and dread us."

By the time of World War II, this new reality of war had been generally accepted by military strategists. From 1944 through early 1945, Allied troops relentlessly attacked German armies, forcing them back to Germany, but Germany finally capitulated only after bombs fell on Dresden and other cities. Similarly, United States armies defeated Japanese armies on the Pacific islands, but victory came only after Hiroshima and Nagasaki were bombed. Lincoln was probably realizing that grim truth about modern war as he marked Sherman's march through the South in 1864 and 1865.

So if Lincoln had occupied the White House in 1945—if he had lived through the devastation wrought by World War I and found himself as commander in chief during this second, even more terrible world war—he certainly would have seriously considered speedily ending this terrible scourge of war with the use of one dreadful weapon. Haggard and war torn, the casualties weighing on him personally, Lincoln, perhaps more reluctantly than Truman, would have ordered those bombs dropped on Hiroshima and Nagasaki. Perhaps he would have carried the burden of the decision with greater apparent suffering than Truman evinced—but surely his decision would have been the same.

And like Truman, Lincoln would have ended this hard war with a soft peace. In Europe and Japan, Truman and his postwar management team implemented a nonretaliatory posture toward their former enemies: they launched the Marshall Plan to rebuild those European nations, friends and foes, and sent an army of occupation to spearhead a rebuilding program in Japan. Surely Truman's program reflected the same spirit Lincoln evoked in his second inaugural, when he promised a month before the war's end "malice toward none"; "charity for all"; and a sincere effort "to bind up the nation's wounds; to care for him who shall have borne the battle, and for his widow, and his orphan—to do all which may achieve and cherish a just, and a lasting peace, among ourselves, and with all nations."

It seems clear that Lincoln would have sent George Tackach home from Okinawa to enjoy that postwar peace. Like Truman, Lincoln would have given George the opportunity to court, to fall in love with, and, in 1948, to marry Loretta Rys. He would have given them the chance to raise two sons, George Jr., born in 1950, and James, born in 1953. George was honorably discharged from the US Army in January 1946, and he lived another thirty-nine years. Harry Truman, whom my father believed gave him those thirty-nine years, remained his favorite US President.

During the spring and summer of 1842, Lincoln exchanged a few letters with his good friend Joshua F. Speed. Speed was engaged to a woman named Fanny but was having second thoughts about the upcoming marriage. Lincoln advised his friend to stay the course; and after the wedding, and a few months of marital bliss, Speed wrote to Lincoln expressing thanks for his advice. Lincoln responded:

I am much pleased with that acknowledgement; but a thousand times more am I pleased to know, that you enjoy a degree of happiness, worthy of an acknowledgement. The truth is, I am not sure there was any merit, with me, in the part I took in your difficulty; I was drawn to it as by fate; if I would, I could not have done less than I did. I always was superstitious; and as part of my superstition, I believe God made me one of the instruments of bringing your Fanny and you together, which union, I have no doubt He had fore-ordained.

By dropping the bombs on Hiroshima and Nagasaki, Harry Truman became an instrument for bringing George Tackach and Loretta Rys together—one tiny, unforeseeable consequence among the millions of outcomes, good and bad, thrown off by the cataclysm of war. Abraham Lincoln would likely have done the same.

LINCOLN'S WORDS

From a Speech at Edwardsville, Illinois (1858)

Lincoln explains the difference between
Republicans and Democrats

I have been requested to give a concise statement of the difference, as I understand it, between the Democratic and Republican parties, on the leading issues of the campaign. This question has been put to me by a gentleman whom I do not know. I do not even know whether he is a friend of mine or a supporter of Judge Douglas in this contest, nor does that make any difference. His question is a proper one. Lest I should forget it, I will give you my answer before proceeding with the line of argument I have marked out for this discussion.

The difference between the Republican and the Democratic parties on the leading issues of this contest, as I understand it, is that the former consider slavery a moral, social and political wrong, while the latter do not consider it either a moral, a social or a political wrong; and the action of each, as respects the growth of the country and the expansion of our population, is squared to meet these views. I will not affirm that the Democratic party consider slavery morally, socially and politically right, though their tendency to that view has, in my opinion, been constant and unmistakable for the past five years. I prefer to take, as the accepted maxim of the party, the idea put forth by Judge Douglas, that he "don't care whether slavery is voted down or voted up." I am quite willing to believe that many Democrats would prefer that slavery should be always voted down, and I know that some prefer that it be always voted up; but I have a right to insist that their action, especially if it be their constant action, shall determine their ideas and preferences on this subject. Every measure of the Democratic party of late years, bearing directly or indirectly on the slavery question, has corresponded with this notion of utter indifference whether slavery or freedom shall outrun in the race of empire across to the Pacific—every measure, I say, up to the Dred Scott decision, where, it seems to me, the idea is boldly suggested that slavery is better than freedom. The Republican party, on the contrary, hold that this government was instituted to secure the blessings of freedom, and that slavery is an unqualified evil to the negro, to the white man, to the soil, and to the State. Regarding it as an evil, they will not molest it in the States where it exists, they will not overlook the constitutional guards which our fathers placed around it; they will do nothing that can give proper offence to those who hold slaves by legal sanction; but they will use every constitutional method to prevent the evil from becoming larger and involving more negroes, more white men, more soil, and more States in its deplorable consequences. They will, if possible, place it where the public mind shall rest in the belief that it is in course of ultimate peaceable extinction in God's own good time. And to this end they will, if possible, restore the government to the policy of the fathers, the policy of preserving the new Territories from the baneful influence of human bondage, as the Northwestern Territories were sought to be preserved by the Ordinance of 1787, and the Compromise Act of 1820. They will oppose, in all its length and breadth, the modern Democratic idea, that slavery is as good as freedom, and ought to have room for expansion all over the continent, if people can be found to carry it. All, or nearly all, of Judge Douglas's arguments are logical, if you admit that slavery is as good and as right as freedom, and not one of them is worth a rush if you deny it. This is the difference, as I understand it, between the Republican and Democratic parties.

September 11, 1858

Lincoln on the battlefield at Antietam,
photographed by Alexander Gardner (October 2, 1862).
Library of Congress

AT THE END OF TWO WARS

1865 and 1945, Lincoln and Roosevelt

Allen C. Guelzo

Allen C. Guelzo is the Henry R. Luce Professor of the Civil War Era at Gettysburg College, where he also directs the Civil War Era Studies Program and the Gettysburg Semester. He is the author of Abraham Lincoln: Redeemer President *(1999 and* Lincoln's Emancipation Proclamation: The End of Slavery in America *(2004), both of which won the Lincoln Prize. He has written essays and reviews for the* Washington Post, *the* Wall Street Journal, Time, *the* Journal of American History, *and many other publications.*

On the 12th of February, 1945, the three heads of the Allied powers—Franklin D. Roosevelt, Winston Churchill, and Joseph Stalin—released a communiqué, summing up the results of their conference at Yalta and laying out the blueprint they had agreed to for the postwar settlement of the world. That blueprint included the unconditional surrender of Nazi Germany, a call for "a conference of United Nations . . . to meet at San Francisco in the United States on April 25, 1945," and the "establishment of order in Europe and the rebuilding of national economic life." For the first time since the Congress of Berlin in 1878, the greatest nations were coming together to sketch the outlines of a new world order. That order would last virtually intact for the next forty-six years, and still largely frames the world we live in today.

The 12th of February also happened to be the birthday of Abraham Lincoln, and Franklin Roosevelt had a word to say on that subject, too. "The living memory of Abraham Lincoln is now honored and cherished by all of our people, wherever they may be," Roosevelt said. Indeed, Lincoln was loved not by Americans only but "by men and women and children throughout the British Commonwealth, and the Soviet Union, and the Republic of China, and in every land on earth where people love freedom."

This statement was not merely an extravagant exaggeration prompted by an anniversary: as a wartime president, Roosevelt lost few opportunities to connect the dots between his and Lincoln's wartime presidency. He introduced the Atlantic Charter with an allusion to Lincoln, and when reporters asked him what he might suggest as a headline, Roosevelt genially responded: "I'd say, 'President quotes Lincoln'—(laughter)—'and Draws Parallel.'"

Similarly, the acceptance speech he gave after the Democratic National Convention nominated him for an unprecedented fourth term in 1944 closed with an invocation of Lincoln's second inaugural as a guide to the path forward into the postwar world. The new world, Roosevelt declared, must be built out of the rubble of war upon "international conferences and united actions," and on "common understanding and co-operative experience" among nations, "which will be so necessary in the world to come." Only by these means could the free nations of the world secure a "lasting peace among ourselves and with all nations."[1]

However, there were at least a few who wondered out loud whether Lincoln really did provide a workable model for the postwar world. Even as a *New York Times* editorial writer asserted in 1941 that, in general, Lincoln "would recognize Hitler and Hitlerism as enemies of every ideal toward which he strove and every truth he cherished," he also conceded that Americans in 1941 "have no right to say that if [Lincoln] were alive now he would support this or that course of action or this or that party." And for anyone who reflected deeply on Lincoln's words and deeds, there was, at numerous points, a struggle to fit the square peg of Lincoln's ideas into the round hole of the new and uncertain future.

After all, Franklin Roosevelt himself had been far more deeply influenced in his development by the "wise counsel" not of Lincoln but of "the great indomitable unquenchable, progressive soul of our Commander-in-Chief, Woodrow Wilson," in whose administration Roosevelt had served as an undersecretary of the navy. Wilson offered a model of what Isaiah Berlin would later call *positive* liberty, which restricts the liberty of some in order to extend liberty to those who had not formerly enjoyed it. Lincoln, on the other hand was a classical nineteenth-century liberal—an exponent of what Berlin called *negative* liberty, which protects individuals from being restricted or impeded by others. As such, Lincoln would have had little interest in laying the foundations for any postwar welfare state, and still less for the *Pax Americana* and the Cold War that Roosevelt himself did not live to see. It is not, in fact, terribly clear that Lincoln would have embraced the transatlantic partnership that developed between Roosevelt and Churchill to defeat Hitler, because Lincoln had never been disposed toward schemes of international intervention and regime change. And, given the reluctance with which Lincoln approached the challenge of dealing with his own domestic rebel leadership once the Civil War was approaching its close, it is not clear either that Lincoln would have been enthusiastic about one of the first manifestations of the new post-1945 era of international cooperation, the Nuremberg trials.

Perhaps, as Lincoln biographer and muck-raking journalist Ida Tarbell warned, "No one can say what Lincoln would have done about unemployment, relief, war debt, prohibition, Manchuria, inflation"—or much else.

* * *

The American economic milieu into which Abraham Lincoln was born in 1809 could not have been more different from the industrial behemoth the United States became by 1945. In the year Lincoln was elected president, corporations represented only 7 percent of the American economy. Most businesses were either sole proprietorships or partnerships and functioned with very small capitalization. In Philadelphia

(which was, with New York, one of the two leading manufacturing centers in the United States), the average size of a manufacturing establishment was only seventeen people. But the forty years that followed
Lincoln's inauguration produced epochal changes in the American
economy. By 1900, corporations represented 66 percent of the national
economy. And *what* corporations they were, too! In 1879, the newly
organized Standard Oil controlled 90 percent of domestic oil production, while, in 1902, US Steel owned 74 percent of all domestic steel
production and manufactured 63 percent of the rails used by American
railroads. US Steel was also very, very well capitalized, at $1.4 billion,
and employed over a hundred thousand workers.

This sea change in the structure of American markets and production also induced a series of social convulsions, reflected by such land-
mark events as the formation of the National Grange in 1867, the
Great Railroad Strike of 1877, the Haymarket Riot in 1886, the
Homestead Strike and the People's Party of 1892, and Coxey's Army
and the Pullman Strike in 1894. The enormous scale of these con-
frontations, and the threat of revolutionary violence that lay behind
them, gave birth to a Progressive movement in American politics that
frankly proclaimed that Americans were no longer living in the age of
the Founders, that the economic environment of their world had
changed, and that Americans must change with it. The Founding Fathers, argued Woodrow Wilson, had lived in a Newtonian era, when
the ideal of government was a precisely balanced machine. "Politics in
their thought was a variety of mechanics. . . . The government was to
exist and move by virtue of the efficacy of 'checks and balances.'" But
"the homely, rural nation" of the revolutionary generation had now
been eclipsed by "a vast and complex urban civilization." An unregu-
lated economy in the new age of the corporation would be too anar-
chistic, too irrational, and too inefficient. The future, said Herbert
Croly, "will have to be planned and constructed rather than fulfilled of
its own momentum." It must become "a workshop in which a purpose
is to be realized." The old hands-off idea of government was proving
rickety and inefficient, and, in its place, Progressives longed for a new
and more direct way of dealing with what John Dewey called "the
problems of men."

Wilson was one of the great shaping influences on Franklin Roosevelt, and that influence was particularly apparent in the outlines Roosevelt sketched in his State of the Union address in 1944 for a new postwar America. "This Republic had its beginning, and grew to its present strength, under the protection of certain inalienable political rights," Roosevelt observed. But "as our Nation has grown in size and stature, however—as our industrial economy expanded—these political rights proved inadequate." What the postwar environment would call for would be "a second Bill of Rights" which would provide for "the right to a useful and remunerative job in the industries or shops or farms or mines of the Nation; the right to earn enough to provide adequate food and clothing and recreation; . . . the right of every family to a decent home; the right to adequate medical care and the opportunity to achieve and enjoy good health; the right to adequate protection from the economic fears of old age, sickness, accident, and unemployment," and "the right to a good education"—all of which would "spell security." And, Roosevelt added, "after this war is won we must be prepared to move forward, in the implementation of these rights, to new goals of human happiness and well-being."

This time, there was no appeal to Lincoln. And with good reason, because Lincoln sat very much on the other side of the great economic divide that separated 1860 from 1944. Adam Smith's *Wealth of Nations*, the great founding document of traditional laissez-faire capitalism, was little more than thirty years old when Lincoln was born, and he remained all his life in the shadow of an economic struggle that cast great metropolitan empires (like Britain) against their colonial peripheries (like America), and pitted an enterprising bourgeoisie against the dead hand of aristocratic landlords. That struggle lent the middle class, with the capitalism they built out of commerce and trade, an enviable reputation as the agents of progress and enlightenment—a reputation they had never before enjoyed and that would soon enough be tarnished by changing circumstances. Merchants "in the Trading World," wrote Joseph Addison in the *Spectator* in 1711, "are what Ambassadors are in the Politick World; they negotiate Affairs, conclude Treaties; and maintain a good correspondence between those wealthy societies of men that are divided from one another by seas and oceans." Capitalist enterprise produced useful men, rather than useless courtiers, "men thriving in their own private fortunes, and at the same time promoting the public stock . . . by bringing into the country whatever is wanting, and carrying out of it whatever is superfluous." In every city, state, or nation where "commerce presented itself" to the people "as their proper object," explained historian William Robertson in 1766, it "opened to them a certain path to wealth and dignity":

> Commerce tends to wear off those prejudices which maintain distinction and animosity between nations. It softens and polishes the manners of men. It unites them, by one of the strongest of all ties, the desire of supplying their mutual wants. It disposes them to peace, by establishing in every state an order of citizens bound by their interest to be the guardians of public tranquility.

Lincoln, whose self-administered reading in political economy included Smith and his disciple John Ramsey McCullough, along with liberal capitalist free marketeers John Stuart Mill and Francis Wayland, could not have agreed more. "We stand at once the wonder and admiration of the whole world," Lincoln said in 1859, and the fundamental reason for this "wonder" was the economic openness of American society. The chief spring "that has given us so much prosperity," Lincoln noted, is "that every man can make himself." Unfettered markets allowed working men to sell their labor freely, allowed employers to hire it, and guaranteed the increase of self-improvement and self-transformation to everyone, and not just a favored elite, whether that elite be "of the British aristocratic sort, or of the domestic slavery sort." Free labor is "the just and generous, and prosperous system, which opens the way for all—gives hope to all, and energy, and progress, and improvement of condition to all."

According to this vision, the task of government in the nation's economy was to clear the field and set the boundaries, although in clearing the field it was allowed to create whatever tilt would best induce prosperity. "The legitimate object of government, is to do for a community of people, whatever they need to have done, but cannot do, at all, or cannot, so well do, for themselves—in their separate, and individual capacities," Lincoln wrote in 1854. This aligned him, from the beginning of his political stirrings in the mid-1830s, with the great Kentucky senator Henry Clay, the founder of the Whig Party (to which Lincoln belonged until its demise in 1856) and the author of the "American System," which envisioned a program of government interventions in the economy to promote growth and expansion. Each of the principal elements of Clay's American System—a national bank, government funding of infrastructure (or "internal improvements"), and tariffs to protect American manufacturing—were endorsed by Lincoln throughout his political career. Tariffs, for instance, would create "a Home demand for the skill and industry of our people . . . and so to foster our manufactures as to make our nation *prosperous* in Peace and *independent* in War."

The Whigs saw themselves as the allies and enablers of "the enterprising mechanic, who raises himself by his ingenious labors from the dust and turmoil of his workshop, to an abode of ease and elegance; the industrious tradesman, whose patient frugality enables him at last to accumulate enough to forego the duties of the counter and indulge a well-earned leisure." And Lincoln was perfectly at home with an economic theory in which

> the prudent, penniless beginner in the world, labors for wages awhile, saves a surplus with which to buy tools or land for himself; then labors on his own account another while, and at length hires another new beginner to help him. This is the just, and generous, and prosperous system, which opens the way to all—gives hope to all, and consequent energy, and progress, and improvement of condition to all.

Although Lincoln abandoned the sinking Whig political ship in 1856 to join the new Republican Party, he (like many other Northern Whigs) merely rolled his economic views over to the Republicans. He did not "believe in a law to prevent a man from getting rich; it would do more harm than good." Far from proposing "any war upon capital," Lincoln wished to "allow the humblest man an equal chance to get rich with everybody else." And if the "humblest man" found that exercising that "equal chance" did not guarantee the production of an equal result—that, in fact, he ran the risk of failure and frustration—Lincoln had no blame for the capitalist system and scant sympathy for the failure. Although it was true that "inequality is certainly never to be embraced for its own sake," every "good thing" is "inseparably connected with some degree of it." Nor is inequality anything but a recognition that some people are more "industrious, and sober, and honest in the pursuit of their own interests" than others. "If any continue through life in the condition of the hired laborer, it is not the fault of the system, but because of either a dependent nature which prefers it, or improvidence, folly, or singular misfortune":

> Some of you will be successful, and such will need but little philosophy to take them home in cheerful spirits; others will be disappointed, and will be in a less happy mood. To such, let it be said, "Lay it not too much to heart." Let them adopt the maxim, "Better luck next time;" and then, by renewed exertion, make that better luck for themselves.

This after all, had been Lincoln's own life story. But in the eyes of Progressives later in the nineteenth century, statements like these made Lincoln appear "strongly conservative and in firm support of vested interests and the conduct of business, unmolested as far as possible, by legislative or any kind of governmental interference." It's hard to imagine a Lincoln in this mold throwing his support behind a Rooseveltian "second Bill of Rights" that placed economic guarantees on the same plane as freedom of speech, press, and religion.

It must be said, too, that Lincoln would surely have proven more resistant than Franklin Roosevelt to American intervention in world conflict, whether in support of "regime change" or a humanitarian "responsibility to protect." Granted, Lincoln neither had to deal with a monomaniac on the order of Hitler nor possessed the technological and military tools required to actually support such interventions. Even so, Lincoln was chary of siding with "every effort of the people to establish free governments, based upon the principles of true religious and civil liberty," no matter how noble or deserving they might be.

This may seem all the more surprising because Lincoln certainly believed in the universality of both human nature and natural rights. Whenever he reflected on "the battle fields and struggles for the liberties of the country" in the American Revolution, he was convinced "that there must have been something more than common that those men struggled for . . . something even more than National Independence; that something that held out a great promise to all the people of the world to all time to come." He could not believe that the sufferings and sacrifices of the revolutionaries were concerned only with "the mere matter of the separation of the colonies from the mother land." There had to be "something in that Declaration giving liberty, not alone to the people of this country, but hope to the world for all future time . . . that in due time the weights should be lifted from the shoulders of all men, and that all should have an equal chance."

In Lincoln's politics, the declaration articulated principles of natural right that were self-evident, and applicable, to everyone. "Perhaps half our people . . . are men who have come from Europe—German, Irish, French and Scandinavian." Coming fresh from Europe, they may not have shared any cultural or historical identity with the American Founders of 1776. But "when they look through that old Declaration of Independence they find that those old men say that 'We hold these truths to be selfevident, that all men are created equal,'" then they feel a universal bond that transcends the trappings of language or tradition and that makes them one in heart and spirit with the American experiment. "They feel that that moral sentiment taught in that day evidences their relation to those men, that it is the father of all moral principle in them, and that they have a right to claim it as though they were blood of the blood, and flesh of the flesh of the men who wrote that Declaration, and so they are." That sense of shared recognition is what trumps nationality, ethnicity, or culture and "links the hearts of patriotic and libertyloving men together, that will link those patriotic hearts as long as the love of freedom exists in the minds of men throughout the world." What began in the American Revolution, then, "is to grow and expand into the universal liberty of mankind."

So Lincoln would have endorsed Roosevelt's assumption that the American yearning for democracy and freedom is, in some sense, universal. But the best expression of that universal solidarity was the movement of those "German, Irish, French and Scandinavian" libertarians to America, not American initiatives to alter their political or social circumstances abroad. For all of Lincoln's universalism about natural rights, he was also very much a nationalist who believed that the American republic was the best expression of a government that honored those rights. Americans had no particular monopoly on understanding the meaning of natural rights, but they also had no reason to seek to export them elsewhere.

Lincoln arrived in Washington in 1847 for his solitary term in the House of Representatives while the Mexican War was still in process, and he attacked American intervention in the affairs of a sister republic as "a war of conquest brought into existence to catch votes." Polk, Lincoln said, could thrash around as he liked, justifying the war on the grounds of "the national honor, the security of the future, the prevention of foreign interference, and even, the good of Mexico herself." But if Mexico was fair game for intervention on those terms today, why not Canada tomorrow? "If . . . he should choose to say he thinks it necessary to invade Canada, to prevent the British from invading us, how could you stop him? You may say to him, 'I see no probability of the British invading us,' but he will say to you 'Be silent; I see it, if you don't.'"

Foreign entanglements became an issue for Lincoln again in 1849, when the Hungarian revolutionary Louis Kossuth was touring America. Lincoln joined in composing a series of resolutions that declared that "in their present glorious struggle for liberty, the Hungarians, command our highest admiration, and have our warmest sympathy." Recognition of an independent Hungary "is due from American freemen, to their struggling brethren" as a recognition of their common dedication "to the general cause of Republican liberty." But the resolutions promptly dialed that endorsement back by adding that "the Government of the United States should acknowledge the Independence of Hungary" only if it is also "consistent with our amicable relations with that Government, against which they are contending" (which in this case was the Austrian empire). And far from welcoming such independence, the Austrian emperor, in league with the czar of Russia, proceeded to put down the Hungarian revolution with singular brutality.

Two and a half years later, Lincoln assisted in drafting another set of Kossuth resolutions, which expansively announced that "we, the American people, cannot remain silent" about the suppression of the Hungarian revolution, "without justifying an inference against our continued devotion to the principles of our free institutions." But passing resolutions was as far as Lincoln was prepared to go in expressing that devotion. Whatever the merits of the Hungarian uprising, "it is the duty of our government to neither foment, nor assist, such revolutions in other governments" or "legally or warrantably interfere abroad, to aid . . . such revolutions." To the contrary, "we should at once announce to the world, our determinations to insist upon . . . nonintervention, as a sacred principle of the international law." In Lincoln's mind, there was no sense of incompatibility between a universalistic concept of democracy and rights and a nationalism willing to single out the United States as "the last, best hope of earth" and God's "almost chosen people."

None of this absolved Lincoln, once he became president, from having to deal with practical political questions involving overseas interventions. The war against the Confederacy forced him to address such issues as the activities of foreign agents abroad, the imposition of a blockade (which ordinarily would have been legal in international law only if it involved two independent nations, whereas Lincoln always maintained that the Confederacy was an insurgency, not a nation), the deployment of British-built Confederate commerce-raiders on the high seas, the attempt at empire building conducted by the French emperor, Napoleon III, in Mexico from 1861 to 1867, and the ever-present possibility that Europe's great powers might intercede to impose binding negotiations on North and South. Lincoln vigorously rebuffed any suggestion that favored international arbitration to settle the Civil War. The Lincoln administration never became a signatory to the first of the great international legal agreements, the 1856 Declaration of Paris, and Lincoln's interaction with the diplomatic corps were remarkably scanty.

Franklin Roosevelt, by contrast, was an early convert to internationalism. In 1920, as the Democratic vice-presidential candidate, Roosevelt was an ardent advocate of the League of Nations and in 1923 designed "A Plan to Preserve World Peace" intended to remedy the defects in the League's charter. In contrast to his predecessor, the hapless Herbert Hoover, Roosevelt committed the United States to the restraint of Japanese expansionism in China in the 1930s and briefly offered in 1938 to act as an arbitrator in the crisis over Czechoslovakia. Once Nazi military might began swallowing France, Belgium, the Netherlands, and Norway whole, he appointed Frank Knox and Henry L. Stimson—both convinced interventionists—as secretary of war and secretary of state in June of 1940.

Roosevelt still had to deal with a recalcitrant and isolationist Congress and a public skeptical of foreign crusades. But he was determined, if necessary, "to improvise a new government within a government" to prepare the United States for the war with Nazi Germany that he was sure must come. "Some of our people like to believe that wars in Europe and in Asia are of no concern to us," Roosevelt said in 1940, and "that we can save our own skins by shutting our eyes to the fate of other nations." This was nonsense: "We must be the great arsenal of democracy." Accordingly, Roosevelt opened up a direct and clandestine correspondence with Winston Churchill on May 15, 1940, shortly after Churchill became prime minister, and began secret joint staff talks between American and British officers in January 1941. By mid-1941, "The United States was no longer neutral in any conventional understanding of the term."

Unlike Lincoln, who could barely be prevailed upon to leave Washington during the Civil War, Roosevelt traveled more extensively outside the United States than any previous president. And, ultimately, Roosevelt was the prime mover in creating "a universal organization" in the United Nations that would be the scaffolding for "a permanent structure of peace" in the world once the Second World War was finished. It would be difficult to imagine Lincoln showing any similar interest. One of his very last remarks to his wife was a wish to visit Jerusalem, as "there was no city on earth he so much desired to see," but this was more in the nature of a personal curiosity rather than a diplomatic ambition.

The single point on which Lincoln was most likely to have differed from the victorious Allies at the close of the Second World War concerned the series of war crimes trials held in Nuremberg and elsewhere to punish the surviving leadership of the Nazi and imperial Japanese governments.

The close of the Second World War was the first occasion in which "war criminals" were brought to trial before an international tribunal. There had been motions of this sort after the First World War, but the United States and the Dutch (who provided asylum for the former German emperor) objected. The Germans themselves held trials in 1921 but convicted only thirteen people and imposed minor sentences. The Allies signaled their intention to pursue Nazi offenders as early as the St. James Declaration of 1942, and by 1943 a list of more than thirty-six thousand names had been assembled for future use. This time, the United States agreed: Roosevelt half joked at Yalta with Stalin, after Stalin proposed executing fifty thousand German leaders, that the Allies might have to settle for forty-nine thousand as a compromise, and Roosevelt's secretary of the treasury, Henry Morgenthau, Jr., seriously proposed a Carthaginian-style settlement for Germany that would reduce the entire nation to rural agriculture. The actual trials, in Nuremburg and in Tokyo, lasted nine months and resulted in the hangings of ten of the defendants (one of them, Hermann Goering, committed suicide; Martin Bormann, who had eluded capture, was condemned in absentia).

The defeated Confederacy in 1865 offered no cast of moral monsters similar to that of the Nazis. But they did have some who approached that level, especially in the cruelty dispensed by two Confederate prison commandants, Henry Wirz at Camp Sumter in Andersonville, Georgia, and David Todd, who was briefly the commandant of Libby Prison in Richmond. (Todd was, ironically, one of Abraham Lincoln's many Todd in-laws.) And there were many Northerners who considered slave-holding itself to constitute enough of a crime to justify treating the South in much the same way as Henry Morgenthau envisioned treating Germany. "In my view, the war has just begun," declared the veteran abolitionist orator Wendell Phillips in 1865. The North, he wrote, must "annihilate" the "social system" built

on slavery and "fill its place with another." "The whole fabric of southern society *must* be changed," pleaded the radical Pennsylvania congressman Thaddeus Stevens, "if the South is ever to be made a safe
Republic let her lands be cultivated by the toil of the owners, or the free
labor of intelligent citizens."

Lincoln's anxieties, however, ran in exactly the opposite direction.
He did not see the war as a crusade by a righteous North against an evil
South: "If it was wrong in the South to hold slaves," Lincoln told his
secretary of state, William H. Seward, "it was wrong of the North to
carry on the slave trade and sell them to the South." And although Lincoln never compromised his insistence on either complete and non-
negotiable reunion under federal authority *or* the emancipation of the
slaves, in the final months of the war Lincoln did make it clear to his
top generals that they might offer whatever terms they thought would
bring about surrender of the Confederate armies as intact bodies, rather
than pressing them so hard that they broke up into innumerable guerrilla bands. They might even offer to recognize the existing rebel state
governments as an inducement to surrender "till Congress could provide others." In February of 1865, Lincoln offered to swap $400 million
in United States bonds if the Confederate states would rejoin the Union
and embrace emancipation *prospectively*, over a period of five years. It
was not uncooperativeness on Lincoln's part but the truculence of the
Confederate leaders that kept this from happening.

Above all, Lincoln wanted no postwar trials, which he believed
would only provide legal martyrdoms for the Confederate leadership.
His hope was that they would simply flee abroad (as many did). When
he was quizzed about arresting one Confederate agent, Jacob Thompson, who had previously held a US cabinet post, Lincoln replied,
"Well, I rather guess not. When you have an elephant on hand, and he
wants to run away, better let him run." In his last cabinet meeting,
Lincoln insisted that "there would be no persecutions, no bloody work
after the war was over." He wanted no part in "hanging or killing" the
rebel generals and politicians, "even the worst of them." If anything, he
"would let down the bars, scare them off," and, to illustrate this, he
waved "his hands as if scaring sheep." In the end, only one war crimes

trial was actually conducted—that of Henry Wirz, the commandant at Andersonville—and that was after Lincoln's death.

Still, Lincoln did make one significant exception to this rule. On August 8, 1860, the United States steam sloop *Mohican* intercepted the slave ship *Erie* off the mouth of the Congo River with almost nine hundred slaves on board—all in violation of international conventions and US laws that made the slave trade a capital offense. The ship's master, Nathaniel Gordon, and his crew were arrested and transported to New York. Considering that New York City allowed more than one hundred slave-trade vessels to operate out of its port in 1860 and that little or nothing was done to punish the captains and crews of American vessels interdicted by British and American naval vessels on the so-called African station, Captain Gordon might have expected little more than a slap on the wrist. But by the time he came to trial in June 1861, Lincoln had become president, and when Gordon was (to the captain's surprise) sentenced to death on November 30, 1861, Lincoln turned aside all appeals for clemency. "There never was a man . . . with such an aversion to bloodshed as I have," Lincoln observed, but he drew the line at the case of "that man who was sentenced for piracy and slave trading on the high seas":

> I believe I am kindly enough in nature and can be moved to pity and to pardon the perpetrator of almost the worst crime that the mind of man can conceive or the arm of man can execute; but any man, who, for paltry gain and stimulated only by avarice, can rob Africa of her children to sell into interminable bondage, I never will pardon, and he may stay and rot in jail before he will ever get relief from me.

Lincoln even refused pleas to commute the sentence to life imprisonment and yielded to only a two-week stay on the grounds that the fruitless appeals "may have prevented the said Nathaniel Gordon from making the necessary preparations for the awful change which awaits him." Otherwise, Gordon was told to dismiss "all expectation of pardon." Gordon was hanged on February 21, 1862, the only execution for the slave trade in American history and the "death blow" to the transatlantic slave trade.

* * *

Lincoln's favorite general, Ulysses S. Grant, once remarked that one of the principle lessons of history is that there may not be many such lessons, or at least, that there might be substantial difficulty in translating the lessons to be learned from one set of historical circumstances to another. "War has responsibilities," Grant said years after the Civil War, "that are either fatal to a commander's position or very successful," adding, "I felt that every war I knew anything about had made laws for itself, and early in our contest I was impressed with the idea that success with us would depend upon our taking advantage of new conditions. No two wars are alike, because they are generally found at different periods, under different phases of civilization."

Perhaps the same practical wisdom should cause us to hesitate in attempting to apply the wisdom of Lincoln to historical challenges from a vastly different set of historical circumstances. Certainly there is much to admire in Lincoln's temperament, resiliency, humor, honesty, and fairness. But those are character traits, not lessons, and there is some debate among the gurus of leadership theory whether those can be studied and absorbed or whether they are peculiar to a certain individual and can only be admired or recognized by others. It's clear that the specific policies that are the hallmarks of Lincoln's presidency—the authorization and funding of a transcontinental railroad, the creation of a national banking system, the privatization of federally owned land through the Homestead Act, protective tariffs—are so tied to the immediate circumstances of the 1860s that it would be hard to know how to copy them for our times or even whether they should be.

Both 1865 and 1945 marked the ends of climactic wars in American history. And it could possibly be said that the pursuit of unconditional surrender and the unquestioned subordination of the US military to civilian authority are two important legacies that tie Civil War and the Second World War together in the American experience. But it is just as true that Abraham Lincoln and Franklin D. Roosevelt represented two vastly different ways of defining the presidency and in two vastly different contexts.

Lincoln was a self-taught lawyer and free-marketeer who was elected in 1860 (as he himself put it) "accidentally," through the splintering of his political opposition and with very little in the way of policy mandates. Franklin Roosevelt was an aristocrat and a Progressive who was driven by the conviction that the evolution of American society had advanced to such a point of complexity and interdependence that social and economic planning was the only way to avoid the chaos of economic depression. Neither Lincoln nor Roosevelt lived to preside over the postwar worlds that followed 1865 and 1945, and there will always be speculation over what might have happened had they lived. One of the most persistently repeated questions I am asked as a historian is what path the Reconstruction era in the South might have followed if Lincoln had dodged John Wilkes Booth's bullet. In Lincoln's absence, the model of reconstruction adopted and applied to the old Confederacy was a clear failure by its end in 1877; it was, nevertheless, a model basically similar to the one that worked spectacularly well in the post-1945 occupation and reconstruction of Germany and Japan—and then backfired again in the attempt to pacify Iraq and Afghanistan sixty years later.

Perhaps, we could say, those rebuilding plans failed in the first instance because Lincoln was no longer in control of the Reconstruction but succeeded in the second because Roosevelt's successors, Harry Truman and the architects of postwar Europe and Asia, were in control. In this case, it was *leadership* that made the difference. Or perhaps, we need to say that the plans failed in one circumstance and succeeded in another because of the *circumstances* themselves—that neither Lincoln nor Roosevelt could have imposed the kind of peace on the Old South that would allow us to call reconstruction a success. On those terms, the identity of the individual who presided over the process—whether Lincoln or Andrew Johnson, Roosevelt or Thomas Dewey—would have been only marginal to the process itself.

There is difficulty enough in recognizing the character of greatness, in 1865 or in 1945, without taking on the deeper difficulty of pasting what may seem to be the lessons of one era onto the blank spaces of another. Perhaps the best lesson is to be grateful that, in 1861 as in 1941, there really was greatness available to guide us.

LINCOLN'S WORDS

From a Speech at New Haven,
Connecticut (1860)

Lincoln as presidential candidate:
"Let us dare to do our duty as we understand it"

It is exceedingly desirable that all parts of this great
Confederacy shall be at peace, and in harmony, one
with another. Let us Republicans do our part to
have it so. Even though much provoked, let us do
nothing through passion and ill temper. Even
though the Southern people will not so much as lis-
ten to us, let us calmly consider their demands, and
yield to them if, in our deliberate view of our duty,
we possibly can. Judging by all they say and do, and
by the subject and nature of their controversy with
us, let us determine, if we can, what will satisfy
them?

Will they be satisfied if the Territories be uncon-
ditionally surrendered to them? We know they will

not. In all their present complaints against us, the Territories are scarcely mentioned. Invasions and insurrections are the rage now. Will it satisfy them if, in the future, we have nothing to do with invasions and insurrections? We know it will not. We so know because we know we never had anything to do with invasions and insurrections; and yet this total abstaining does not exempt us from the charge and the denunciation.

The question recurs, what will satisfy them? Simply this: we must not only let them alone, but we must, somehow, convince them that we do let them alone. [Applause.] This, we know by experience, is no easy task. We have been so trying to convince them, from the very beginning of our organization, but with no success. In all our platforms and speeches, we have constantly protested our purpose to let them alone; but this has had no tendency to convince them. Alike unavailing to convince them is the fact that they have never detected a man of us in any attempt to disturb them.

These natural and apparently adequate means all failing, what will convince them? This, and this only; cease to call slavery *wrong*, and join them in calling it *right*. And this must be done thoroughly—done in *acts* as well as in *words*. Silence will not be tolerated—we must place ourselves avowedly with them. Douglas's new sedition law must be enacted and enforced, suppressing all declarations that Slavery is wrong, whether made in politics, in presses, in pulpits, or in private. We must arrest and return their fugitive slaves with greedy pleasure. We must pull down our Free State Constitutions. The whole atmosphere must be disinfected of all taint of opposition to Slavery, before they will cease to believe that all their troubles proceed from us. So long as we call Slavery wrong, whenever a slave runs away they will overlook the obvious fact that he ran because he was oppressed, and declare he was stolen off. Whenever a master cuts his slaves with the lash, and they cry out under it, he will overlook the obvious fact that the negroes cry out because they are hurt, and insist that they were *put up to it by some rascally abolitionist.* [Great laughter.]

I am quite aware that they do not state their case precisely in this way. Most of them would probably say to us, ``Let us alone, do nothing to us, and say what you please about Slavery." But we do let them alone—have never disturbed them—so that, after all, it is what we say, which dissatisfies them. They will continue to accuse us of doing, until we cease saying.

I am also aware they have not, as yet, in terms, demanded the overthrow of our Free State Constitutions. Yet those Constitutions declare the wrong of Slavery, with more solemn emphasis than do all other sayings against it; and when all these other sayings shall have been silenced, the overthrow of these Constitutions will be demanded, and nothing be left to resist the demand. It is nothing to the contrary, that they do not demand the whole of this just now. Demanding what they do, and for the reason they do, they can voluntarily stop nowhere short of this consummation. Holding as they do, that Slavery is morally right, and socially elevating, they cannot cease to demand a full national recognition of it, as a legal right, and a social blessing.

Nor can we justifiably withhold this, on any ground save our conviction that Slavery is wrong. If Slavery is right, all words, acts, laws, and Constitutions against it, are themselves wrong, and should be silenced, and swept away. If it is right, we cannot justly object to its nationality—its universality; if it is wrong, they cannot justly insist upon its extension—its enlargement. All they ask, we could as readily grant, if they thought it wrong. Their thinking it right, and our thinking it wrong, is the precise fact upon which depends the whole controversy.

Thinking it right as they do, they are not to blame for desiring its full recognition, as being right; but, thinking it wrong, as we do, can we yield to them? Can we cast our votes with their view, and against our own? In view of our moral, social, and political responsibilities, can we do this?

Wrong as we think Slavery is, we can yet afford to let it alone where it is, because that much is due to the necessity arising from its actual presence in the nation; but can we, while our votes will prevent it, allow it to spread into the National Territories, and to overrun us here in these Free States?

If our sense of duty forbids this, then let us stand by our duty, fearlessly and effectively. Let us be diverted by none of those sophistical contrivances wherewith we are so industriously plied and belabored—contrivances such as groping for some middle ground between the right and the wrong, vain as the search for a man who should be neither a living man nor a dead man—such as a policy of "don't care" on a question about which all true men do care—such as Union appeals beseeching true Union men to yield to Disunionists, reversing the divine rule, and calling, not the sinners, but the righteous to repentance—such as invocations of Washington, imploring men to unsay what Washington did.

Neither let us be slandered from our duty by false accusations against us, nor frightened from it by menaces of destruction to the Government, nor of dungeons to ourselves. Let us have faith that right makes might; and in that faith, let us, to the end, dare to do our duty, as we understand it.

March 6, 1860

A contemporary print depicting Lincoln reading the
Emancipation Proclamation to his cabinet, based on a painting by
Francis Bicknell Carpenter (1864). *Library of Congress*

8

ABRAHAM LINCOLN

The President as Outlaw

JAMES MALANOWSKI

James Malanowski has been a writer and editor at Time, Es-
quire, Spy, *and other publications. His lifelong interest in
the Civil War came to fruition in 2010, when he became the
lead writer of the* New York Times' *award-winning* Disunion *series. His articles for* Disunion *were collected in the
book* And the War Came. *Jamie has also written for the*
New Yorker, Vanity Fair, *the* Washington Monthly, *and
many other publications and is the author of the novels* Mr.
Stupid Goes to Washington *and* The Coup.

In American mythology, there are two kinds of heroes: the official
hero and the outlaw hero. The official hero is the cop, the fireman,
the G.I., the teacher, the parent, the builder, the defender. He or
she believes in and supports the community, the system, and the common good. The country was built by official heroes: the Pilgrims who
landed at Plymouth Rock, the Founding Fathers, the hardy western
pioneers.

Yet at the core, however, the official hero is often a rebel or a misfit,
someone who stands in opposition to the norm. The Pilgrims were a

religious minority who sought freedom from official persecution. Before the Founding Fathers established a new nation, they were traitors to their king. As for the pioneers, they were often driven by a yearning for wide-open spaces and the freedom—not to say lawlessness—they promised. Scratch an official hero, and underneath there often lies someone who opposes the established order. An outlaw hero.

The outlaw hero is an outsider, a maverick, a nonconformist who cannot appreciate society without also understanding its shortcomings and failures. Sometimes these heroes are rugged individualists, like Davy Crockett. Sometimes they just can't be hemmed in, like Huck Finn or Holden Caulfield. Some are critics or artists, like Bob Dylan. And some are action heroes, like Batman or Dirty Harry. But most outlaw heroes agree with Dylan when he said, "A hero is someone who understands the degree of responsibility that comes with his freedom," and nearly all of them, facing a conflict between the moral law and the written law, would subscribe to Crockett's famous maxim "be sure that you are right, and then go ahead."

Martin Luther King Jr., arguably the most influential American of the twentieth century, led a movement that fought state-sanctioned segregation, often from jail. He was an outlaw hero, but one driven by deep ethical and religious convictions. Scratch an outlaw hero, and underneath there often lies someone with a powerful sense of morality.

Official hero, outlaw hero—often they are two sides of the same coin. In no case is that more true than that of Abraham Lincoln. Certainly Lincoln is an official hero. He's the figure sitting in the big chair in that temple in Washington, he's one of the giant heads on Mount Rushmore, his face is on our money, and he's the man who scribbled on an envelope the great short speech that generations of schoolchildren have memorized. Hey—he's the man who saved the Union, a conserver, a protector, a father figure par excellence.

Except that Abraham Lincoln didn't save anything. More properly, he transformed it: he entered a broken political system and combatted the crisis of its fracture by seizing powers previously unrecognized in the system. The results were astounding. By the end of the war, the institution of slavery was finished. The rich and powerful class of slaveholders who had dominated the country since its inception was eliminated, the source of their wealth wiped out with the stroke of Lincoln's pen. Black Americans were on the path to full citizenship. And the Union? It was intact as a legal entity, but it was destroyed as a concept. The Civil War made the idea passé. We were no longer states that had entered into a union; instead, we were a country, a nation, led by a president and a central government stronger than it had ever been. And it was Abraham Lincoln who shattered the roadblock of ineffectual laws and dysfunctional politics and inadequate options that had stymied lesser men. Lincoln made sure he was right, then went ahead—and transformed America.

* * *

To understand Lincoln's singular achievement, one first has to understand how dire and dreadful was the situation as he was assuming office. Secession threatened the American union, and (still worse) the potential triumph of a slaveholding aristocracy threatened the very future of democratic government throughout the world. Congress had run out of patchwork solutions as well as the will to enact them. Lincoln did not come into the presidency as a firebrand; the most moderate of the candidates who had sought the Republican nomination, he campaigned against a further expansion of slavery but promised that it would remain untouched where it already existed. Moreover, he had no mandate to make changes; he had won only 40.1 percent of the vote, and his party did not control Congress. But, even though Lincoln was politically weak, the secessionists would not give him a chance to govern, immediately spreading panic about what he *might* do. The day after Lincoln was elected in November 1860—the very next day!—forces in South Carolina began a fevered campaign to take the state out of the Union, an objective they accomplished only seven weeks later. Within another six weeks, six other states joined them. The very few voices in the South that urged people to give Lincoln a chance were shouted down.

The best example of the federal government's inability to deal with this challenge was the man who still stood at its head, President James Buchanan. At sixty-nine, Buchanan was sauntering through the last lap of a career that had given him one of the most distinguished résumés of any man in the history of the young republic: soldier in the War of

1812, congressman, minister to Russia, senator, secretary of state, minister to the court of St. James, and finally the presidency. Alas, Buchanan did little to distinguish himself in any of these posts, and his presidency was defined by a poor economy and the country's slide toward Civil War.

Buchanan made two attempts to cope with secession before any states broke away. In November, he met with his cabinet and floated an idea that might have enabled the nation to sidestep the war: he would call a national constitutional convention to consider an amendment that would allow secession. This was not an absurd idea: The Constitution was silent on the question of whether states could withdraw from the Union, and a convention would provide a democratic process that would enable people to debate the issue. The idea wasn't really to figure out how to allow secession; it was to give people a chance to talk, to let passions cool, to give Lincoln a chance, and to give Southerners time to consider what they risked by secession.

Unfortunately, the idea got no support in his cabinet. Secretary of State Lewis Cass vehemently opposed the idea because he refused to even countenance the idea of secession. He was joined in his opposition by three Southern members of the cabinet who behaved dishonestly, deceitfully, perhaps even traitorously. Two of them, Interior Secretary Jacob Thompson of Mississippi and Treasury Secretary Howell Cobb of Georgia, were already maneuvering with allies back home to secure positions with the new Confederate government. The third, Secretary of War John Floyd, would, within the next month, be revealed as, first, complicit in a scandal to enrich himself with government bonds and, second, to be shipping rifles and cannon to US installations in the South, where, Floyd knew, they were likely to fall into the hands of secessionists. The corrupt and traitorous Floyd joined his duplicitous, self-serving colleagues in arguing that the time for such a convention had passed. A disappointed Buchanan concluded that the only thing left for him to do was to spell out his position in his final State of the Union address, which he did in the first week of December.

Buchanan's argument was lawyerly, scholarly, and completely devoid of leadership. Faced with an epidemic of secession in the deep

South, Buchanan put the blame squarely on the North. "The long-continued and intemperate interference of the Northern people with the question of slavery in the Southern States has at length produced its natural effects. . . . [It has] produced its malign influence on the slaves and inspired them with vague notions of freedom. Hence a sense of security no longer exists around the family altar." If the radical abolitionists up north would only stop provoking the South, in other words, all this talk of secession would stop. "All that is necessary to accomplish the object, and all for which the slave States have ever contended, is to be let alone and permitted to manage their domestic institutions in their own way. As sovereign States, they, and they alone, are responsible before God and the world for the slavery existing among them."

But after expressing his sympathy with the South, Buchanan denied that they had any right to secede. If that were so, he said, the Union would be "a rope of sand, to be penetrated and dissolved by the first adverse wave of public opinion in any of the States." Buchanan then went through the Constitution, and showed, article by article, where the individual states had ceded their authority in commerce, foreign relations, and other matters to the central government in order to form "a more perfect union." "The framers [of the Constitution] never intended to implant in its bosom the seeds of its own destruction." Secession, he declared, "is neither more nor less than revolution."

Finally, dramatically, Buchanan noted that he had sworn a solemn oath to take care that the laws be "faithfully executed." But then Buchanan waffled. Because every federal official in South Carolina (except the postmaster) had joined the secessionists, Buchanan said he lacked any mechanism for enforcing the law and was therefore helpless. And not only was *he* helpless, but so was Congress. "Has the Constitution delegated to Congress the power to coerce a State into submission which is attempting to withdraw or has actually withdrawn from the Confederacy?" he asked. (Confusingly, Buchanan here referred to the United States using the word "confederacy" that would soon be adapted by the Southern states to designate their new would-be nation.) He answered his rhetorical question with a no—Congress did not have the power to prevent secession.

Secessionists took great confidence from Buchanan's irresolution. "There will be no war," said Senator Alfred Iverson of Georgia, disdainfully measuring the administration's lack of resolve. "In less than 12 months, a Southern Confederacy will be formed, and it will be the most successful government on earth."

Meanwhile, in the North, there was no agreement about what to do. There were hard-liners who believed that secession meant the nullification of the ballot box and the end of democracy. They were willing to fight for the Union. But businessmen in New York and Boston and Philadelphia knew that war would disrupt commerce and therefore preferred compromise or, if necessary, a peaceful separation of the states that wouldn't hurt profits. Abolitionists like Wendell Phillips also favored letting the South go, the better to remove the moral taint of slavery from the republic. So did William Seward, the future secretary of state, who was willing to let the slave-holding states go because he was sure they would fail and would soon come crawling back.

As was the custom of the president-elect, Lincoln was officially silent during the postelection period, but he made it clear that he did not take the threat of secession very seriously. Lincoln knew that the South had bluffed about secession before. More important, he believed that there was enough pro-Union sentiment in the South to withstand a wave of secession fever. Even in late February 1861, as he made his way from Springfield to Washington for his swearing-in, he tried to drain some of the tension from the situation. "Why all this excitement?" he said in Cleveland. "Why all these complaints? As I said before, this crisis is all artificial. It has no foundation in facts. . . . Let it alone and it will go down itself."

By that point, seven states had seceded, and Lincoln was soon persuaded to drop this sanguine approach.

When Lincoln next spoke on the subject of secession, it was in his inaugural address on March 4, and he was far more tough-minded. Absent was the vacillation of Buchanan. Ignored was the readiness of the business community to embrace appeasement. Disregarded were the moralistic fervor of Phillips and the too-clever-by-half maneuverings of Seward. Most notably, gone was the search for a compromise that had marked more than forty years of sectional struggle. Abraham Lincoln did not quite say to the South, "Go ahead, make my day," as another outlaw hero did—he was far too subtle and too generous of spirit—but he was as unyielding:

> In your hands, my dissatisfied fellow countrymen, and not in mine, is the momentous issue of civil war. The government will not assail you. You can have no conflict, without being yourselves the aggressors. You have no oath registered in Heaven to destroy the government, while I shall have the most solemn one to preserve, protect and defend it.

Buchanan acknowledged that he, too, had taken that oath, but he'd seen no mechanism for enforcing federal rule. Lincoln located that power in himself—in his power to act as the commander in chief. It was a bold assertion. For decades, the policy of the government had been confused, weak, vacillating, and eager to accommodate; in one speech, Lincoln drew a line in the sand.

Just because Lincoln took a stand, however, didn't mean that he wanted war or that he had the apparatus to wage it. The entire US Army consisted of fewer than twenty thousand men, most of whom were stationed on the frontier. Lincoln knew that he would have to rely on the states that remained in the Union to supply him troops, and it was far from certain that they would all comply. Some states would be as uncertain as Buchanan about the right of one state to use arms against another.

Lincoln's policy, therefore, was to hold and maintain—to continue to protect federal military installations in the South and to deny the seceded states any recognition of independent status. If he was firm, he believed, secession fever would burn itself out, and the rebellious states would come around. But almost immediately upon taking office, Lincoln learned that this policy was dead on arrival. In three weeks, the garrison at Fort Sumter in Charleston Harbor would be out of food. Lincoln faced a hard choice: reinforce and replenish the garrison, which would invite the opening of hostilities, or give up the fort and, with it, any hope of an effective presidency.

As the days counted down, Lincoln's key advisors told him to give up the fort. After General Winfield Scott told Lincoln that it would take an invasion force of twenty thousand men to subdue the batteries trained on Fort Sumter, nearly the entire cabinet was ready to throw in the towel. Surrender of Sumter was "an inevitable necessity," said Simon Cameron of the War Department. We should treat the seceded states "as an accomplished revolution," said Salmon P. Chase of Treasury. "I would not initiate a war to regain a useless position on the soil of the seceded States," said Seward of the State Department. "I would not provoke a war in any way *now*."

But one man, Postmaster General Montgomery Blair, urged the president to fight for the Union, and another man, a former naval officer named Gustavus Fox, developed a plan to get fresh supplies to Sumter. Buoyed by their encouragement, Lincoln once again escaped the unsatisfactory choices that were being foisted upon him. Unlike Buchanan, Lincoln would not be mired in his cabinet's irresolution. He would send Sumter provisions, but not troops or ammunition. This would allow him to adhere to his policy of hold and maintain, while throwing the responsibility for starting the war onto the Southerners.

The newly formed Confederate government didn't see things the same way, of course. In their eyes, whether the soldiers in the fort were behaving aggressively was beside the point, because federal occupation of a fort in Charleston Harbor was on its face a threat and had to be removed. On April 12, the Confederate forces began bombardment, and the next day, the fort was surrendered.

The attack on Sumter and the insult inflicted on Old Glory unified and inspired the North in a way that nothing else could have. "All squeamish sentimentality should be discarded, and bloody vengeance wreaked upon the heads of the contemptible traitors," said the Columbus, Ohio, *Daily Capital City Fact*. Said Senator Stephen A. Douglas, the president's onetime electoral rival, "There can be no neutrals in this war, only patriots or traitors." In the North, flags and bunting were hung from every window and porch rail; in Pittsburgh, lampposts sported nooses, sashed with the slogan "Death to Traitors!" On Monday the 15th, Lincoln called upon the state militias to provide seventy-thousand men for federal service, and the Northern states responded with determination.

In office just over a month, Lincoln had broken the logjam in Washington, created a clear and coherent policy, unified the North behind it, and raised an army to enforce it. Action hero, indeed.

But Lincoln didn't stop there. In the next eighty days, between his call for troops and the official convening of a special session of Congress on July 4, 1861, Lincoln took a series of actions on no authority other than the powers he asserted as president. He called forth the militia, ordered the rebels "to disperse and retire peacefully" to their homes, increased the size of the army and navy, spent government funds to buy weapons, ordered a blockade of Southern ports, suspended the writ of habeas corpus, and empaneled military tribunals to try civilians in occupied or contested areas, all without congressional approval (although Congress would approve all the steps retroactively). He did these things, he said, not to wage a "civil war" but to suppress a rebellion. The language was important: the Constitution leaves it up to Congress to declare war, but the executive acting alone can suppress a rebellion. Knowing the difference is what separates the outlaw from the outlaw hero.

Of all the measures that Lincoln took, the one that still creates the most unease is his decision to suspend the writ of habeas corpus, the Constitutional guarantee traced back to English common law that holds that a person who has been imprisoned can be immediately released if his imprisonment is found not to conform to law.

After hostilities commenced in April 1861, Lincoln found himself in a perilous position. The center of government, Washington, DC, sat between Virginia, a state that had just seceded, and Maryland, a slave-holding state that was teetering on the verge of joining the Confederacy. If Maryland left the Union, it would be nearly impossible to defend Washington. To suppress rebel agitation there, Lincoln suspended habeas corpus and began arresting secessionists. One of them, John Merryman, had not only advocated secession but tried to recruit a company of soldiers for the Confederate army. On May 25, Merryman was locked up in Fort McHenry in Baltimore. Ignoring Lincoln's edict, his lawyer sought a writ of habeas corpus from Roger B. Taney, the chief justice of the US Supreme Court. Taney concurred, ordering the fort's commander, George Cadwalader, to produce Merryman before the court the next day. Cadwalader refused.

Taney then issued an attachment that held Cadwalader for contempt, but Cadwalader simply refused to allow the US marshal to enter the fort to serve the attachment. Taney, recognizing that the president had an army at his disposal while he had just a handful of marshals, sat down and wrote the now-famous opinion, *Ex Parte Merryman*, in which he argued that Congress alone possessed the power to suspend the writ of habeas corpus.

Taney's argument was technically correct on the issue of congressional versus presidential power, but it seemed blind to the fact that a rebellion was in progress, people were dying, and the fate of the nation was up for grabs. In an address to Congress, Lincoln explained his reasoning in pragmatic terms that are beyond contradiction: "The whole of the laws which I was sworn to [execute] were being resisted . . . in nearly one-third of the states. . . . Are all the laws but one to go unexecuted, and the government itself go to pieces, lest that one be violated?" Two years later, Congress resolved the ambiguity in the Constitution and permitted the President the right to suspend the writ while the rebellion continued.

Although Lincoln's actions in Maryland seem justified, there were other suspensions of habeas corpus later in the war, under circumstances that rendered the act far less defensible. After widespread protests greeted the establishment of the first military draft in July 1862, Secretary of War Stanton suspended habeas corpus nationwide, a huge expansion of the power. Stanton issued the excessively broad mandate that anyone "engaged, by act, speech, or writing, in discouraging volunteer enlistments, or in any way giving aid and comfort to the enemy, or in any other disloyal practice against the United States" was subject to arrest and trial before a military commission. Under this order, local sheriffs and constables had the latitude to decide who was loyal or disloyal, and there was considerable abuse. More than ten thousand people were incarcerated without a prompt trial. Even so, Lincoln dismissed the idea that his suspension of the writ would have any long-term effects on American liberties. That's certainly a debatable point.

The third major instance when Lincoln violated the Law of Conventional Wisdom was his issuance of the Emancipation Proclamation. This decision represents a great leap in Lincoln's thinking—about the war, about slavery, and about race.

During the first year of the war, there were a number of significant military actions. But the truth is that neither side was fully committed to a battlefield solution. Neither side believed that the other side had much fight in them; both sides were convinced that their opponents, if pushed, would yield. The South believed that the North would not fight over slavery and that, once they suffered a few setbacks, it would be clear that Northern troops lacked the same will to fight as Southerners possessed. In the North, the belief was that, in the face of the hardships caused by the blockade, Southerners would see the foolishness of secession and would seek to rejoin the Union under terms that would preserve slavery.

The fierce and bloody Battle of Shiloh, in April 1862, began to disabuse leaders on both sides of these opinions, and, over the summer as confederate armies won significant victories in Virginia, both Lincoln and Jefferson Davis of the Confederacy began to focus more seriously on what it would take to win the war.

In Lincoln's mind, the abolition of slavery began to grow in importance both as a war aim and as a method of victory. Confederate armies were able to take the field in part because black slaves continued to produce the crops that fed the soldiers and that financed weapons and supplies bought from Europe. Ending slavery would hurt the Southern military effort directly and could also be used to weaken the rebellion among its main sponsors.

More important, abolishing slavery was also a moral good. When Lincoln ran for president, he said he personally opposed slavery but did not believe that he or any other president had any power to do away with it. But the commencement of war changed things. Several Union generals had freed the slaves in the districts they commanded, declaring them contraband of war that they were under no obligation to return. Lincoln began to see that, as a commander in chief in wartime, he did possess the power to free the slaves.

But not everywhere. Lincoln did not feel that his powers as commander in chief applied in places that were not at war. Lincoln would not free the slaves in Maryland, Kentucky, Missouri, or Delaware, the four states where slavery was legal that did not secede, nor in Tennessee or New Orleans or western Virginia, which had already passed back into federal control. Still, more than three million slaves lived in the states under Confederate control; after the issuance of the Emancipation Proclamation on January 1, 1863, as the Union armies advanced, those people became free, which permanently turned the tide against slavery. Moreover, this also turned the tide of the war. The lack of slaves to work the fields hurt the Southern war effort, just as the two hundred thousand former slaves who now joined the Union army further strengthened the North's manpower advantage.

Lincoln made the decision to free the slaves on a moral basis. In this, he was ahead of many of his fellow Northerners, who were willing to fight for the Union but who did not really care about slavery one way or the other and who certainly believed the white race to be superior to blacks. New York newspaper editor Horace Greeley in August 1862 called for immediate emancipation: "On the face of this wide earth, Mr. President," Greeley had written, "there is not one . . . intelligent champion of the Union cause who does not feel . . . that the rebellion, if crushed tomorrow, would be renewed if slavery were left in full vigor." In his famous reply, Lincoln seemed to reject that advice:

> If there be those who would not save the Union unless they could at the same time destroy slavery, I do not agree with them. My paramount object in this struggle is to save the Union, and is not either to save or to destroy slavery. If I could save the Union without freeing any slave I would do it, and if I could save it by freeing all the slaves I would do it; and if I could save it by freeing some and leaving others alone I would also do that. What I do about slavery, and the colored race, I do because I believe it helps to save the Union; and what I forbear, I forbear because I do not believe it would help to save the Union. . . . I have here stated my purpose according to my view of official duty; and I intend no modification of my oft-expressed personal wish that all men everywhere could be free.

But as Lincoln scholar Harold Holzer has pointed out, when the president wrote this letter, his mind was made up to do what Greeley was advising; the president had already drafted a preliminary version of the Emancipation Proclamation, which he had determined to issue after the next Union military victory. "This letter," writes Holzer, "was in truth an attempt to position the impending announcement in terms of saving the Union, not freeing slaves as a humanitarian gesture. It was one of Lincoln's most skillful public relations efforts, even if it has cast longstanding doubt on his sincerity as a liberator."

Ahead of his time and many of his countrymen, Lincoln optimized his presidential powers, enlarged his war aims, developed a strategy that undermined his adversary, and brought into being the modern United States—in the process skirting, bending, or outright breaking many of the laws and customs that had constrained his less effectual predecessors.

* * *

Since then, many presidents have made similar attempts to expand their powers to cope with crises, but not all have been as successful. Franklin Roosevelt was the most activist of America's twentieth-century presidents, but his willingness to expand the role of government and the scope of his executive powers had mixed results. Many of FDR's innovative federal programs to fight the Depression were popular and effective, but others were struck down by the Supreme Court, and his subsequent retaliatory efforts to "pack the court" marked the low point of his administration.

FDR was more successful, however, in foreign affairs. FDR was a staunch supporter of Great Britain's opposition to Nazi Germany from the outset of the Second World War, even as most Americans wanted to avoid US involvement in the conflict. The United States continued to sell arms and supplies to Great Britain and other countries, but eventually those countries began to run out of money. FDR would have been willing to extend credit to Britain, but the Neutrality Act prohibited the sale of arms to a belligerent power except on a cash basis, and Roosevelt did not believe that the isolationist Republicans in Congress would make an exception for Britain. Instead, Roosevelt and his advisors came up with the lend-lease program, under the provisions of which Britain received our aging battleships and cruisers in return for access to various British bases in the Atlantic.

The fact that Roosevelt didn't tell Congress about the arrangement until the deal was finalized earned him sharp Republican criticism. His presidential opponent, Wendell Willkie, called the deal "the most arbitrary and dictatorial action ever taken by any president in the history of the United States," and Republican congressman George Tinkham of Massachusetts said "there is no difference between his [FDR's] action from either Hitler, Mussolini, and Stalin." But opponents were unable to block the deal, and before long Congress blessed it by appropriating funds to improve the bases that the United States had received access to.

In doing what he thought was right, FDR found a way to sidestep a law and implicitly expanded the power of his office. In doing so, he provided Great Britain with the means to hold out against Germany until American's formal entry into the war. No doubt Lincoln would have admired FDR's courage and finesse.

Other presidents who have attempted to expand their power have been rebuffed. Richard Nixon clearly overstepped his authority in authorizing a cover-up of the crimes committed by his subordinates during Watergate, and he was never able to persuade his fellow citizens of the legitimacy of his view, which he summarized after his resignation as, "When the president does it, that means that it is not illegal."

Ronald Reagan's presidency came close to ruin during the Iran-Contra Affair, when in an attempt to secure the release of hostages held by Iran, senior officials defied an official arms embargo, sold weapons to Iran, and then used the proceeds to fund Nicaraguan contras in direct violation of the Boland Amendment. Reagan denied having firsthand knowledge of these activities, but fourteen members of his administration were indicted and eleven convicted, although some of those convictions were vacated on appeal.

And in the aftermath of 9/11, President George W. Bush attempted to indefinitely detain without trial American citizens who were designated enemy combatants, but the Supreme Court said that they were still entitled to due process.

Sometimes, of course, a lawbreaker is simply a lawbreaker—not an outlaw hero. "We are a nation of laws, not of men," John Adams memorably said, and that succinct formulation has usually served the country well. Usually, but not always. What the presidency of Abraham Lincoln teaches us is that laws and institutions and procedures are necessary and vital, but they are not always sufficient. Sometimes, in fact, they are obstacles to solutions. Sometimes, particularly during times of crisis, we need leaders who can grasp the essential challenges of a situation and maintain the highest ideals while breaking through the obstacles to address the issues at hand. Recognizing those times when they arise and being neither too quick nor too tardy to assume the mantle of outlaw is one of the supreme challenges faced by the leader.

It was his ability to overcome the limits imposed by old laws and tired thinking while upholding honored principles in devising new solutions that made Abraham Lincoln our greatest president.

LINCOLN'S WORDS

To Horace Greeley (1862)

Lincoln's response to a leading abolitionist:
"I would save the Union"

Executive Mansion, Washington, August 22, 1862.

Hon. Horace Greeley: Dear Sir.

I have just read yours of the 19th. addressed to myself through the New-York Tribune. If there be in it any statements, or assumptions of fact, which I may know to be erroneous, I do not, now and here, controvert them. If there be in it any inferences which I may believe to be falsely drawn, I do not now and here, argue against them. If there be perceptable in it an impatient and dictatorial tone, I waive it in deference to an old friend, whose heart I have always supposed to be right.

As to the policy I "seem to be pursuing" as you say, I have not meant to leave any one in doubt.

I would save the Union. I would save it the shortest way under the Constitution. The sooner the national authority can be restored; the nearer the Union will be "the Union as it was." If there be those who would not save the Union, unless they could at the same time *save* slavery, I do not agree with them. If there be those who would not save the Union unless they could at the same time *destroy* slavery, I do not agree with them. My paramount object in this struggle *is* to save the Union, and is *not* either to save or to destroy slavery. If I could save the Union without freeing *any* slave I would do it, and if I could save it by freeing *all* the slaves I would do it; and if I could save it by freeing some and leaving others alone I would also do that. What I do about slavery, and the colored race, I do because I believe it helps to save the Union; and what I forbear, I forbear because I do *not* believe it would help to save the Union. I shall do *less* whenever I shall believe what I am doing hurts the cause, and I shall do *more* whenever I shall believe doing more will help the cause. I shall try to correct errors when shown to be errors; and I shall adopt new views so fast as they shall appear to be true views.

I have here stated my purpose according to my view of *official* duty; and I intend no modification of my oft-expressed *personal* wish that all men every where could be free.

Yours, A. Lincoln.

In Mathew Brady's photography studio with son Tad (1864).
Library of Congress

9

PRESIDENT ABRAHAM LINCOLN CONFRONTS THE WAR ON TERROR

The Honorable Frank J. Williams

Frank J. Williams served as chief justice of the Supreme Court of Rhode Island from 2001 until his retirement in 2008. On December 30, 2003, the president of the United States, through the secretary of defense, invited Chief Justice Williams to be a member of the Military Commission Review Panel for tribunals to be held in Guantanamo Bay, Cuba, with the rank of major general. The Military Commissions Act of 2006 created the Court of Military Commission Review on which Justice Williams served as a civilian judge. On November 21, 2007, the secretary of defense appointed Chief Justice Williams chief judge of the United States Court of Military Commission Review, where he served until December 2009. Chief Justice Williams is also a nationally recognized expert and author on the life and times of Abraham Lincoln. The author wishes to acknowledge Nicole J. Benjamin, Esq., for her assistance with this chapter.

The events of September 11, 2001, were as inhumane as they were unanticipated by most Americans and individuals throughout the world. On that cloudless autumn morning, nineteen Islamic terrorists hijacked four commercial jet airliners, intentionally flying two of the planes into the twin towers of New York

City's World Trade Center and one into the Pentagon in Arlington, Virginia. The fourth plane, believed to have been aimed at the White House in Washington, DC, crashed in Shanksville, Pennsylvania, when its passengers attempted to retake control of the plane to avert further mass murder. In one morning, almost three thousand innocent civilians perished on American soil as victims of horrific depredations committed by nihilistic barbarians.

The threat that the attacks of 9/11 posed to the nation was severe but not unprecedented. Throughout the history of this nation, its security has, at times, been in jeopardy. Most notably, in the days and months following the beginning of the Civil War, a comparable national emergency caused the nation's sixteenth president to take immediate steps to safeguard the nation and its capital.

In April 1861, on the heels of the bombardment of Fort Sumter in Charleston Harbor by Confederate forces, Lincoln called for seventy-five thousand troops to protect Washington, DC, and put down the rebellion. Responding to Lincoln's call for state militias, the Sixth Massachusetts Regiment arrived in Baltimore, where riots congested the streets and pro-Confederate "bullies" attempted to prevent troops from reaching Washington. The regiment forced its way from one railroad station to another, sustaining four deaths and several injuries. Twelve civilians were killed.

By then, the Civil War was under way. The nation's capital was in jeopardy, given that it was bordered on one side by Virginia, a secessionist state, and on three sides by Maryland, whose threats to secede were widely known. In the days and weeks that followed, the city of Washington was isolated and virtually severed from the states of the North. Troops stopped arriving, telegraph lines were slashed, and postal mail from the North reached the city only infrequently.

Lincoln immediately perceived the grave danger to national security if the Confederates seized the capital or caused it to be completely isolated. In the eighty days between the April 1861 call for troops and the convening of Congress in special session on July 4, 1861, Lincoln performed a whole series of important acts by sheer assumption of presidential power. He increased the size of the army and navy, appropriated money for the purchase of arms and ammunition without congressional authorization, claimed the right to review private telegrams and censor the mail, and suspended the writ of habeas corpus. Lincoln also declared a blockade of the Southern coast, an act of war that, arguably, recognized the status of the Confederacy as a belligerent nation rather than as a mere mass of individuals in rebellion against the Union (which Lincoln insisted they were).

The suspension of habeas corpus was perhaps the most constitutionally significant of these acts. Often known as the Great Writ of Liberty, habeas corpus is the constitutionally authorized means by which a court may immediately assume jurisdiction over an arrested individual and inquire into the legality of the detention. If a court concludes that the detention is unlawful, it is empowered to immediately release the individual. In suspending the writ, Lincoln relied on the constitutional authorization that the framers had perceptively included years before in Article I, Section 9 (which reads, in part, "The privilege of the Writ of Habeas Corpus shall not be suspended, unless when in Cases of Rebellion or Invasion the public Safety may require it"). However, the Constitution implies that congressional action is required for such suspension. Despite the fact that Congress was in session at the time, Lincoln did not request its approval but personally authorized General Winfield Scott to suspend the writ along the railroad from Philadelphia to Washington, believing that his duty was to protect the capital and that the Union required such action.

Lincoln's unilateral suspension of habeas corpus was instrumental in securing communication lines and the movement of troops to the nation's capital. The effect was to enable military commanders to arrest and detain individuals indefinitely in areas where martial law had been imposed. Many of those detained had been attempting to halt military convoys by destroying bridges and telegraph lines. Lincoln saw that immediate action, even without the rights explicit in our usual judicial process, was necessary to divest civil liberties from those who were disloyal and whose overt acts against the United States threatened the nation's survival. For Lincoln, this was not a matter of abrogating the Constitution but rather of applying it appropriately in extreme circumstances. As he explained in his letter of June 29, 1863, to Matthew Birchard, "the constitution is different, in its application in cases of

Rebellion or Invasion, involving the Public Safety, from what it is in times of profound peace and public security."[1]

Much like the dark days of the spring of 1861, the fall of 2001 presented a similar, albeit arguably more perilous, threat to national security. Again, the nation's capital was in jeopardy, and the savage attacks sent a clear message that the nation was at war. It seems overwhelmingly likely that if Lincoln had been in the White House on 9/11 his response would have resembled that of President George W. Bush. Aware of his solemn duty to take action to defend and protect the United States, Bush responded to the attacks with a series of steps that, taken together, have come to be referred to as the War on Terror.

Three days after the 9/11 attacks, President Bush declared a national emergency. Congress responded by enacting an Authorization for Use of Military Force (AUMF) on September 18, 2001. Thus, unlike Lincoln, Bush had congressional authorization for his actions in immediate response to the crisis. The AUMF empowered the president to "take action and prevent acts of international terrorism against the United States." It further authorized the President to "use all necessary and appropriate force against those nations, organizations, or persons he determines planned, authorized, committed, or aided the terrorist attacks." Congress's authorization was, in all respects, a ratification of the President's actions as commander in chief and legally pre-empted any potential criticism he might have otherwise received for acting unilaterally.

It seems inevitable that Lincoln's response to the 9/11 terror attacks would have mirrored his response to the situation in Baltimore in April 1861. Following Lincoln's acts in the months after the commencement of civil war, he explained what was at stake as he sought congressional ratification in his message of July 4, 1861:

> This issue embraces more than the fate of these United States. It presents to the whole family of man, the question, whether a constitutional republic, or a democracy—a government of the people, by the same people—can, or cannot, maintain its territorial integrity, against its . . . foes. It presents the question, whether discontented individuals [can with or] without any

pretence, break up [a] Government, and thus practically put an end to free government upon the earth. It forces us to ask: "Is there, in all republics, this inherent, and fatal weakness?" "Must a government, of necessity, be too strong for the liberties of its own people, or too weak to maintain its own existence?"

So viewing the issue, no choice was left but to call out the war power of the Government; and so to resist force, employed for its destruction, by force, for its preservation.

The importance of Lincoln's words has not lessened over the past 150 years. They remain as true today as they were in 1861.

Approximately two months after the 9/11 attacks, President Bush issued an order permitting the establishment of military commissions to detain and prosecute suspected terrorists. The effect of that order was to convene the first United States military commission in more than fifty years. In doing so, President Bush emphasized that trial by military commission was necessary "in light of grave acts of terrorism and threats of terrorism . . . to protect the United States and its citizens." His order made it clear that it was not practical for such tribunals to apply without modification the principles of law and the rules of evidence generally recognized in the trial of criminal cases in the federal courts. The decision to authorize military commissions was, in effect, a decision to restrict unlawful enemy combatants' access to the writ of habeas corpus.

In ordering the establishment of military commissions, President Bush took his cues from history. Almost 150 years earlier, Lincoln had authorized the use of military commissions to try those disloyal to the Union. Many were civilians who were believed to be "guilty of disloyal practice" or who "afforded aid and comfort to Rebels." In total, during the Civil War, the Union army conducted at least 4,271 trials of US citizens by military commission and another 1,435 during the Reconstruction period that followed. Most of those tried by military commission were charged with guerrilla activities, including tearing down telegraph lines, bridge burning, and horse stealing.

Lincoln defended his authorization of military commissions on both practical and legal grounds. In Lincoln's opinion, the president in his role as commander in chief has the authority to choose the forum in which those detained during war will be tried. As Lincoln wrote in his June 12, 1863, letter to Erastus Corning (more commonly known as the Corning letter):

> Nothing is better known to history than that courts of justice are utterly incompetent to such cases. Civil courts are organized chiefly for trials of individuals, or, at most, a few individuals acting in concert; and this in quiet times, and on charges of crimes well defined in the law. Even in times of peace, bands of horse-thieves and robbers frequently grow too numerous and powerful for the ordinary courts of justice. But what comparison, in numbers, have such bands ever borne to the insurgent sympathizers even in many of the loyal states? Again, a jury too frequently has at least one member, more ready to hang the panel than to hang the traitor. And yet again, he who dissuades one man from volunteering, or induces one soldier to desert, weakens the Union cause as much as he who kills a union soldier in battle. Yet this dissuasion, or inducement, may be so conducted as to be no defined crime of which any civil court would take cognizance.

Lincoln recognized that the laws of war are different from the laws that apply in ordinary circumstances. Different rules are essential in the midst of a national emergency. Lincoln recognized the threat to national security that would result if insurrectionists were not tried and convicted for their actions. In Lincoln's mind, a weakened Union army was a substantial threat to national security.

For similar reasons, Lincoln would surely have defended the use of military commissions by President Bush (and later President Obama) to try those accused of terrorism. Although the American civilian criminal justice system requires the government to indict suspects, arrest them without the use of excessive force, and fully Mirandize them by formally notifying them of their rights under the Constitution, such protocol is not practicable during times of war. As Professor Ruth Wedgwood has observed, "U.S. Marines may have to burrow down an Afghan cave to smoke out the leadership of al Qaeda. It would be ludicrous to ask that they pause in the dark to pull an Afghan-language Miranda card from their kit bag. This is war, not a criminal case."

Lincoln, an experienced lawyer, would be keenly aware that the procedural rules characteristic of our criminal justice system could further complicate the trial of suspected terrorists and thereby jeopardize our nation's security. Most notable are the rules of discovery, which mandate that the government disclose to a criminal defendant any information in its possession that can be deemed material to the accused, in addition to any potentially exculpatory evidence. To provide a suspected terrorist with such extensive information could be deadly. For this reason, the Military Commissions Act of 2009 provides that such information may be given only to a detainee's counsel, not the detainee himself.

Furthermore, if Lincoln were in office today, he would probably be adamant that preventative detention measures are necessary to hold members of foreign and domestic terrorist organizations before they are able to carry out attacks. During the Civil War, Lincoln preemptively detained between thirteen and twenty-eight thousand citizens in Northern states—not even foreign detainees—under the fear that they would either engage in or encourage guerrilla acts against the Union. In the Corning letter, he defended these detentions with his ever keen understanding of military necessity:

> Must I shoot a simple-minded soldier boy who deserts, while I must not touch a hair of a wiley agitator who induces him to desert? This is none the less injurious when effected by getting a father, or brother, or friend, into a public meeting, and there working upon his feelings, till he is persuaded to write the soldier boy, that he is fighting in a bad cause, for a wicked administration of a contemptable government, too weak to arrest and punish him if he shall desert. I think that in such a case, to silence the agitator, and save the boy, is not only constitutional, but, withal, a great mercy.

As he did during the Civil War, Lincoln likely would distinguish between American citizens who have rights specified under the United States Constitution and those alien combatants who have no such rights. As Senator Charles Sumner, a sometime Lincoln supporter, explained in 1862,

If the enemies against whom we are now waging war were not our own fellow-citizens—if they were aliens unhappily established for the time on our territory—there would be no finespun question of constitutional immunities. . . . If the war on our part were . . . in subordination to those provisions of the Constitution which were devised for peace, it is evident that our Government would be unable to cope with its enemy. It would enter battle with its hands tied behind its back. Of course, in warfare with people of another country, Senators would not require any such self-sacrifice.

In addition to authorizing the use of military commissions to try enemy combatants, Lincoln would have taken an active role in reviewing the detentions of those held at centers like the one in Guantanamo, Cuba. Although legislation in place during the Bush administration permitted the president to designate detainees as "enemy combatants," that administration was also sharply criticized for its failure to speedily exercise that authority. Lincoln would surely have recognized the importance of a presidential check on the military commission system, because such a check was prominent in his administration.

President Lincoln personally reviewed certain cases that came before the military commissions during the Civil War. After the Sioux uprising in Minnesota that killed hundreds of white settlers in 1862, the military court had sentenced 303 Sioux to death. Those cases came before Lincoln to review as final judge. Yet, despite great pressure to approve the verdicts with minimal review, Lincoln insisted that the complete records of the trial be sent to him. Working deliberately, Lincoln reviewed the cases one by one, spending a month carefully working through the transcripts to sort out those who were guilty of serious crimes. Ultimately, Lincoln commuted the sentences of 264 defendants, and only 39 of the original 303 were executed. Although Lincoln was criticized for this act of clemency, he responded, "I could not afford to hang men for votes."

Lincoln also reviewed courts-martial during the Civil War. Lincoln would carefully review the death sentences of sleeping sentinels, homesick Union soldiers, and deserters that he called his "leg cases." In many of these cases, Lincoln mercifully pardoned the accused soldiers.

However, he more frequently sustained sentences for slave traders, those convicted of robbery, and those who committed sexual offenses.

As a lawyer, Lincoln was accustomed to sets of rules prescribing codes of proper behavior. Recognizing the value of such rules, Lincoln sought to codify the laws and usages of war that Union forces were expected to follow. On April 24, 1863, at the recommendation and urging of General of the Army Henry W. Halleck, Lincoln approved a set of instructions on how soldiers should conduct themselves in wartime that had been drafted by Dr. Francis Lieber, a political philosopher and a political science professor who had immersed himself in the study of early nineteenth-century warfare. Dr. Leiber's *Instructions for the Government of Armies of the United States in the Field*, which was released as Army General Orders No. 100, is now commonly referred to as the Lieber Code. The first comprehensive list of instructions on the laws of war, the Lieber Code included ten sections and 157 articles covering topics that ranged from martial law to property of the enemy and insurrection. The code was intended to be malleable enough so that wars could be won while also upholding more rigid standards designed to protect basic human dignity.

The Lieber Code recognized military commissions as the appropriate forum for trying "cases which do not come within the 'Rules and Articles of War,' or the jurisdiction conferred by statute on courts-martial." Importantly, the Lieber Code reflected Lincoln's belief that "military necessity does not admit of cruelty—that is, the infliction of suffering for the sake of suffering or for revenge, nor of maiming or wounding except in fight, nor of torture to extort confessions." The Lieber Code was used as a guide and template for the Hague Conventions of 1899 and 1907 and remained in force until World War I.

Today, the corollary to the Lieber Code's comprehensive set of instructions is the Military Commissions Act of 2009, a 281-page set of procedures for conducting military commissions. The act mirrors in many respects the provisions of the Uniform Code of Military Justice, which governs courts-martial for uniformed service members. One notable feature of the act is its intolerance for cruelty and torture. Under the act, statements obtained through torture or through cruel, inhuman, or degrading treatment are not admissible as evidence in the later trial of the detainee. This aspect of the act would have been critically important to Lincoln, who believed that cruelty and torture were intolerable and could not be justified in the name of military necessity.

If this were Lincoln's War on Terror, the sixteenth president would also be a likely proponent of the Military Commissions Act's appellate review process. As we've seen, during the Civil War, Lincoln found it necessary to suspend the writ of habeas corpus altogether. However, resources available today, and perhaps the hindsight of history, have made it possible to supplant the right to habeas corpus with an intricate appellate review process, including eventual review in an Article III forum, a federal civil court.

If Lincoln were alive in the aftermath of 9/11, he would have vigorously defended what some today decry as the expansion of executive power and war powers of the commander in chief. Indeed, although Lincoln lamented his own use of executive power during the Civil War, he also defended it as unavoidable in his July 4, 1861, message to Congress:

> It was with the deepest regret that the Executive found the duty of employing the war-power, in defence of the government, forced upon him. He could but perform this duty, or surrender the existence of the government. . . . As a private citizen, the Executive could not have consented that these institutions shall perish; much less could he, in betrayal of so vast, and so sacred a trust, as these free people had confided to him. He felt that he had no moral right to shrink; nor even to count the chances of his own life, in what might follow. In full view of his great responsibility, he has, so far, done what he has deemed his duty. You will now, according to your own judgment, perform yours. He sincerely hopes that your views, and your action, may so accord with his, as to assure all faithful citizens, who have been disturbed in their rights, of a certain, and speedy restoration to them, under the Constitution, and the laws.

Thus, in most ways Lincoln's management of the War on Terror would likely mirror that of Presidents Bush and Obama. However, it is unlikely that Lincoln would fully appreciate and protect the right to freedom of speech as we understand it. Historical circumstances explain this fact. Although the First Amendment was always an important part of the bill of rights, modern First Amendment law was not born until after World War I. For this reason, Lincoln and his subordinates imposed restrictions on speech during the Civil War that he likely would not have imposed if he had the benefit of the next 150 years of First Amendment jurisprudence.

For example, on September 24, 1862, responding to the grave political and military climate, Lincoln issued a proclamation declaring martial law and authorizing the use of military tribunals to try civilians within the United States who were believed to be "guilty of disloyal practice" or who "afford[ed] aid and comfort to Rebels." The following March, Major General Ambrose Burnside assumed command of the Department of the Ohio and issued General Order No. 38, authorizing imposition of the death penalty for those who aided the Confederacy and who "declared sympathies for the enemy."

When Democratic congressman Clement L. Vallandigham, perhaps Lincoln's sharpest Northern critic, referred to Lincoln in a public speech as a political tyrant and called for his overthrow, he was arrested by 150 Union soldiers at his home in Dayton at 2:40 a.m. on May 5, 1863. He was escorted to Kemper Barracks, a military prison in Cincinnati, brought before a military tribunal a day after his arrest, found guilty, and sentenced to imprisonment for the duration of the war. Eventually, President Lincoln, concerned about the harshness of Vallandigham's punishment and its potential to inspire criticism and even political turmoil, commuted his sentence to banishment to the Confederacy. It's difficult to imagine that Lincoln would consider the imprisonment of Vallandigham justified today. In fact, he did not believe at the time that the imprisonment of Vallandigham was justified. But he stood by Major General Ambrose Burnside and used Vallandigham's arrest as another opportunity to defend his suspension of certain civil liberties as he had done in the Corning Letter. Likewise, the political background against which President Bush grappled and President Obama continues to grapple with national security issues during the War on Terror is something that was not at issue for Lincoln. The Civil War was confined to American soil. Today, however, we live in a global village, and the War on Terror is being fought on the soils of many nations. For that reason, if

Lincoln were in the White House today, he would need to learn to be sensitive to the global issues implicated by the War on Terror.

If the War on Terror were Lincoln's war, it seems likely that it would have been conducted much as it has been conducted under the administrations of Presidents Bush and Obama. Lincoln understood the importance of history and the need for each generation to look back on the successes and failures of past generations for guidance and wisdom. Responding to a serenade by supporters on November 10, 1864, he observed that "in any future great national trial, compared with the men of this, we shall have as weak, and as strong; as silly and as wise; as bad and good. Let us, therefore, study the incidents of this, as philosophy to learn wisdom from, and none of them as wrongs to be revenged."

Less than 150 years later, the nation did confront another "great national trial" in which Lincoln's philosophy and policy decisions have continued importance and meaning. A democratic nation at war must always struggle to maintain a delicate balance between protecting the nation and safeguarding civil liberties. Lincoln wrote in an April 4, 1864, letter to Albert G. Hodges that as president he "did understand . . . that my oath to preserve the constitution to the best of my ability, imposed upon me the duty of preserving, by every indispensable means, that government—that nation—of which that constitution was the organic law." To Lincoln, it would be simply intolerable to lose the nation and yet preserve the Constitution. As he explained, "by general law life and limb must be protected; yet often a limb must be amputated to save a life; but a life is never wisely given to save a limb." Thus, Lincoln believed that measures otherwise unconstitutional might become lawful in those times when they were indispensable to the preservation of the Constitution because they preserve the nation itself.

The United States lost 620,000 people over the four years of the Civil War. It could lose that many people in one day if it were to suffer a nuclear, chemical, or biological attack at the hands of terrorists. The horrific events of 9/11 are a stark reminder that such attacks are a real possibility. In times like these, small sacrifices of personal freedoms are necessary. As Lincoln believed, it would simply be intolerable to lose our great nation rather than recognize and accept the necessity of such sacrifices.

LINCOLN'S WORDS

To James C. Conkling (1863)

Lincoln on emancipation and the enlistment of black soldiers:
The promise being made, must be kept"

Executive Mansion, Washington, August 26, 1863.

Hon. James C. Conkling.

My Dear Sir.

Your letter inviting me to attend a mass-meeting of unconditional Union-men, to be held at the Capitol of Illinois, on the 3d day of September, has been received.

It would be very agreeable to me, to thus meet my old friends, at my own home; but I can not, just now, be absent from here, so long as a visit there, would require.

The meeting is to be of all those who maintain unconditional devotion to the Union; and I am sure my old political friends will thank me for tendering, as I do, the nation's gratitude to those other noble men, whom no partizan malice, or partizan hope, can make false to the nation's life.

There are those who are dissatisfied with me. To such I would say: You desire peace; and you blame me that we do not have it. But how can we attain it? There are but three conceivable ways. First, to suppress the rebellion by force of arms. This I am trying to do. Are you for it? If you are, so far we are agreed. If you are not for it, a second way is to give up the Union. I am against this. Are you for it?

If you are, you should say so plainly. If you are not for *force,* nor yet for *dissolution,* there only remains some imaginable *compromise.* I do not believe any compromise, embracing the maintenance of the Union, is now possible. All I learn, leads to a directly opposite belief. The strength of the rebellion, is its military—its army. That army dominates all the country, and all the people, within its range. Any offer of terms made by any man or men within that range, in opposition to that army, is simply nothing for the present; because such man or men, have no power whatever to enforce their side of a compromise, if one were made with them. To illustrate. Suppose refugees from the South, and peace men of the North, get together in convention, and frame and proclaim a compromise embracing a restoration of the Union; in what way can that compromise be used to keep Lee's army out of Pennsylvania? Meade's army can keep Lee's army out of Pennsylvania; and I think, can ultimately drive it out of existence. But no paper compromise, to which the controllers of Lee's army are not agreed, can at all affect that army. In an effort at such compromise we should waste time, which the enemy would improve to our disadvantage; and that would be all. A compromise, to be effective, must be made either with those who control the rebel army, or with the people first liberated from the domination of that army, by the success of our own army. Now allow me to assure you, that no word or intimation, from that rebel army, or from any of the men controlling it, in relation to any peace compromise, has ever come to my knowledge or belief. All charges and insinuations to the contrary, are deceptive and groundless. And I promise you, that if any such proposition shall hereafter come, it shall not be rejected, and kept a secret from you. I freely acknowledge myself the servant of the people, according to the bond of service—the United States Constitution; and that, as such, I am responsible to them.

But to be plain, you are dissatisfied with me about the negro. Quite likely there is a difference of opinion between you and myself upon that subject. I certainly wish that all men could be free, while I suppose you do not. Yet I have neither adopted, nor proposed any measure, which is not consistent with even your view, provided you are for the Union. I suggested compensated emancipation; to which you replied you wished not to be taxed to buy negroes. But I had not asked you to be taxed to buy negroes, except in such way, as to save you from greater taxation to save the Union exclusively by other means.

You dislike the emancipation proclamation; and, perhaps, would have it retracted. You say it is unconstitutional—I think differently. I think the constitution invests its Commander-in-chief, with the law of war, in time of war. The most that can be said, if so much, is, that slaves are property. Is there—has there ever been—any question that by the law of war, property, both of enemies and friends, may be taken when needed? And is it not needed whenever taking it, helps us, or hurts the enemy? Armies, the world over, destroy enemie's property when they can not use it; and even destroy their own to keep it from the enemy. Civilized belligerents do all in their power to help themselves, or hurt the enemy, except a few things regarded as barbarous or cruel. Among the exceptions are the massacre of vanquished foes, and non-combatants, male and female.

But the proclamation, as law, either is valid, or is not valid. If it is not valid, it needs no retraction. If it is valid, it can not be retracted, any more than the dead can be brought to life. Some of you profess to think its retraction would operate favorably for the Union. Why better *after* the retraction, than *before* the issue? There was more than a year and a half of trial to suppress the rebellion before the proclamation issued, the last one hundred days of which passed under an explicit notice that it was coming, unless averted by those in revolt, returning to their allegiance. The war has certainly progressed as favorably for us, since the issue of proclamation as before. I know, as fully as one can know the opinions of others, that some of the commanders of our armies in the field who have given us our most important successes believe the emancipation policy and the use of the colored troops constitute the heaviest blow yet dealt to the Rebellion, and that at least one of these important successes could not have been achieved when it was but for the aid of black soldiers. Among the commanders holding these views are some who have never had any affinity with what is called abolitionism or with the Republican party policies but who held them purely as military opinions. I submit these opinions as being entitled to some weight against the objections often urged that emancipation and arming the blacks are unwise as military measures and were not adopted as such in good faith.

You say you will not fight to free negroes. Some of them seem willing to fight for you; but, no matter. Fight you, then exclusively to save the Union. I issued the proclamation on purpose to aid you in saving the Union. Whenever you shall have conquered all resistence to the Union, if I shall urge you to continue fighting, it will be an apt time, then, for you to declare you will not fight to free negroes.

I thought that in your struggle for the Union, to whatever extent the negroes should cease helping the enemy, to that extent it weakened the enemy in his resistence to you. Do you think differently? I thought that whatever negroes can be got to do as soldiers, leaves just so much less for white soldiers to do, in saving the Union. Does it appear otherwise to you? But negroes, like other people, act upon motives. Why should they do any thing for us, if we will do nothing for them? If they stake their lives for us, they must be prompted by the strongest motive—even the promise of freedom. And the promise being made, must be kept.

The signs look better. The Father of Waters again goes unvexed to the sea. Thanks to the great Northwest for it. Nor yet wholly to them. Three hundred miles up, they met New England, Empire, Key-stone, and Jersey, hewing their way right and left. The Sunny South too, in more colors than one, also lent a hand. On the spot, their part of the history was jotted down in black and white. The job was a great national one; and let none be banned who bore an honorable part in it. And while those who have cleared the great river may well be proud, even that is not all. It is hard to say that anything has been more bravely, and well done, than at Antietam, Murfreesboro, Gettysburg, and on many fields of lesser note. Nor must Uncle Sam's web-feet be forgotten. At all the watery margins they have been present. Not only on the deep sea, the broad bay, and the rapid river, but also up the narrow muddy bayou, and wherever the ground was a little damp, they have been, and made their tracks. Thanks to all. For the great republic—for the principle it lives by, and keeps alive—for man's vast future—thanks to all.

Peace does not appear so distant as it did. I hope it will come soon, and come to stay; and so come as to be worth the keeping in all future time. It will then have been proved that, among free men, there can be no successful appeal from the ballot to the bullet; and that they who take such appeal are sure to lose their case, and pay the cost. And then, there will be some black men who can remember that, with silent tongue, and clenched teeth, and steady eye, and well-poised bayonnet, they have helped mankind on to this great consummation; while, I fear, there will be some white ones, unable to forget that, with malignant heart, and deceitful speech, they strove to hinder it.

Still, let us not be over-sanguine of a speedy final triumph. Let us be quite sober. Let us diligently apply the means, never doubting that a just God, in his own good time, will give us the rightful result.

Yours very truly,
A. Lincoln

A hostile cartoon from the campaign of 1864, depicting an aloof Lincoln making a mockery of the nation's war dead. *Library of Congress*

10

"PUBLIC OPINION IS EVERYTHING"

Lincoln the Communicator

DOUGLAS L. WILSON

Douglas L. Wilson is George A. Lawrence Distinguished Service Professor Emeritus and codirector of the Lincoln Studies Center at Knox College in Galesburg, Illinois. His work on Abraham Lincoln has appeared in the Atlantic Monthly, American Heritage, Time, *the* American Scholar, *as well as other magazines and scholarly journals, and has resulted in six books.* Lincoln Before Washington: New Perspectives on Lincoln's Illinois Years *(Champaign: University of Illinois Press, 1997) is a collection of essays on Lincoln's prepresidential years.* Herndon's Informants: Letters and Interviews about Abraham Lincoln *(1998),* Herndon's Lincoln *(2006), and* The Lincoln-Douglas Debates *(2008), were all coedited with Rodney O. Davis and published by the University of Illinois Press. Wilson's book on Lincoln's early life,* Honor's Voice: The Transformation of Abraham Lincoln *(New York: Knopf, 1998), and* Lincoln's Sword: The Presidency and the Power of Words *(New York: Knopf, 2007), a study of Lincoln's presidential writings, were both awarded the Lincoln Prize.*

B ecause Abraham Lincoln successfully presided over a desperate effort to keep the United States united and simultaneously engineered the demise of slavery, there is overwhelming agreement in our own time that he was a great American president. That he was also a great communicator would seem to be a common presumption, though his modern admirers are less certain about the evidence for that. Wasn't he known as a great speaker? Didn't his performances in the legendary debates against Stephen A. Douglas catapult him to national status? Wasn't his Cooper Union address crucial in positioning him as a leading candidate for the presidency? And didn't some of his speeches as president, like the Gettysburg Address and the second inaugural, inspire and thus help to preserve the nation?

Well, not exactly. Lincoln's rise to power was indeed facilitated by the power of his oratory. But, as president, he deliberately limited himself to a very small handful of public speeches, and the address at Gettysburg, as well as the second inaugural, became widely admired and sources of national inspiration only decades after their delivery. Nonetheless, the presumption that Lincoln was a great communicator is historically correct, even if how this might translate into a modern context is far from clear.

Part of the difficulty is that his modern admirers tend to be as much, if not more, interested in what Lincoln might do in *their* milieu as in how he actually operated in his own. "How might Lincoln cope with the 'sound bite' culture of TV news?" they ask. "How would his humor serve him as a guest of Jay Leno or Jon Stewart?" "Would Lincoln talk with Oprah about the troubles of his boyhood and early manhood?" Provocative questions like these not only invite but *demand* speculation. But in order to speculate about Lincoln the communicator in a modern setting, it is necessary to start with a sense of what the historical Lincoln was like, what he thought about communication issues, and how he actually performed.

Unfortunately, the more one knows about Lincoln, the more problematic the hypothetical questions become. Contrary to what one might expect from a man who had built his reputation in politics almost exclusively as a speaker, Lincoln's policy as president was to avoid the public rostrum, and the exceptions to this rule were few. Perhaps even more stringently followed was his policy against speaking in public without a prepared text. This rule of his was both unusual and unpopular, for it meant he was constantly disappointing groups that turned out to pay homage to him or demonstrate their support and hoped to hear a few words in return. But Lincoln had his reasons, which he explained at least partially to a crowd of serenaders at Gettysburg on the night before his famous address. In response to their predictable cries for a speech, he explained that he had no speech to give and would therefore have to decline. "In my position it is sometimes important that I should not say foolish things," Lincoln said. A wag in the crowd shouted, "If you can help it," to which Lincoln replied, "It very often happens that the only way to help it is to say nothing at all."

This is precisely what he did on this and like occasions. In addition, Lincoln's closest friends testified that for all of his folksy openhandedness and affability, he was an unusually reticent, essentially secretive man where his private life and personal feelings were concerned, sure to deflect any inquiries into such matters. And just here is the difficulty. To suppose that the superreticent Lincoln would open up to Oprah or that Honest Abe would appear with Stephen Colbert to banter about "truthiness" are both engaging prospects, but both require that we throw the historical Lincoln out the window.

A willingness to change the historical equation by positing a fictitious twenty-first-century Lincoln indicates that the object is less enlightenment than entertainment, which is why most historians shy away from it. Not that there is anything wrong with entertainment. Lincoln's high place in the national pantheon has made him a perennial subject of American humor, and probably always will. The comedian Bob Newhart, for example, succeeded brilliantly with a famous sketch in which Lincoln's familiar style of dress and personal eccentricities were crafted by a press agent using modern methods. Much of Newhart's humor revolves around the press agent's frustration in attempting to pass off a witless bumbler as an authentic statesman, which is summed up in a line about changes his client wants to make in the Gettysburg Address: "Abe, do the speech the way Charlie wrote it, would you?"

Instead, suppose, in the hope of enlightenment, we reverse the historical polarity and ask what Lincoln's actual performance as a political communicator as president has to tell us, if anything, about the contemporary media and the way modern politicians currently use it. What might we learn from this exercise?

To begin with, some modern forms of communication were already in operation in Lincoln's day, such as newspapers. Far more limited in scope and circulation than their modern counterparts, they were, nonetheless, even more closely tied to politics and very often owed their existence to a political party or partisan cause. As a young man breaking into politics in the 1830s, Lincoln wrote scores of editorials for the local Whig newspaper, a practice that he seems to have continued throughout his pre-presidential career. Most of these efforts were either unsigned or pseudonymous and therefore difficult to identify, though the evidence of this activity is clear enough. As an office seeker and party publicist, Lincoln certainly knew how to plant stories and solicit editorial support from newspaper editors. It is perhaps instructive that his private papers include fragments of unpublished articles he worked on in the months before his election to the presidency. And as president, he cultivated newspaper editors and journalists, allowing them access to the White House and other favors, fully expecting favorable treatment in return. In these respects, Lincoln was perhaps as much involved with the media as any of his modern counterparts, always keeping in mind that the "media" of his day were almost exclusively newspaper editors and reporters.

One of the features of American political life that has remained fairly constant over time and that offers opportunities for interesting and sometimes arresting comparisons is every president's need to come to terms with public opinion. So much is made in our own time of scientifically designed public opinion polls, especially in election years, that one might be tempted to assume that in Lincoln's day, long before such tools were available, politicians paid less heed to public opinion. With Lincoln, at least, we can be sure that this was not the case. A number of specific remarks made in the years before he become president show that Lincoln was intently focused on public opinion. "Our government rests in public opinion," he told his fellow members of the new Republican party in 1856, "Whoever can change public opinion, can change the government, practically just so much." This was in direct contrast to the approach of his great adversary, Stephen A. Douglas, who professed to champion "popular sovereignty," which seemed to mean giving the public whatever it wanted, as opposed to consciously seeking to reshape those preferences. A minority party, but a fast-growing one, Lincoln's Republicans were out to win converts, to change people's minds, and so alter the nation's political direction. They were still a minority party in the 1860 election, but the fractious divisions in the majority Democratic Party enabled the Republicans to gain the presidency, which in turn precipitated the secession of Southern states and, ultimately, the Civil War.

As president, Lincoln continued to focus on public opinion, and for good reason. Still relatively little known and taking command at a time of extreme crisis, he was received with grave misgivings in the press and among the leadership of his own party. After the immediate gush of patriotism in response to the firing on Fort Sumter, the Northern public grew less and less patient with a president who seemed to move slowly, who appeared vacillating and irresolute, and whose military produced few victories. A deep suspicion pervaded the country that the amiable prairie politician with no executive experience was in over his head. He was also widely suspected of having more than one motive in prosecuting the war—the preservation of the Union, which was popular, and the abolition of slavery, which was not.

In the late summer of 1862, faced with these widespread doubts, with the war going badly for the Union and with Northern morale sorely undermined, Lincoln did something entirely unexpected. He appealed directly to the public by answering one of his critics in the newspapers.

Horace Greeley, a prominent editor and nominally a supporter of the administration, had run an ill-tempered front-page editorial scolding the president at great length for ineffective leadership and for having no discernible policy. As it happened, Lincoln had just drafted a piece that was intended to be something of a trial balloon on the issue of emancipation, and he was, at that moment, casting about for a means of getting it before the public. Within a few days, Lincoln had adapted his piece as an answer to Greeley's attack and had it published in a Washington newspaper not Greeley's. Its core message was brief and memorable:

> My paramount object in this struggle *is* to save the Union, and is *not* either to save or to destroy slavery. If I could save the Union without freeing *any* slave I would do it, and if I could save it by freeing *all* the slaves I would do it; and if I could save it by freeing some and leaving others alone I would also do that. What I do about slavery, and the colored race, I do because I believe it helps to save the Union; and what I forbear, I forbear because I do *not* believe it would help to save the Union.

The national press was aghast, and its response was swift and severe. A sitting president's responding directly to editorial criticism was unprecedented; it was beneath the dignity of the presidential office to bicker with a journalist in the newspapers. What's more, the journalists fulminated, Lincoln's prose was "peculiar" and unpresidential; the episode showed yet again that Lincoln was out of his depth and did not understand how the nation's first magistrate was expected to behave.

And yet, as Lincoln hoped, this very clamor heightened attention to his message, which was so strategically compact and well phrased that it could almost be recited after a single reading. It forced itself into public notice and incited widespread comment and discussion. This much-criticized gambit was, in short, a wildly successful effort to engage the public's attention. Perhaps even more remarkable was its forceful tenor. It radiated determination and purpose, while leaving the critical options open. Was the president planning to act on the wishes of the radicals of his party and emancipate all the slaves? Only if it would save the Union. Would he be willing to free slaves in some parts of the country but not in others? Yes, but only if that would help to save the Union.

We know in retrospect, of course, that Lincoln had already informed his cabinet that he had decided upon the latter—a carefully calculated measure that would emancipate slaves in those parts of the country that were in rebellion, but not elsewhere, such as the loyal border states. The reply to Greeley was, as noted, a trial balloon, whose purpose was to test the reaction of the public to these alternatives.

The success of this novel venture emboldened the president to repeat it when he came under fire some months later, having been accused of acting too aggressively against critics of his administration, a concern for the infringements of civil liberties that was not merely partisan but alarmingly widespread. Lincoln later described how he had prepared for this second public letter by making notes whenever an idea "would occur to me which seemed to have force and make a perfect answer" to his critics. One of these emerged as the much-quoted highlight of a markedly effective defense of his actions: "Must I shoot a simple-minded soldier boy who deserts, while I must not touch a hair of a wiley agitator who induces him to desert?"

This public letter was followed by two more in succeeding months, the second of which was the so-called Conkling (or Springfield) letter, perhaps the hardest-hitting and, in the end, most effective all of Lincoln's public letters. In it he confronted the stubborn resistance of Northern whites to the Emancipation Proclamation and, in particular, their resentment of black soldiers, whose inclusion in the army had been a controversial provision of the Proclamation. The language of Lincoln's letter, without being harsh or disrespectful, was direct, and his logic relentless:

> I thought that in your struggle for the Union, to whatever extent the negroes should cease helping the enemy, to that extent, it weakened the enemy in his resistance to you. Do you think differently? I thought that whatever negroes can be got to do as soldiers leaves just so much less for white soldiers to do, in saving the Union. Does it appear otherwise to you? But negroes, like other people act upon motives. Why should they do any thing for us, if we will do nothing for them? If they stake their lives for us, they must be prompted by the strongest motive— even the promise of freedom. And the promise being made, must be kept.

Of the Conkling letter, his private secretaries later observed: "Nothing he ever uttered had a more instantaneous success."

With the appearance of this string of noteworthy letters, it began to dawn on Lincoln's critics that they had either misjudged him or, more likely, that someone else was writing these public letters. Some suspected Lincoln's secretary of state, William H. Seward, while others thought they recognized the capable hand of his secretary of war, Edwin M. Stanton. One of Stanton's former colleagues at the bar went so far as to compliment him on being the president's ghostwriter. Stanton not only denied the attribution but admitted that the talents of his unprepossessing chief had been grossly underrated, even by himself.

What neither his critics nor his supporters realized was that the president had been a gifted and dedicated writer from childhood. His stepmother testified that as a boy he kept a notebook of his reading and trial compositions, reflecting his obsession with words and their meanings, with the problem of ambiguity in language, and with the need for clarity of expression. Close friends would report that, even as a successful politician in later life, Lincoln assiduously wrote and rewrote passages for later use in his stump speeches and debates to assure that his message would be clearly understood and would appeal to ordinary citizens.

In an age that expected politicians to discourse in ornamental language and lofty expression, he took a distinctly different tack and worked toward a style of plain speaking and ordinary language. In writing, he constantly revised, but, in addition to being a *re*-writer, he was also a *pre*-writer. He formed a habit of writing down on scraps of paper words, phrases, and ideas that occurred to him. His law partner William H. Herndon described how he accumulated many such scraps for his famous House Divided speech, storing them in his hat. One day he dumped the scraps on the table in their law office, sorted, organized, and numbered them and proceeded to write out his speech. There is conclusive evidence that he followed this same procedure in the preparation of some of his most consequential presidential writings.

That Lincoln's very considerable talent as a writer was almost entirely unknown when he became president must be regarded as something of an advantage to him. The standard response of his political adversaries to his presidential writings was, at first, automatic ridicule, but it eventually became evident that his public letters were generally persuasive and well received. Later in his presidency, after he had written another impressive public letter—the one that contained the line "If slavery is not wrong, nothing is wrong"—Horace Greeley finally acknowledged that the president was an able and effective advocate and advised his fellow critics that, in these circumstances, it was counterproductive to treat these powerful writings as if they were the inept work of a simpleton.

What Greeley recognized, and was implicitly admitting, was that Lincoln's newspaper letters were working as intended: they were reshaping public opinion. George Templeton Strong, the astute New York diarist, wrote in 1864:

> The change of opinion on this slavery question since 1860 is a great historical fact, comparable with the early progress of Christianity and of Mahometanism. Who could have predicted it, even when the news came that Sumter had fallen, or even a year and a quarter afterwards, when Pope was falling back on Washington, routed and disorganized? I think this great and blessed revolution is due, in no small degree, to A. Lincoln's sagacious policy.

Soon after Strong entered this in his diary, *Harper's Weekly* zeroed in on the role of Lincoln's writing in this same process:

> He wrote the Greeley letter, the Vallandigham letter [on civil liberties], the Springfield [Conkling] letter, simple, plain, direct; letters which the heart of every man in the land interpreted, and, unlike any other instance in our political annals, every letter he wrote, every speech he made, brought him nearer to the popular heart.

Lincoln came to the presidency believing that "Public opinion in this country is everything," and his efforts to influence it went well beyond his successful series of public letters. At the outbreak of hostilities, knowing that his annual report to the Congress would give him the opportunity to define the terms and lay out the rationale for the oncoming conflict, he worked on it assiduously over a period of two months. "This is essentially a People's contest," he wrote. "On the side of the Union, it is a struggle for maintaining in the world, that form, and substance of government, whose leading object is, to elevate the condition of men—to lift artificial weights from all shoulders—to clear the paths of laudable pursuit for all—to afford all, an unfettered start, and a fair chance, in the race of life." Lincoln seized the moment to explain not only what must be done, but why.

***

What, then, does Lincoln's experience in shaping public opinion have to tell us, if anything, about political communication at the presidential level in the vastly different world of the twenty-first century?

Given the extraordinary sophistication and complexity of the present-day media, Lincoln's public letters and incidental writings may appear primitive indeed, but their overall effectiveness at critical moments should command our attention. Without doubt, that effectiveness owed much to Lincoln's skill as a writer, but here one needs to say a word about "Charlie," Bob Newhart's press agent stand-in for the team of writers that is now an indispensable part of a modern presidency. Given the voracious demands of the modern media and the range of issues that the presidential office must address, it is not reasonable to expect a twenty-first-century president to do all his own writing. And it must be said that, in general, Charlie's writing (as reflected in speeches by presidents from Franklin D. Roosevelt to Ronald Reagan and beyond) has generally proven to be adequate to the task, in most cases clearly superior to what his chief would be capable of.

The comparison that concerns us here is less about literary ability than it is about other notable qualities that contributed to Lincoln's success in shaping public opinion. Perhaps the first is that he did the unexpected: he defied tradition and openly courted censure for doing so. Further, by insisting on performing this time-consuming literary labor himself (for there were Charlies available even then), he demonstrated that he regarded the shaping of public opinion as a top priority—something too sensitive and too important to delegate. This, in itself, would appear to be a telling characteristic.

Another is that even with the mind-boggling prolixity of politically-related news stories, television programs, talk radio shows, editorials, blogs, Twitter feeds, and so much more competing for our attention today, a president speaking directly to the public on an important topic still attracts massive national and international attention. Although not highly controversial as in Lincoln's day, a presidential statement still turns on red lights because of the risks involved—of saying something that turns out to be disadvantageous or harmful, as well as the additional hazard of overexposure.

This opens the subject of Lincoln's presidential risk taking, which was much more considerable than the legend allows, even as his public communication was carefully calibrated and hedged. At the same time, Lincoln's risk taking as a communicator is a useful model for presidents in search of effective strategies, as well as for observers in need of standards of comparison. Times of crisis demand decisive action, and the boldness of Lincoln's communication gambits may recommend itself to future leaders when they face similarly historic turning points.

But perhaps the most significant and consequential of all the qualities Lincoln displayed in his public communications was an unwillingness to demonize his adversaries. Brought up on bare-knuckled frontier politics, Lincoln eventually came to the belief that treating your opponent with respect rather than demeaning him was not only more becoming but improved your prospects for making points with your audience as well. Strongly principled himself, he urged ideologues who were unwilling to compromise to rethink the alternatives with open minds. "Much as I hate slavery," he said in 1854, "I would consent to the extension of it rather than see the Union dissolved, just as I would consent to any GREAT evil to avoid a GREATER one."

With the outbreak of civil war, this practice stood out in stark relief when it concerned those who were, in his view, out to destroy the Union. Although resorting in certain situations to stern language, such as "treason" and "traitor," for the most part Lincoln treated those in rebellion as errant brothers of whom he asked only that they lay down their arms and renew their allegiance to their common country. This set him apart from the many Northern politicians who insisted upon harsh treatment of the rebels. Lincoln's benign attitude permeated his public discourse about the war and constituted one of the major differences between himself and other Unionists. One has only to compare what Lincoln wrote in this regard with the public utterances of members of his own cabinet and the Republican leaders in Congress, nearly all of whom wanted vengeance, up to and including capital punishment, for the crimes of rebellion.

Nowhere is this dramatic contrast more profoundly reflected than in the sharply differing views of national reconstruction being proposed as the war drew to a close. This is the context for what is perhaps Lincoln's most ambitious effort to shape public attitudes, his second inaugural address. How Lincoln would have handled the reconstruction of the South has always been the great historical "what if," but his basic theme is enunciated in the sonorous conclusion of this famous address: "With malice toward none; with charity for all; with firmness in the right, as God gives us to see the right, let us strive on to finish the work we are in; to bind up the nation's wounds; to care for him who shall have borne the battle, and for his widow, and his orphan— to do all which may achieve and cherish a just, and a lasting peace, among ourselves, and with all nations."

Abraham Lincoln was, by any measure, a great communicator and a skillful shaper of public opinion. In one respect, his example is exasperatingly out of reach for most modern politicians, because his ability to move ordinary people, to affect their feelings and attitudes, and to alter their political convictions, is almost without parallel in American or even in world history. But there are still many valuable insights that modern politicians can glean from his example.

For instance, when the fortunes of his administration were at their nadir in August 1862, and his fellow Republican, Horace Greeley, chose this moment to rake him over the coals on the front page of his influential newspaper, Lincoln responded to the message by writing, "If there be in it any statements, or assumptions of fact, which I may know to be erroneous, I do not, now and here, controvert them. If there be in it any inferences which I may believe to be falsely drawn, I do not now and here, argue against them. If there be perceptible in it an impatient and dictatorial tone, I waive it in deference to an old friend, whose heart I have always supposed to be right."

With this self-imposed civility, Lincoln did more than demonstrate restraint; he laid the basis for gaining a sympathetic hearing from a greatly discouraged and discontented public by appealing to what he had memorably called, in his first inaugural address, "the better angels of our nature." Thus, what is arguably the most important lesson Lincoln has to teach is as simple as it is difficult: refuse to demonize your opponent, even if (or especially if) he has demonized you.

LINCOLN'S WORDS

Speech to the 166th Ohio Regiment, Washington, D.C. (1864)

Freedom and Equality, the "Inestimable Jewel"

SOLDIERS—I suppose you are going home to see your families and friends. For the services you have done in this great struggle in which we are engaged, I present you sincere thanks for myself and the country.

I almost always feel inclined, when I say anything to soldiers, to impress upon them, in a few brief remarks, the importance of success in this contest. It is not merely for the day, but for all time to come, that we should perpetuate for our children's children that great and free government which we have enjoyed all our lives. I beg you to remember this, not merely for my sake, but for yours. I happen, temporarily, to occupy this big White House. I am a living witness that any one of your children may look to come here as my father's child has. It is in order that each one of you may have, through this free government which we have enjoyed, an open field, and a fair chance for your industry, enterprise, and intelligence; that you may all have equal privileges in the race of life with all its desirable human aspirations—it is for this that the struggle should be maintained, that we may not lose our birthrights—not only for one, but for two or three years, if necessary. The nation is worth fighting for, to secure such an inestimable jewel.

August 22, 1864

Long ABRAHAM LINCOLN a Little Longer.

Cartoonist Frank Bellew in *Harper's Weekly* celebrates Lincoln's victory in the 1864 election by depicting "Long Abraham Lincoln" becoming "a Little Longer." *The Granger Collection, New York*

11

"THE ALMIGHTY HAS HIS OWN PURPOSES"

Abraham Lincoln and the Christian Right

RICHARD CARWARDINE

Richard Carwardine is the president of Corpus Christi College, Oxford University. Elected a fellow of the British Academy in 2006, he is the author of Transatlantic Revivalism: Popular Evangelicalism in Britain and America 1790–1865 *(1978) and* Evangelicals and Politics in Antebellum America *(1993). His analytical political biography of Abraham Lincoln,* Lincoln: A Life of Purpose and Power, *won the Lincoln Prize in 2004. He is currently working on a study of religion in American national construction between the Revolution and the Civil War.*

I n 1993, the *Weekly World News*, a semisatirical tabloid newspaper featuring outlandish fictional "news," reported that Abraham Lincoln's body, injected with a miracle drug, had come briefly back to life. The amazed scientists who clustered round his stirring corpse heard Lincoln utter just a few words. "Gentlemen," he inquired, "where am I?" Then he returned to oblivion.[1]

The story is joyfully ludicrous, but Lincoln's question, though banal, reminds us that he would find much to shock and perplex him in the modern world. In an encounter with massive corporate power, finance capitalism, unceasing revolutions in technology and communications, upheavals in global power, and reconstructed gender and race relations—including an African American in the White House, serving not as a menial but as president—what continuities, if any, might Lincoln discern between his own time and ours?

Were he to return today, Lincoln would at least recognize the names of the two parties that have dominated American electoral politics since the mid-1850s, when he embarked on his pursuit of high national office. But he would discover that, although their labels have gone unchanged, the parties' constitutional bearings and philosophical outlooks have not. Democrats have long abandoned their forebears' defining agenda of states' rights and white racial supremacy. Modern-day Republicans' language of hostility to big government shows how far they, too, have traveled since the Civil War era, when they looked keenly to the federal government as a primary agent of economic and social improvement. Indeed, the evolution in the two parties' postures has allowed each to appropriate the sixteenth president as their talisman and symbolic ally.

Still, in one respect at least, the party of Lincoln gives the appearance of clear continuity over time. The Republicans remain the party most likely to trumpet their religious values and in particular their kinship with evangelical Protestantism. The elements that coalesced during the 1850s into the Republican opposition of the dominant Democratic Party included an army of activist evangelicals who were determined to mold their new political party into an agency of righteousness. They shaped its values, program, and electoral energy— and they gloried in their self-identification as "the Christian party." Their modern descendants are the chief beneficiaries of the culture wars that have polarized the parties since the 1970s.

In this latter-day conflict, Republicans have defended traditional moral values and sheltered conservative religionists. In the South, this has helped destroy the Democrats' century-long regional supremacy.

Republicans win votes from—amongst others—Catholics, Jews, and Mormons, but their largest religious constituency is that of conservative evangelicals. White evangelical voters constituted 23 percent of the electorate in the presidential contest of 2004. Of these, 78 percent voted for George W. Bush.

Not all evangelicals are fundamentalists and biblical literalists, but those who are provide the backbone of the so-called Christian Right. In their approach to public issues, conservative Christians present no uniform or consolidated policy agenda, but their various concerns have become the coin of politics. The Constitution may prevent the federal government from sponsoring a particular church or religion, but—religious fundamentalists maintain—the separation of church and state was never intended to secularize politics or remove religious values from the domain of public policy. In the field of education, they support school prayer, the teaching of creationism and "intelligent design" as alternatives to evolution, and abstinence-based sex education. They speak out against premarital sex, homosexuality, civil unions and gay marriage, adoption by same-sex couples, and employment of gays and bisexuals in the classroom, the church ministry, and the armed forces. They mostly support capital punishment, but oppose abortion and the destruction of human embryos in medical research. Generally favoring laissez-faire economics and tax cuts, they distrust welfare legislation and "socialized" medical care (a term flexible enough to embrace even the free-market-based program promoted by Barack Obama in the Affordable Care Act of 2010). On foreign issues, a broad skepticism over international cooperation has not prevented a firm commitment to the state of Israel as a bulwark against Islam.

To ask how Lincoln would view this fusion of conservative religion with conservative politics is, of course, to seek the unknowable. There are obvious hazards in questions like this. One wise scholar, when asked how Lincoln would have addressed the issue of school busing, avoided fatuous anachronism by replying: "I guess he'd have said, 'what's a bus?'" Lincoln would be likely to express similar mystification over civil unions, human embryos, and other issues addressed in the social conservative agenda. It is, however, possible to investigate the complicated development of Lincoln's personal faith and cast of mind, what he accepted as the legitimate linkage between religion and politics in his own time, and in particular how he dealt with the powerful evangelical forces of the day. Taken together, this evidence invites some informed speculation about how Lincoln might respond to an encounter with today's Christian Right.

"Not a Technical Christian": Lincoln's Faith

Given that one of Lincoln's close legal and political associates, Judge David Davis, described him as "the most reticent—Secretive man I Ever Saw—or Expect to See," what can be said with certainty about Lincoln's personal faith?[2] Was he "eminently a Christian President . . . who thought more of religious subjects than of all others," and "had an undying faith in the providence of God," as a fellow lawyer contended after his death?[3] Yes indeed, declared other acquaintances, who included the pastor of the First Presbyterian Church in Springfield, where the Lincoln family worshiped. Not so, countered some other Illinois associates, who recalled an essentially godless man. According to James Matheny, Lincoln had been an open infidel in his youth, when he called Christ "a bastard," "ridiculed the Bible" as self-contradictory and irrational, and wrote "a little Book on Infidelity." He learnt to be discreet, however, "as he grew older [and] . . . didn't talk much before Strangers about his religion." During the 1850s, as "a rising man" in politics, he had "played a sharp game" on the Christian community and duped pious voters into believing he was "a seeker after Salvation &c in the Lord."[4]

   Neither of these verdicts stands up to close scrutiny. Lincoln was not faithless, but neither was he a Christian. In his youth he read the Bible but grew away from the "hard-shell" Calvinism of his Baptist upbringing, though that strict faith left its legacy in his continuing fatalism. "What is to be will be," he told congressman Isaac Arnold, in words he often repeated to his wife Mary: "I have found all my life as Hamlet says: 'There's a divinity that shapes our ends, Rough-hew them how we will.'"[5] He told his law partner William Herndon that "all things were fixed, doomed in one way or the other, from which there was no appeal" and that "no efforts nor prayers of ours can change, alter, modify, or reverse the decree."[6] Throughout his life he would speak of the determining power of "Divine Providence."

Leaving his parental home, Lincoln relished the opportunity for intellectual inquiry. Settling in New Salem, he had no time for rural hell-fire itinerants or the revivalist enthusiasms of polemical Methodists and Baptists. Rather, he turned to rationalist critiques of Scripture, notably Thomas Paine's *Age of Reason*. He loved Robert Burns' satire on Calvinist self-righteousness. If, as is likely, he questioned the status of the Bible as divine revelation, this does not mean, as one of his acquaintances asserted, that his views "bordered on absolute Atheism."[7] His skepticism easily embraced belief in a Creator. This God, though, was not quixotic or impulsive, or one who consigned souls to endless punishment, as in the conventional Protestant theology of Lincoln's day.

Lincoln's views continued to evolve throughout his lifetime. Private reflection on matters of ethics and ultimate reality came naturally to him. As a Springfield lawyer with family responsibilities, he encountered a more intellectual and searching Protestantism. Following the death in 1850 of Eddie, their three-year-old son, Abraham and Mary migrated from the Episcopal to the First Presbyterian Church, whose sympathetic pastor, James Smith, had conducted the funeral ceremony. Lincoln himself attended irregularly. Smith was a well-educated Scot ready to take on freethinkers. In *The Christian Defense*, a substantial work of theology, Smith marshaled historical and natural sciences in the service of orthodoxy. He gave a copy to Lincoln, who, he maintained, gave the arguments a "searching investigation."[8]

Later, as president during a time of civil war, Lincoln found himself drawn toward even more profound inquiry. Not only did he feel a sense of personal responsibility for the savage struggle, but the conflict brought him trials closer to home: the death of friends and colleagues and the loss through typhoid of a dear son, Willie. He attended public worship more habitually than before, at the Old School Presbyterian

Church on Washington's New York Avenue. He found in his darkest nights increasing solace in the Scriptures, including the Psalms and the book of Job.

Lincoln, however, was at no time in his adult life an evangelical or even, strictly speaking, a Christian. His faith was never Christ-centered, and his implicit questioning of the divinity of Jesus placed him closer to Unitarianism—with its honoring of the Fatherhood of God and the brotherhood of man—than to Trinitarian Christianity. Before the war, their conversations about religion had convinced Jesse Fell, a Bloomington lawyer, that Lincoln "did not believe in what are regarded as the orthodox or evangelical views of Christianity."[9] Springfield's New School Presbyterian minister, Albert Hale, regretted that Lincoln was not "born of God."[10] During his presidency, when he embraced a more interventionist and personal God, still Lincoln never spoke of "my Saviour" as an evangelical might, only of "the Saviour." Reminiscing after his death, the president's widow was sure he had not been "a technical Christian": he had, Mary said, "no hope—& no faith in the usual acceptation of those words."[11]

Religion and Politics: Lincoln's Experience

Lincoln entered young manhood at the same time that American mass democratic politics came of age. The world's first broad-based political parties—notably the Democrats and Whigs of the 1830s and 1840s—learned much about popular mobilization from the nation's fast-growing evangelical churches, the most influential subculture in the United States. During the first half of the nineteenth century, the proportion of Protestant evangelicals in the overall population more than doubled: By the 1850s, at least four in every ten Americans belonged to one or another of a range of evangelical denominations, from high-status Presbyterians and Congregationalists to the self-proclaimed churches of the plain folk, notably the Methodists and Baptists. Religious identities, issues, and language did much to shape party loyalties, political agendas, and the tone of political discourse.

Lincoln was personally affronted by religious sectarianism, but he recognized that religious identity and animosities helped shape Illinoisans' party choices. He knew about religion's electoral significance though unhappy personal experience. In 1843 he failed to get the Whig nomination for the Eighth Congressional District. Afterward, he ruefully explained why: "it was everywhere contended that no Christian ought to go for me, because I belonged to no church, [and] was suspected of being a deist." These influences, he judged, "were very strong" and "levied a tax of considerable per cent upon my strength throughout the religious com[m]unity."[12]

Three years later, he again sought the nomination. His opponent was a combative and formidable Methodist circuit rider, Peter Cartwright, whose supporters put it about that Lincoln was "an open scoffer at Christianity." Alarmed, Lincoln published a handbill seeking to limit the damage. He conceded that he was "not a member of any Christian Church," but, he insisted, "I have never denied the truth of the Scriptures," "'I have never spoken with intentional disrespect of religion in general, or of any denomination of Christians in particular," and "I do not think I could myself, be brought to support a man for office, whom I knew to be an open enemy of, and scoffer at, religion." Lincoln described this as "the whole truth, briefly stated, in relation to myself, upon this subject." But it was scarcely full disclosure. He avoided any statement of positive belief: "the higher matter of eternal consequences," he judged, should remain an issue between man and his Maker.[13] This time, Lincoln secured the nomination.

Lincoln had learned a defining lesson. He would not again expose himself to the charge of irreligion. When he returned to active politics in 1854, spurred by the passage of Stephen A. Douglas's Kansas-Nebraska Act, he addressed the ethical challenge of slavery expansionism with a set of arguments that spoke to the moral outrage of antislavery Protestants. This is not to imply that Lincoln cynically manipulated his language in order to capture the support of progressive Christians. But, over the next six years, by invoking the principles of the Declaration of Independence and setting them within a framework of right and wrong, he delighted those antislavery Christians who brought to the infant Republican party a mix of the Enlightenment idealism of the Founding Fathers with New Testament theology. Lincoln's religious correspondents in 1858, when he ran against Douglas for the US Senate seat, encouraged him to hold on to "high ground . . . up to the standard of the Christianity of the day."[14] They left him confident in his ability to inspire churchgoing Republicans.

In 1860, running for the presidency, Lincoln and his party again touched a religious nerve. The Republicans' campaign, promising an end to slavery's further expansion, blended the economic, the political, and the moral: free soil and free labor, under threat from an unscrupulous "slave power," were not only an economic good, they were essential means of moral advance for the nation. Crusading Republicans rallied millennialist Protestants, describing the irrepressible conflict between free and slave labor as "Christ's doctrine of righteousness conflicting with evil."[15] They presented their candidate as a man of sound Protestant faith: "He is a regular attendant upon religious worship, and though not a communicant, is a pew-holder and liberal supporter of the Presbyterian church in Springfield, to which Mrs. Lincoln belongs";[16] he had "always held up the doctrines of the Bible, and the truths and examples of the Christian religion, as the foundation of all good."[17] He would rescue the nation from the rule of a Godless administration. Lincoln himself never sought to exploit religious sectarianism for electoral gain, but these scruples did not trouble Republican campaigners, who played on popular anti-Catholicism and branded Stephen A. Douglas, his Democratic opponent (whose second wife, Adele Cutts, was Catholic), with the mark of the beast.

Across the North, Republicans extended their influence within evangelical communions. Lincoln ran impressively among German Protestant voters who previously had been alienated by the party's anti-immigrant elements, and at the same time he made gains at the expense of the nativist and anti-Catholic American (Know-Nothing) Party. Although his party did not command a unified evangelical vote, it did organize the moral energies of evangelical churches better than ever before in the cause of political antislavery and national purification. Republicans were both more and less than "the Christian party in politics," but in the eyes of antislavery voters they deserved that label better than any previous political force. Combining constitutional conservatism and ethical earnestness, Lincoln gave the Republicans a standard-bearer who admirably met the needs of both political pragmatists and high-minded crusaders.

When war came, Lincoln was diligent in keeping the key elements of Northern evangelical Protestantism loyal to the Republican-Unionist coalition. He frequently emphasized three lines of thought: every nation was a moral being; the Almighty's purposes were wise, if mysterious; and the American Union, under God, promised to be an agent of moral and political transformation. These theological themes (expressed most notably just weeks before his death in his sermonic second inaugural address) were in such harmony with the thinking of mainstream evangelical Christians that Lincoln, as a fellow Illinoisan put it, came to be seen as "a sort of halfway clergyman."[18] He fostered good relations with church leaders—preachers, newspaper editors, and representatives of the welfare agencies—and gave them ready access to the Executive Mansion (as the White House was then formally known).

Together, Lincoln's encouragement of loyal religious constituencies and their mutual confidence contributed signally to the Union's mobilization. These Protestants acted as ideological warriors, recruiting volunteer soldiers, stiffening the Republican-Union party in the politics of national defense, and defending the administration's strong-arm tactics against draft resisters and dissenters. Lincoln's re-election campaign in 1864 witnessed the most complete fusing of religious crusade and political mobilization in America's electoral experience. Clergy gave election speeches, addressed troops, and editorialized. Churches became Union-Republican clubs. Lincoln won in large part thanks to those who saw themselves as agents of God as well as the president: the leaders of the mainstream evangelical churches.

Lincoln and the Christian Right

Lincoln, then, though no evangelical Christian himself, worked in concert with evangelicals in energizing the young Republican Party and in defending the Union. On the face of it, this offers parallels—and even points of real kinship—between his experience and that of today's Republicans, with their electoral embrace of Bible-based insurgents. Lincoln would surely not be taken aback by the current interpenetration of religion and politics and would see the energetic political engagement of evangelical Christians as wholly legitimate. He knew firsthand all about evangelicals' efforts to assert themselves in the public arena and to legislate a program based on their values and principles. During his political career, he observed evangelical campaigns for, inter alia, the protection of Native Americans, Sabbath observance, restrictions on the use of alcohol, opposition to the public funding of Catholic schools, and the abolition of slavery. More often than not, those who mounted these campaigns were numbered among his partners in the coalition of interests that comprised his Whig and Republican Parties.

Beyond that, we should note that Lincoln shared with the evangelicals of his own time, as of today, an admiration for individual self-discipline, sobriety, and thrift. His own early history was a chronicle of ambitious self-improvement. Well before reaching the age of majority in 1830, he had had enough of the hard life of the midwestern farmer. He left his family home, hired himself out as a Mississippi flatboat man, and then, in the aspiring commercial hamlet of New Salem, progressed through a sequence of occupations: clerk, mill manager, store owner, postmaster, surveyor, and self-taught lawyer. By the time he joined a law practice in Springfield, in 1837, he had acquired a reputation for diligence, ingenuity, and conscientious self-education. If not an evangelical Christian, he shared evangelicals' sense that alcohol, tobacco, and gambling were an affront to self-command and obstacles to achievement.

Nothing better illuminates these values than Lincoln's 1848 letter to his feckless stepbrother, John Johnston, who had asked for yet another loan. "Your request for eighty dollars, I do not think it best, to comply with now," he wrote. Johnston's repeated requests could only be the result of "some defect in your *conduct.* . . . You are not *lazy,* and still you *are* an *idler.* I doubt whether since I saw you, you have

done a good whole day's work in any one day. . . . This habit of use-
lessly wasting time, is the whole difficulty; and it is vastly important
to you, and still more so to your children that you should break this
habit." Lincoln urged his stepbrother to hire himself out for work.
"And to secure you a fair reward for your labor, I now promise you,
that for every dollar you will . . . get for your own labor . . . I will then
give you one other dollar." By these means "you will soon be out of
debt, and what is better, you will have a habit that will keep you from
getting in debt again." Johnston had said that he would "almost"
trade his place in heaven for seventy or eighty dollars. "Then you
value your place in Heaven very cheaply for I am sure you can with
the offer I make you get the seventy or eighty dollars for four or five
months work."[19]

This, however, is the strongest case that can be made in the cause
of tying Lincoln to today's conservative evangelicals. The fact remains that the overwhelming logic of Lincoln's relations with the religious world of his own day sets him far apart from today's Christian
Right.

The case for this line of argument is twofold. First, the evangelical Protestants of the Civil War era represented a wide cross-section
of religious opinion, much of it deeply conservative and hostile to
the new Republican Party. Those with whom Lincoln was allied politically, and with whom he personally had most in common, clustered at the other end of that spectrum; they were Christians who
carried into the public sphere a zeal for social progress and national
modernization. Second, Lincoln's own intellectual journey reveals
his profound distrust of religious dogmatism and what he saw as self-
righteousness. He was always open to philosophical inquiry and rational thought. We may reasonably suppose he would be alienated
by what can seem the closed-minded certainties of modern conservative evangelicals and their political program. These claims require
some elaboration.

It is essential to recognize, first, that the evangelicals who brought so
much moral energy to Lincoln's Republican Party in its early days were
among the most progressive forces of the time. Disproportionately

drawn from New England and its wide diaspora, and alive with millennialist expectations, they championed religious activism, so-called New School theology, personal civic responsibility, economic progress, and intellectual inquiry. Their educational institutions set the pace in the encouragement of science and the improvement of human capabilities. They saw their American republic and its institutions of popular, democratic government threatened by what they deemed the social and economic archaism of slaveholders and the medieval temper of Roman Catholicism. They were hardly conservatives in any helpful meaning of that term. When confronted over time by the challenges of modern science and secularism, many of them, and their descendants, followed a path of liberal Christianity that kept them loyal to their faith, as well as confident in—and stimulated by—intellectual and scientific inquiry.

Lincoln shared with these evangelicals a sense of the enormous potential for humankind under the ordered freedom of the American Union. Some of the most radical of them—United States congressmen Joshua Giddings and Owen Lovejoy, for example—were numbered among his admirers. The most committed antislavery evangelicals rallied to Lincoln as a dependable representative of a particular variety of progressive Protestantism, represented by Quakers, Freewill Baptists, Wesleyan Methodists, and Free Presbyterians.

At the same time, to Lincoln's distress, he also knew that there were battalions of other evangelicals, and Christians more generally, who drew on Scripture to sustain a deeply conservative view of the social order. Very many evangelicals of Lincoln's time, including significant numbers in the North, were strongly proslavery and grounded their position on a literal interpretation of Biblical texts; while abolitionists generally argued from the *spirit* of Christ's teaching, defenders of the South's peculiar institution invoked the *letter* of both Old Testament and Pauline texts. During the 1860 election campaign, Lincoln pored over the results of a canvass of Springfield opinion and shared with a colleague his frustration that so many God-fearing Christians seemingly did not care whether slavery was voted up or down: "Here are twenty-three ministers of different denominations, and all of them are against me but three; and here are a great many prominent members of the churches, a very large majority of whom are against me."[20]

Lincoln reserved his particular scorn for Southern conservative theologians. He chided the Presbyterian author Frederick A. Ross for concluding that "it is better for *some* people to be slaves; and, in such cases, it is the Will of God that they be such." The fact that determining God's will was to be left to Dr. Ross, who "sits in the shade, with gloves on his hands, and subsists on the bread that Sambo is earning in the burning sun," gave Lincoln little confidence that he would "be actuated by that perfect impartiality, which has ever been considered most favorable to correct decisions."[21] Late in 1864, the wife of a Confederate prisoner of war pressed the president to release him, partly on the grounds of her husband's piety. Lincoln granted her request but in complying delivered a "political sermon" for publication under his heading of "The President's Last, Shortest, and Best Speech": "You say your husband is a religious man; tell him . . . that . . . I am not much of a judge of religion, but that, in my opinion, the religion that sets men to rebel and fight against their government, because, as they think, that government does not sufficiently help some men to eat their bread on the sweat of other men's faces, is not the sort of religion upon which people can get to heaven!"[22]

Nowhere did Lincoln more eloquently describe this conflict within Christianity than in his second inaugural. In both the Union and the Confederacy, he noted, nominally similar churches, reading the same Bible and sharing evangelical convictions, "pray to the same God; and each invokes His aid against the other." Reflecting on this paradox, he gave voice to a sentiment that marked him out from the majority, certain they knew God's will: "Let us judge not that we be not judged. The prayers of both could not be answered; that of neither has been answered fully. The Almighty has His own purposes."[23]

As this reveals, Lincoln's faith was marked by caution, a deep sense of the mystery of God, and a distrust of the self-righteous dogmatism that he saw in so many of his contemporaries. He was especially dismayed by the nativist intolerance of the Know Nothings toward immigrants and Catholics. He was cool toward the moral absolutism of teetotalers and abolitionists, despite his personal disrelish of alcohol and his view of slavery as an unequivocal wrong: the victims of drink and the prisoners of the slave system—white as well as black— merited understanding as victims of unbreakable habit and embedded environments. White Southerners did just what the people of the free states would have done in their situation. "No man was to be eulogized for what he did or censured for what he did not do," his law partner Herndon noted. "I never heard him censure anyone but slightly."[24]

When, early in the war, his friend Orville Browning urged him to strike against slavery as the means of securing divine assistance for the Union, Lincoln replied, "Browning, suppose God is against us in our view on the subject of slavery in this country, and our method of dealing with it?"[25] In similar vein, he asked a visiting delegation of emancipationist Quakers to consider that, possibly, "God's way of accomplishing the end which the memorialists have in view may be different from theirs."[26] In a remarkable private expression of his thinking—his "meditation on the divine will"—Lincoln offered a startling hypothesis: "In the present civil war it is quite possible that God's purpose is something different from the purpose of either party. . . . I am almost ready to say this is probably true—that God wills this contest, and wills that it shall not end yet." God *chose* to let the contest begin. "And having begun He could give the final victory to either side any day. Yet the contest proceeds."[27]

These were the words of a man whose ideas on divine intervention indicated some kinship with the evangelical mainstream but one whose hesitancy over equating the Union cause with God's will, or with Christian holiness, set him apart from it. How exactly could one know what God wanted? Lincoln would remark that "from the beginning" he had seen that "the issues of our great struggle depended on the Divine interposition and favor. If we had that all would be well."[28] But he remained ever cautious and reluctant to claim he had heard the voice of God. "I hope," he told a delegation from the Chicago churches, "it will not be irreverent for me to say that if it is probable that God would reveal his will to others, on a point so connected with my duty, it might be supposed he would reveal it directly to me; for . . . it is my earnest desire to know the will of Providence in this matter. *And if I can learn what it is I will do it!*"[29] But in the absence of miracles or direct revelation, he had to use the only means available: observation and rational analysis.

It was Lincoln's appetite for prioritizing reason that above all marked his intellectual and spiritual life. He never lost the spirit of free inquiry that he brought to his exploration of ideas, technological innovation, and scientific advance. Essentially he was a child of the Enlightenment and remained so even when in the midst of a terrifying war, when he came to feel, much more than he had done before, the mystery of God's purposes.

We can only speculate—and that with caution—on how his Enlightenment temper would serve him in a confrontation with, for example, modern-day evolutionary science. In his own day, as the historian Daniel Walker Howe has noted, "virtually everyone," Christians and deists alike, believed in intelligent design: belief in the rational design of the universe was a staple of the worldview of the Enlightenment.[30] Lincoln's own reading included Robert Chambers's analysis of Christianity and evolutionary science. We can reasonably suppose that his criticism of the self-serving Biblical literalism of the proslavery South and his open-minded quest for an understanding of human development would make him ready to engage with Darwinian theory. It is only conservative fundamentalists who find evolutionary theories incompatible with religious faith; Christians and others of a nonfundamentalist persuasion find no necessary contradiction between Darwinian science and religious belief. Given Lincoln's distaste for literalist dogma, it is much easier to envisage him today standing against, not alongside, creationists.

Equally, though we cannot know what he would say about abortion or gay marriage or stem cell research, we can at least note his aloofness from movements in his own time—notably temperance reform—that called for the statutory control of personal morality. Finally, and with more confidence, we might conclude that Lincoln's

Enlightenment rationalism, which he fused with a religious sensibility, would leave him not just frustrated but mystified by the chasm
that separates the certainties of the Christian Right from the spirit of
liberal inquiry that animates those of other religious persuasions as
well as those with none.

LINCOLN'S WORDS

Memorandum on Probable Failure
of Re-election (1864)

In an unpublished, private memo,
Lincoln prepares for the worst

Executive Mansion
Washington, Aug. 23, 1864.

This morning, as for some days past, it seems
exceedingly probable that this Administration will
not be re-elected. Then it will be my duty to so
co-operate with the President elect, as to save the
Union between the election and the inauguration;
as he will have secured his election on such ground
that he can not possibly save it afterwards.

A. Lincoln

Last known photo of Lincoln, taken by Alexander Gardner
(April 10, 1865). *Library of Congress*

THE REAL LINCOLN
IS THE ICON

An Interview with
ANDREW FERGUSON

Andrew Ferguson, a senior editor at the Weekly Standard, *is the author of three books:* Fools' Names, Fools' Faces *(1996), a collection of essays;* Land of Lincoln: Adventures in Abe's America *(2007), named by the* Wall Street Journal *and the* Chicago Tribune *as a Book of the Year; and* Crazy U: One Dad's Crash Course in Getting His Kid into College *(2011).*

Formerly a senior writer for the Washingtonian *magazine, he has been a contributing editor to* Time *magazine, as well as a columnist for* Fortune, TV Guide, Forbes FYI, National Review, Bloomberg News, *and* Commentary. *He has also written for the* New Yorker, New York *magazine, the* New Republic, *the* American Spectator, *the* Los Angeles Times, *the* New York Times, *the* Washington Post, *and many other publications. In 1992, he was a White House speechwriter for President George H. W. Bush. Ferguson lives in suburban Washington, DC, with his wife and two children. In July 2012, editor Karl Weber interviewed him there.*

KW: *Your book* Land of Lincoln, *which explores the varying legacies of Lincoln for contemporary Americans, is a very entertaining book, filled with funny stories and witty observations. But I gather you also had a serious intention in writing it.*

AF: Yes—several intentions, in fact. One was to suggest the— futility is too strong a word—but the crippling difficulty of trying to pin down exactly who Lincoln was and the precise meaning of his life. In the book, I describe the years I spent trying to learn all I could about Lincoln, which demonstrated to me just how little is really known with certainty about the inner man. I made a joke out of it by using the phrase "Scholars differ" as a kind of mantra, but it's all true—you can't delve very deeply into the story of Lincoln without encountering one serious area of disagreement after another. And, as I recount in the book, I visited countless historic settings from Springfield to Washington, looking for Lincoln, and, every time I thought I was about to grasp him, he vanished. The real Lincoln is terribly elusive.

Of course, that doesn't stop people from defining Lincoln for themselves. I was on a panel once with a poet and novelist who is very interested in Lincoln. When I said, "I think Lincoln is essentially unknowable," he reacted as if he felt personally insulted, because he'd just written a fictionalized biography of Lincoln. He said, very indignantly, "Well, I know who Lincoln was!" And it's true that, in his novel, he had created a very plausible Lincoln. But it wasn't the Lincoln. It was his Lincoln.

KW: *And I suppose we each have our own Lincoln. So who is your Lincoln?*

AF: I'm fascinated by so many things about Lincoln. One of the things that first attracted me to him was his stature as a literary figure. I think he may be the greatest prose stylist that America has ever produced.

KW: *How did that awareness hit you?*

AF: Well, from my childhood, my father and mother made me very conscious of how people write. My father was a lawyer in the firm of

Isham, Lincoln, and Beale, which was actually founded in 1872 by Lincoln's son Robert, and my mother was a homemaker. Both of them were the first ones in their family to go to college, and they really prized the intellectual life. My father in particular loved the clarity of great legal writing, and Lincoln has that quality above all, as well as that slightly biblical, King-Jamesian spin that he can put on a sentence. My father gave me a copy of Jacques Barzun's famous essay about Lincoln as a stylist—a very perceptive and deep piece of writing that really gets at something important about Lincoln's character and the habits of his mind.[1] So from an early age I was very conscious of Lincoln's greatness as a writer.

KW: *What do you consider to be Lincoln's supreme literary works?*

AF: The second inaugural address, which I think is what most people would say, and, of course, the Gettysburg Address. I think the first inaugural address is also brilliant, although kind of hard for people today, and so is the message to Congress that he wrote in 1861. Then there's a beautiful letter he wrote in 1863 to respond to people who were protesting the enlistment of freed black men into the US Army. It was written to a political figure named James C. Conkling, and it's just so brilliant, so beautiful, as well as very pointed and witty. Maybe the most famous line in it is the one where Lincoln remarks, "You say you will not fight to free negroes. Some of them seem willing to fight for you; but, no matter." Using irony like a stiletto—it's classic Lincoln.

When Lincoln's prose is at its best, I feel about it the way I feel about poetry. Of course, H. L. Mencken saw those same poetic qualities and used them as evidence of Lincoln's cynicism. He said the Gettysburg Address, for example, was nonsense—but beautiful nonsense.

KW: *Do you agree—is it beautiful nonsense?*

AF: No, I think it's the most profound statement anyone could have made at that point in history. If you respect what Lincoln did for the country—which I do—then you take the meaning of the Gettysburg Address quite seriously. It's beautiful, but it's not nonsense.

There's a wonderful book called *How to Do Things with Words* by a British philosopher named John Austin. His point is that words can do more than just describe reality. Sometimes, by using words to say something, you can actually *do* something. He calls this a "performative utterance." So, for example, when the minister says to a couple, "I now pronounce you husband and wife," he is actually accomplishing something just by uttering the words. In the same way, when Lincoln reframed the country and the country's mission in the Gettysburg Address, he made it true simply by uttering it. In a sense, he remade the country just by speaking the words.

KW: *I suppose his power to do that derived from his being president. Although I guess that Martin Luther King Jr. did something similar in his I Have a Dream speech—he redefined the mission of the country despite not having any legal mandate to speak on the nation's behalf.*

AF: And of course Lincoln didn't reshape the country primarily through legislation or an edict or even through military might. He did it by changing the way people think about the country—and that means predominantly through the power of words.

KW: *So Lincoln as a writer is a figure who means a lot to you. What about Lincoln as a politician? I find myself drawing comparisons between Lincoln and President Obama, not in terms of historical stature, of course, but in the way Obama is being attacked from both left and right while trying to walk a tightrope between conciliation and conflict.*

AF: Well, I think that's what all "conviction politicians," as they call them, have to do. There are entire college courses that focus on analyzing Lincoln's political skill—his ability to keep one set of supporters happy while simultaneously trying to satisfy their opponents, and then committing to one or the other at just the right moment. And he had a profound understanding of how public opinion ebbs and flows.

KW: *I guess that's one of the themes of Doris Kearns Goodwin's book.*

AF: Yes, and of Richard Carwardine's. He is a brilliant writer. But I think the greatest political biography of Lincoln is by another Englishman, Lord Charnwood, written way back in 1917. Of all the biographers up to that time, Lord Charnwood, who was himself a professional politician, was the one who took Lincoln most seriously as a politician/philosopher. One of his themes is how Lincoln recalled the country to its founding conception of equality.

Charnwood thought Lincoln was a genius as a politician, and I guess he was. Though I'm also sympathetic to some people who think some of this genius talk is a little overdone. Lincoln certainly blundered at times, most obviously in his choice of generals. It's very easy in hindsight to look at the course of history and impose a clear pattern, a clear intention on his actions that might not have been present at the time.

KW: *Lincoln said as much, didn't he?*

AF: Yes—in a letter to Albert G. Hodges, he famously wrote, "I claim not to have controlled events, but confess plainly that events have controlled me." But I think, in that instance, most people believe he was being a bit disingenuous. He was very good at that, too.

KW: *So is Charnwood's biography the one you'd recommend to readers who are new to the Lincoln literature?*

AF: Well, I have two sentimental favorites, the Charnwood biography and one by Benjamin P. Thomas, who was an amateur historian, as so many of the greatest Lincoln historians are. He wrote it back in 1952.

KW: *The fact that you cite a couple of older books suggests to me that your feeling is that scholarship in the last several decades hasn't added anything profoundly new to our understanding of Lincoln.*

AF: I think that's probably true. The great, brute facts of his life are pretty settled now. The rest of it is either matters of interpretation or scholastic bickering—how many angels are dancing on the head of the pin? And lots of these are problems of historiography. Doug Wilson gives a brilliant example in the first chapter of his book *Honor's Voice*, where he lays out a set of facts about a particular incident and then shows us several different ways people have interpreted those facts. Rather than just a work of history, Wilson's book is almost an introductory course in the kinds of problems that historians face.

KW: *So one of those imponderables that make Lincoln so difficult to pin down is the question of the degree to which he controlled events as opposed to being controlled by them. If Lincoln hadn't come along, what would have happened? How would American history have been different? What if someone like Andrew Johnson had served in Lincoln's place?*

AF: Shudder. Johnson was so incompetent, and he combined his incompetence with a terrible temperament—a deadly combination. I suppose if he'd taken office in 1861, the country would have just continued to muddle along for a while, with the conflict over slavery becoming more and more intense. And eventually the Union would have collapsed, and the South would have somehow tried to go its own way. The problem was that there wasn't anywhere to go. The Confederacy probably would have become a client state of the North, as a weaker country will with a stronger country, essentially living in a dependent relationship with it. Which just compounds the resentment and hostility on both sides.

More significant, since there would have been no established principle against secession, either the Union or the Confederacy could have broken up again the next time a sectional dispute arose. At some point, the West probably would have broken away. There would be some advantages to that—we wouldn't have California to deal with, for example! (Just kidding.) But the upshot is that the whole notion of a united country based on the concept of democracy would have been damaged seriously, maybe irreparably, and the Founders would have been doing somersaults in their tombs.

KW: *And so you share Lincoln's conviction that a permanent split between North and South would have spelled the demise of democracy, at least as we understand it—is that correct?*

AF: Well, nothing can kill the *idea* of democracy. But it would have been greatly weakened without the United States as the exemplar.

KW: *So Lincoln was concerned not just with the significance of the Union for Americans but for its importance in the sweep of world history. I find it interesting that the two most touching stories in your book are about foreigners for whom Lincoln is a profound symbol—one a couple from Thailand that settled in Chicago and created a little shrine to Lincoln in the back of their restaurant, the other a Holocaust survivor who says he had a vision of Lincoln while in his cell in a concentration camp. Those stories really brought home for me the meaning of Lincoln for the rest of the world—not just for us Americans.*

AF: I'm glad those stories had that effect on you. I wanted to emphasize the fact that, for Lincoln, democratic equality was a universal proposition. He believed that it applied to all people everywhere—that ordinary people around the world could govern themselves and had a right to do so. He derives a lot of his power as a symbol from his understanding of that idea's universality.

Which is one reason why I think it's kind of silly when people try to appropriate Lincoln on behalf of a particular political cause or partisan ideology. I also think it's silly to try to apply his own actions to specific events from different historical eras—to play the "What would Lincoln do?" game.

KW: *Although that is what the other contributors to our book are doing. . . .*

AF: Is it? Me and my big mouth.

KW: *Yes—they're offering their thoughts about how Lincoln might have addressed the issue of women's suffrage, or the problems of the*

Great Depression, or the decision about using the atom bomb at Hiroshima. . . .

AF: Well, those exercises can be fun and sometimes illuminating. But I think they're not quite fair to Lincoln. Lincoln is bigger than that, I think.

KW: *How do you mean?*

AF: Well, we have to begin by thinking about him in the context of his time, and we don't always do that when approaching those kinds of "What if?" questions. Lincoln was an extremely partisan politician himself, for example. He was capable of genuine deviousness, underhandedness, subterfuge, and all the other qualities that you ascribe to a fierce partisan. But when we try to apply him to contemporary events, all those qualities of his, which were very deeply rooted, drop away, and he winds up as something he wasn't.

KW: *That political side of Lincoln comes out in the screenplay that Tony Kushner wrote for Spielberg's movie. The focus is largely on Lincoln as a practical politician. He's depicted as having idealistic aims—mainly to free the slaves—but also as being very pragmatic, even ruthless at times about the means he used.*

AF: That was Gore Vidal's idea, too. But those are matters of means. The means make Lincoln interesting for historians. What makes Lincoln special for everyone else are the ends—the purposes he worked toward. No one else understood what was at stake in the survival of the country quite the way he did, and that's what makes him iconic. That's the reason we remember him—not because of his political skills or his military prowess or his literary talent. It's because he always kept his vision of the end in view, and the end turned out to be an end that we can all share and partake in.

For us to ignore that special gift, and instead ask a question like, "What would Lincoln think about raising the marginal tax rate on capital gains?" is just so belittling, so trivializing. When we use him simply to validate our own views—"Lincoln would have agreed with me about everything!"—we reduce a great man to the measure of our own petty vanity.

I also think that it's telling that, although Lincoln is clearly one of the grand figures in world history, in so many ways he *wasn't* grand. He wasn't a man of general culture. He had no interest in the visual arts. His taste in literature was highly questionable, with the exception of the King James Bible and Shakespeare. His favorite play was *Macbeth*, but it seems that there were a vast number of Shakespeare plays that he'd never read—and in his letters he mentions that he read *Macbeth* over and over again. I mean, couldn't he have found time for *King Lear*? Apparently his favorite piece of music was "Jimmy Crack Corn." So here you have a man who was pedestrian in so many ways, and yet he changed the course of history.

KW: *So if what made Lincoln great was his clear understanding of the ends for which he was working, then maybe the only real answer to the question of "What Would Lincoln Do?" is to say that he would have thought deeply and seriously about where America and the world were going and then tried to accommodate his strategies to that overarching vision.*

AF: That's a good way to say it. And, in a sense, I think he believed that the end, the objective, was ready-made. It was given to us by the Founders through the Declaration of Independence and the Constitution. In that sense, the end is permanent and doesn't have to be reinvented every time we face a crisis.

KW: *But didn't Lincoln have to reinvent or reshape the end, in the sense that the vision of the Founders accommodated slavery? By Lincoln's day, it was clear that that wasn't going to work much longer.*

AF: I think Lincoln's argument, which he tried to establish through meticulous research, was that the Founders deliberately placed slavery on a path to its ultimate extinction. I don't think he could have abided a vision of a country in which slavery was permanently accommodated. I think he believed that it wouldn't be true to the Founders' intent to have a country in which slavery would flourish forever. Lincoln saw himself as being true to the Founders' original vision—not altering it. He didn't necessarily want to remake the country. He just wanted it to be more of what it already was.

KW: *Which raises, for me, this question. In the century and a half since Lincoln, many Americans who consider themselves progressive or liberals have tried to extend Lincoln's project into the present by saying that the fulfillment of the vision of the Founders involves various items on the liberal agenda—the Civil Rights movement of the 1960s, the women's rights movement, and now the gay rights movement. The demands of these movements clearly go beyond what the founders envisioned. Does that mean they're not true exemplars of the Lincoln vision?*

AF: Well, I'm not sure that it's legitimate in a Lincolnian sense to invent new categories of human beings and then extend rights to these individuals based on their specific distinguishing characteristics. On the other hand, it's clear that all Americans *as Americans* are entitled to their full civil rights. Nobody believes that the right to habeas corpus or the right to free assembly should be taken away from a person because he is gay.

KW: *So when it comes to same-sex marriage—*
    AF: Lincoln would have just been agog.

KW: *He was a man of his time, obviously.*
    AF: I can't imagine that he would accept the notion of same-sex marriage. I can't really say that that part of the progressive project is a natural outgrowth of Lincoln's way of looking at the country. Though it's certainly something people could debate about with great benefit to understanding Lincoln.

KW: *What about Jim Crow? It seems pretty clear that, by the time he died, Lincoln was prepared to give voting rights at least to some blacks, but social equality for the races may have been a different matter. And what would have happened had Lincoln lived to be eighty or ninety years old? It's hard to picture Lincoln being happy with a South ruled by Jim Crow and the Ku Klux Klan.*

AF: I'm sure Lincoln would not have allowed the reign of terror that white supremacists inflicted upon the South, especially during the 1880s and 1890s. It would have offended his sense of justice to see millions of citizens denied their basic rights—and just the spastic cruelty of it would have horrified him. I can't imagine him not using the federal government to make it stop—although, again, we can't say things like this with any real certitude.

KW: *You've mentioned the concept of equality as being important to Lincoln. One of today's biggest debates is about the growth of income inequality. I wonder whether Lincoln would have been troubled by that. In fact, closer to his own time, if Lincoln had survived into what Mark Twain called the Gilded Age, I wonder how he would have viewed what we now think of as the rampant and exploitative capitalism of the 1880s and '90s.*

AF: Now that would be a very illuminating discussion to have—although, again, you'd never arrive at anything definitive. Lincoln strongly believed in what we now call free enterprise, and he recognized the essential importance of capital, although he thought labor was "prior to capital" in economic and even moral terms.

KW: *Lincoln didn't know anything about Marx, did he?*

AF: No, although they were contemporaries and Marx himself wrote admiringly about—and even to—Lincoln. (Marx wrote Lincoln a letter in 1864 congratulating him on his re-election.) But the question Marx wrestled with and the one that people today are asking is, What if the free enterprise system inevitably leads to drastic inequality—does that create not just a political problem but a philosophical problem and eventually a potential threat to the social order and to free enterprise itself? That's a legitimate question, and we can't know what Lincoln's answer would have been.

Lincoln wasn't a redistributionist. He clearly believed that people should have the right to keep the fruits of their labor. But he was a politician who'd built his early career around the need for public works, which are redistributionist by their very nature—extracting revenue from one group of citizens for the benefit of another. One of the reasons he got into politics was that floods in central Illinois were hurting commerce. Nobody could make a living, so the government needed to step in and canalize the waterways to regulate flooding. There's no indication that Lincoln would have been a libertarian in today's sense—an opponent of any and all government intervention in the economy. And one of his reasons for opposing the extension of slavery, which he shared with other Republicans, was that it lessened the value of free labor.

KW: *Given all this, isn't it hard to imagine a Lincoln who would have permitted the exploitation of workers who were relatively helpless to defend themselves? For example, wouldn't Lincoln have supported labor unions in trying to bring about collective bargaining and improve the lot of workers as a class?*

AF: Maybe. But, on the other hand, it's hard for me to see how Lincoln would even think of workers as a class. His whole vision, as he explained very eloquently, is that the working person begins by working for somebody else so that, in time, he doesn't have to work for anybody else and ultimately is able to hire people to work for him. In a sense, the distinction between boss and worker would have been alien to him, because he focused on social and economic fluidity. The historian Gabor Boritt coined the phrase "the right to rise," which is a beautiful summation of what Lincoln thought about economics.

KW: *But how he would have reacted to the vast corporations of today, or even of the Gilded Age, is purely speculative.*

AF: I think he would have sensed that the best argument against huge corporations is that they can sometimes inhibit the right to rise by crowding out other kinds of enterprise. But would he have been in favor of antitrust laws? Would he have thought and governed like the trust-busting progressive Theodore Roosevelt? I just can't imagine one way or the other, really.

There's no question that the Lincoln of history was a capitalist, a corporate guy. The people he liked best and the people who supported him financially were corporate people, and the business milieu is where he clearly felt most comfortable. This is one of the many senses in which Lincoln represents a classic American type—the poor boy made good.

Lincoln thrived as what we now call a knowledge worker—to make another connection to our own time. In his own person he embodied the rise from yeoman labor—doing work that puts calluses on your hands—to getting paid for sitting around a table and thinking. That is the way millions of people have risen in the United States—first in fields like the law, engineering, and banking, and more recently in the sciences, academia, and information technology.

KW: *So a Lincoln arriving at adulthood today might find himself gravitating toward Silicon Valley.*

AF: Yeah, I can just see him with an iPad.

KW: *I can, too. It's quite an image. And even more fun than imagining him wrestling with the great political issues of later times is imagining Lincoln in dialog with a Teddy Roosevelt, a Franklin D. Roosevelt, a Ronald Reagan, or a Barack Obama.*

AF: Who knows if they'd even have anything to talk about? The frames of reference are so different.

KW: *If Lincoln were to travel to today via time machine, you'd probably need to start by taking a week or two just to tour modern*

America with him, doing your best to explain what it's like. It would be pretty fascinating to see how he would gradually take it all in and react to it.

AF: One of the most atrocious things I've heard anybody say about Abraham Lincoln came from Malcolm Gladwell, the pop science writer. He was on TV and he said that, though Lincoln was clearly a genius in his own time, if he were alive today, he would be just above the idiot level, because he couldn't handle the modern pace of life and the speed at which we process information. If there's a better example of the solipsism of our generation, I can't imagine it. Lincoln couldn't have gotten past the first level of Angry Birds, so what good was he?

We've talked about this tendency to trivialize Lincoln, to patronize him, and to use him to support our own pet projects and perspectives. But at least some people are still passionate about Lincoln and what he represents, whether for good or ill. In *Land of Lincoln*, I devote the first chapter to the world of the neo-Confederates—people, mostly Southerners, who regard Lincoln as an arch-villain, a tyrant, and a destroyer of a peaceful, pastoral way of life. It's all baloney, but at least these guys recognize history as a living thing. They sense that they are part of a long stream of events that connects Lincoln's day to our own. It's an understanding that I find totally absent in many Lincoln admirers. They're interested in Lincoln so they can downsize, appropriate, and sentimentalize him.

In that same first chapter, I talk about meeting Robert Kline, founder of the United States Historical Society. He's the guy who got the idea to erect a statue of Lincoln in the heart of the old Confederacy at the Tredegar Ironworks in Richmond, Virginia. The neo-Confederates went berserk. Mr. Kline wasn't a historian. He was a businessman who made his money by manufacturing little patriotic tchotchkes—collectible dolls and plaques and miniatures and replicas depicting everybody from JFK to Chuck Yeager to Elvis to John Paul Jones to Pocahontas—and, of course, Abe Lincoln. He sold them all as interchangeable symbols of the good ol' USA.

KW: *Does that sort of downsizing of Lincoln offend you?*

AF: Not much. Let me put it this way: It offends me in the same way that saying Lincoln would support a zero capital gains rate offends me. It's trying to bring him down to our level.

That seems to be the contemporary approach to Lincoln. While doing interviews for the book, I kept hearing the same thing: "We've got to move beyond the icon, the plaster saint, the symbol. We want to be in touch with Lincoln the man." That's one reason why I stress the unknowability of Lincoln the man. I wanted, at least for a moment, to redirect our focus away from questions like, "Was Lincoln really in love with Ann Rutledge?" "Did he suffer from Marfan syndrome?" "Did he try to commit suicide?" They're all fascinating questions, and I can get as lost in the details about them as anybody else. But focusing on these questions is, unintentionally, a disservice to what Lincoln means to the country and what he meant to earlier generations, including the people who built that big temple for him over by the Potomac River.

I go there sometimes just to hang out. I'm always struck by the way that place demands our reverence, our awe. When people walk up those steps and into that marble sanctuary, the temperature drops about ten degrees and they just shut up. They stare at that immense statue, they read the inscriptions, and they stand there for ten minutes just quietly reading, thinking, and pondering.

KW: *It's a very powerful experience.*

AF: It really is. I worry that we may lose that experience by trying to say, "Let's get past Lincoln the icon and focus on the flesh-and-blood Lincoln." I think Lincoln the icon is a precious inheritance.

So maybe that takes us back to the first question you asked me—who is *my* Lincoln? My Lincoln is the man who renewed the country. I don't think he invented a "new country" the way some people say—Gary Wills, for example—but he revived it, and he shifted its center of gravity back to the proposition that all men are created equal. That proposition has always been true, but Lincoln is the one who made it the principle that we all have to deal with, struggle with, and work to embody as Americans.

That's why loving Lincoln is a way of loving America. This is what can get lost amidst all our little, personal Lincolns—Lincoln the racist, Lincoln the left-winger, Lincoln the conservative, Lincoln the jokester, Lincoln the manic-depressive—even Lincoln the literary artist. We need Lincoln the lodestar, Lincoln the icon. He is the *real* Lincoln, the Lincoln that matters. Everything else is nuance.

LINCOLN'S WORDS

Second Inaugural Address (1865)

"With malice toward none, with charity for all"

Fellow-Countrymen:

At this second appearing to take the oath of the Presidential office there is less occasion for an extended address than there was at the first. Then a statement somewhat in detail of a course to be pursued seemed fitting and proper. Now, at the expiration of four years, during which public declarations have been constantly called forth on every point and phase of the great contest which still absorbs the attention and engrosses the energies of the nation, little that is new could be presented. The progress of our arms, upon which all else chiefly depends, is as well known to the public as to myself, and it is, I trust, reasonably satisfactory and encouraging to all. With high hope for the future, no prediction in regard to it is ventured.

On the occasion corresponding to this four years ago all thoughts were anxiously directed to an impending civil war. All dreaded it, all sought to avert it. While the inaugural address was being delivered from this place, devoted altogether to saving the Union without war, insurgent agents were in the city seeking to destroy it without war—seeking to dissolve the Union and divide effects by negotiation. Both parties deprecated war, but one of them would make war rather than let the nation survive, and the other would accept war rather than let it perish, and the war came.

One-eighth of the whole population were colored slaves, not distributed generally over the Union, but localized in the southern part of it. These slaves constituted a peculiar and powerful interest. All knew that this interest was somehow the cause of the war. To strengthen, perpetuate, and extend this interest was the object for which the insurgents would rend the Union even by war, while the Government claimed no right to do more than to restrict the territorial enlargement of it. Neither party expected for the war the magnitude or the duration which it has already attained. Neither anticipated that the cause of the conflict might cease with or even before the conflict itself should cease. Each looked for an easier triumph, and a result less fundamental and astounding. Both read the same Bible and pray to the same God, and each invokes His aid against the other. It may seem strange that any men should dare to ask a just God's assistance in wringing their bread from the sweat of other men's faces, but let us judge not, that we be not judged. The prayers of both could not be answered. That of neither has been answered fully. The Almighty has His own purposes. "Woe unto the world because of offenses; for it must needs be that offenses come, but woe to that man by whom the offense cometh." If we shall suppose that American slavery is one of those offenses which, in the providence of God, must needs come, but which, having continued through His appointed time, He now wills to remove, and that He gives to both North and South this terrible war as the woe due to those by whom the offense came, shall we discern therein any departure from those divine attributes which the believers in a living God always ascribe to Him? Fondly do we hope, fervently do we pray, that this mighty scourge of war may speedily pass away. Yet, if God wills that it continue until all the wealth piled by the bondsman's two hundred and fifty years of unrequited toil shall be sunk, and until every drop of blood drawn with the lash shall be paid by another drawn with the sword, as was said three thousand years ago, so still it must be said "the judgments of the Lord are true and righteous altogether."

With malice toward none, with charity for all, with firmness in the right as God gives us to see the right, let us strive on to finish the work we are in, to bind up the nation's wounds, to care for him who shall have borne the battle and for his widow and his orphan, to do all which may achieve and cherish a just and lasting peace among ourselves and with all nations.

Saturday, March 4, 1865

"The Apotheosis of Lincoln," a popular print reflecting public sentiment in the wake of Lincoln's assassination. *Library of Congress*

13

LINCOLN—
THE UNLIKELY CELEBRITY

HAROLD HOLZER

Harold Holzer is one of the country's leading authorities on Abraham Lincoln and the political culture of the Civil War era. A prolific writer and lecturer and frequent guest on television, Holzer serves as chairman of The Lincoln Bicentennial Foundation, successor organization to the US Abraham Lincoln Bicentennial Commission (ALBC), to which he was appointed by President Clinton in 2000 and which he cochaired from 2001 to 2010. President Bush, in turn, awarded Holzer the National Humanities Medal in 2008.

Holzer has authored, coauthored, and edited forty-two books. His latest is Emancipating Lincoln: The Emancipation Proclamation in Text, Context, and Memory *(Harvard University Press), which Henry Louis Gates Jr. called an "essential guide to Lincoln's Emancipation Proclamation." His other recent books are* The New York Times Complete Civil War, *coedited with Craig L. Symonds;* Lincoln on War, *a special collection of the sixteenth president's letters and speeches; an edited volume called* Hearts Touched By Fire: The Best of Battles and Leaders of the Civil War; *and an award-winning young readers' volume on the Lincoln family entitled* Father Abraham: Lincoln and His Sons.

No matter how many speeches I make on Abraham Lincoln and no matter where I make them, no matter how many queries I field on radio and television, at colleges and clubs, at Lincoln groups and Civil War round tables, the question I most often get—right up there with "Was Lincoln gay?" "Did Lincoln suffer from depression?" and "Did Lincoln have a fatal disease?"—is "Could Abraham Lincoln have succeeded in the modern political arena?"

In today's image-suffused political culture, the issue seems especially relevant. Could a manifestly talented but homely, awkward, bearded, thickly-accented giant saddled with a midwestern drawl and a high nasal voice, sporting perennially bad hair and pock-marked skin, armed with a bottomless store of (sometimes inappropriate) jokes and stories, unable to mask a fondness for blackface minstrel shows, and constantly lapsing into melancholia—could such a collection of damaged goods possibly win election today even for sheriff of Maricopa County, much less for President of the United States?

Who can really know for sure? But *my* answer is always the same: of course.

And that is because Lincoln was much more than the sum of his ill-fitting parts. He was much more than "the homeliest man in Illinois,"[1] as he once joked to an artist painting his portrait. He was much more than an ardent antislavery man, an indefatigable reader, an intelligent lawyer, and a shrewd politician. And so he was much more than a gifted nineteenth-century statesman. One can scarcely imagine any of his talented contemporaries making a mark in twenty-first-century politics. Could the fierce, racist champion of state rights John C. Calhoun have become a leader of today's Tea Party? Might Thaddeus Stevens, with his uncorrectable limp and African American mistress, have fought Nancy Pelosi for leadership of congressional progressives? Such antique figures are inexorably locked in their own time and place, but not Lincoln. And the difference is that Lincoln was something more than a politician. He was also a celebrity. And one can only conclude he would have been a celebrity had he lived in ancient Greece or modern America.

Yet to fully appreciate Lincoln's potential as a twenty-first-century celebrity still requires a huge leap of historical imagination. It asks us to take a quintessentially nineteenth-century character—most frequently pictured in a black broadcloth frock coat and a tall stovepipe hat—and place him in a modern milieu that more often than not inspires its presidential candidates to wear blue jeans (albeit of the designer variety) and split hairs, not rails. The exercise calls on us to make the unprovable assumption that Lincoln would have easily adapted to the requirements of modern communications, image making, and political organizing, requirements he could never have even dreamed about. And it asks us to assume that a modern Lincoln would have been willing and able to master the talents and techniques required of today's political aspirants: fundraising, tweeting, blogging, conducting television and radio interviews, and mass advertising. The scrupulous historian is always reluctant to transfer Lincoln into his future—our present—because it requires speculation about his adaptability to circumstances he never even imagined.

But where Lincoln is concerned, there may be ample justification for what otherwise might be a foolhardy leap of faith. For Lincoln was not only a master politician and a brilliant executive, he was also a genuinely irresistible character—and was so regarded almost wherever he lived and worked, for at least the last twenty-five years of his life, first on a local level, later in a statewide and regional arena, and ultimately throughout the entire nation. Much as his reputation soared retrospectively after his assassination and martyrdom, there can be little doubt that a day or a week or a year before his fateful visit to Ford's Theatre on April 14, 1865, Abraham Lincoln was already the most famous man in America. And much of that renown had less to do with his political record and more to do with the intangible qualities of leadership and personality that today we characterize as celebrity. Lincoln had it—from the beginning.

To reach this level of fame, it should be noted, Lincoln overcame in his own time deficiencies and handicaps that would have thwarted less determined men of any era. For one thing, reports of his ugliness were in no way exaggerated. Lincoln not only had massive, flapping ears, a prominent nose that looked as if it were perennially pointed to the wind in search of some revealing aroma, and a crooked if generous mouth that appeared to be smiling on one side and frowning on the other. He looked even worse than these ill-fitting attributes suggest. Lincoln's law partner and later biographer William H. Herndon described his skin as "coarse, pimply, dry-hard no blood seemingly in it." His head sat on a scrawny, dark totem pole of a neck and was topped with chronically "disordered" hair, as he himself put it. His pockmarked and mole-suffused face bore the unmistakable evidence of untreatable adolescent acne. Seeing the president for the first time in 1862, British journalist Edward Dicey described him this way:

> To say he is ugly is nothing; to add that his figure is grotesque is to convey no adequate impression. Fancy a man about six feet high, and thin in proportion, with long bony arms and legs, which somehow seem always to be in the way; with great rugged furrowed hands, which grasp you like a vice when shaking yours; with a long scraggy neck and a chest too narrow for the great arms at his side. Add to this figure a head, coconut shaped and somewhat too small for such a statue, covered with rough, uncombed hair, that stands out in every direction at once; a face furrowed, wrinkled, and indented as though it has been scarred by vitriol; a high narrow forehead, sunk beneath bushy eyebrows, two bright, somewhat dreamy eyes, that seem to gaze through you without looking at you; a few irregular blotches of black bristly hair, in the place where beard and whiskers ought to grow; a close-set, thin-lipped, stern mouth, with two rows of large white teeth, and a nose and ears which have been taken by mistake from a head twice the size. Clothe this figure then in a long, tight, badly-fitting suit of black, creased, soiled, and puckered up at every salient point of the figure (and every salient point of this figure is salient,) put on large, ill-fitting boots, gloves too long for the long bony fingers . . . and you will have the impression left upon me by Abraham Lincoln.

The disquieting package that Dicey described would have been more than enough to inhibit the political and social aspirations of most men—then or now—but early in life, Lincoln learned to use his uniquely disquieting personal appearance to his advantage. Accused by a rival politician of being two-faced, he turned the charge on its ear by commenting self-deprecatingly: "If I were two-faced, would I be wearing this one?" To the amusement of many audiences, he enjoyed telling the story of the hideously ugly woman who once confronted him in some remote forest and unexpectedly aimed a shotgun at his chest. When a frightened Lincoln asked the woman why she was threatening him, she replied: "I swore if I ever met a person uglier than I was, I would shoot him on the spot." Lincoln shrugged and replied: "Madam, if I am uglier than you, fire away."

Saddled with incurable physical homeliness, Lincoln made a concerted effort to develop other attractive qualities. He devoured and digested every book he could lay his hands on and showed an extraordinary ability to commit what he read to memory. He could entertain friends with a spontaneous recital of a Shakespearean soliloquy or a long passage from the Bible. Lincoln grew far taller than his peers—six feet four, not merely six feet, as Dicey acknowledged—in an age when most men were a foot shorter. He also made himself stronger than most men. From early adolescence, he could chop trees, split rails, and build wooden fences faster and more efficiently than many adults. When challenged by town rowdies after moving to his first home as an adult in New Salem, Illinois, Lincoln defeated the local champion in what became a legendary wrestling match. He established himself as a leader among men—the old-fashioned way, by defeating the leader of the pack. He could also outrace all his friends and lift greater weight than two men combined.

From early adulthood, Lincoln demonstrated other attributes that built his legend—thereby adding new layers to his multifaceted and irresistible personality. Whereas most of his contemporaries hunted game for both food and recreation, Lincoln eschewed blood sport. He was more sensitive than most. For reasons historians are still debating, he did not chase women with the same lusty abandon as his peers (though he had fondness enough for ribald stories and, by some accounts, for the services of prostitutes). His first serious crush was on a chaste New Salem girl named Ann Rutledge, who was safely engaged to another suitor who had left town for a trip to New York. Her untimely death sent Lincoln into a deep depression, but he later recovered enough to halfheartedly pursue a portly but well-to-do woman named Mary Owens, who ultimately rejected him for his chronically indifferent behavior.

When he finally lost his heart, not surprisingly it was to Mary Todd, an attractive, mercurial, demanding Kentucky-born belle, who probably pursued him more ardently than he pursued her. The legend of their subsequent unhappy marriage, probably exaggerated, added the title of "giant sufferer" to his expanding personal résumé. Herndon nurtured this particular legend by arguing that his friend's life with Mary became a domestic hell, making his public achievements all the more remarkable. Mary's defenders later contended that the vengeful Herndon chafed because Mary never invited him to the house for dinner. Whatever reality, in terms of building a cult of sympathetic personality, it did not hurt matters that Herndon depicted Lincoln as the all-time champion of long-suffering husbands. To add yet another layer to this tragic image, the Lincolns endured the loss of two sons during their tempestuous marriage—a common enough bereavement, sadly, in that era of primitive medical science, elevated to the level of grand tragedy because it concerned the already melancholic Lincoln.

Lincoln's evolving career provided grist for the cult of personality, too. He was a sociable character, fond of jokes, storytelling, and sports—one of the boys, as people say—but, unlike most of his colleagues in the legal profession, he eschewed liquor. He did not swear. He ate abstemiously and never touched tobacco. He read more often and more widely than his peers but never put his superior knowledge on display. Instead, his lack of ostentation put his contemporaries, from fellow citizens to legal and political rivals, at ease. He was everybody's favorite colleague at the Illinois bar. He told the best stories, took the worst clients, and made the fewest demands of any of the lawyers who crowded together in the same awful country inns, sometimes several in a bed, in pursuit of business on the judicial circuit in and around Sangamon County. Although professional colleagues like William Herndon tut-tutted over Lincoln's lack of interest in legal research and study (a fact that only increases his appeal in an era as chronically suspicious as our own of intellectual superiority), they also spoke admiringly of his spellbinding power over juries. Like no other lawyer of his day, Lincoln could make a bad case seem irresistibly attractive to an enthralled panel of twelve by drawling a few well-chosen jokes and aphorisms. If contemporary reports are to be believed, he won some cases by force of personality alone.

Even as his renown increased, Lincoln remained appealingly modest. He described himself as "humble Abraham Lincoln" in his first appeal for votes in Illinois, declaring matter-of-factly, "If the good people in their wisdom shall see fit to keep me in the background, I have been too familiar with disappointments to be very much chagrined." From the beginning of his adult life, Lincoln also developed a well-earned reputation for unblemished honesty. Indeed, when he was a boy he had agreed to work in a neighbor's field to pay the cost of a borrowed book damaged in a rainstorm. The book turned out to be the very biography of George Washington that had introduced the legend of the "I cannot tell a lie" chopping down of the cherry tree. There was significant historical irony in the fact that Lincoln later told his neighbor the truth about damaging the volume—and that he probably had to chop down a few trees of his own to pay it off. "He never to my knowledge told a willful falsehood," testified one of his New Salem neighbors. Added one of his later political confidantes, "If there were any traits of character that stood out in bold relief, in the person of Mr. Lincoln, it was that of truth and candor. He was utterly incapable of insincerity." Supposedly Lincoln came to detest the nickname of Honest Abe. But it served him extremely well in his subsequent campaigns for elective office. No one ever doubted his absolute truthfulness—an attribute rare among politicians, then as now.

Even before he relocated to Springfield, Illinois, Lincoln had achieved enormous popularity among his neighbors. No one in New Salem seemed to mind when they received their newspaper subscriptions preread and carelessly refolded. They assumed that village postmaster Lincoln had opened and perused them first—and, after all, though too poor to pay for newspapers of his own, Lincoln was the best-informed man in town. When he enlisted in the local militia to fight an Indian invasion in 1832, Lincoln claimed he was surprised when his comrades elected him company captain. But in retrospect he seemed an obvious choice—a man looked to for leadership from the beginning not because of intellectual ability or political zeal but because of the more generic and universally appealing virtues of physical strength, genuine modesty, and unimpeachable honesty. Being elected captain of volunteers, he allowed himself to suggest—as close as he would come to a boast—was "a success which gave me more pleasure than any I have had since."

As Lincoln learned painfully after his election to Congress in 1846, political controversy created as many liabilities as opportunities. Lincoln spent his one and only term in Congress vigorously opposing the Mexican-American War and voting for every resolution that promised to prohibit slavery in the vast territories acquired from Mexico. Whether his position cost him renomination for a second term has remained a matter of dispute since. Most historians agree that Lincoln had agreed by prearrangement to serve only once and then rotate the seat to another equally ambitious local Whig. Whatever the truth, the experience may have taught Lincoln and his supporters a valuable lesson. In future campaigns they would de-emphasize divisive issues and stress the personal attributes that had made Lincoln so successful in the first place.

To be sure, Lincoln re-entered the political arena in 1854 "aroused" back into the fray by a most serious and divisive issue: slavery. Senator Stephen A. Douglas's new Nebraska law gave white settlers the right to vote either to welcome or ban slavery in the country's new western territories. Now Lincoln wrapped his arms around an issue that would carry him all the way to the White House: His seemingly curious insistence that, although slavery could continue to exist in the Southern states where it had thrived so long, it could not be permitted under any circumstances to expand into even one acre of new western land. Merely restricting the spread of slavery, he insisted, would drive the institution toward "ultimate extinction."

Lincoln never really explained how slavery would die out while slaves themselves continued to reproduce, but his argument caught on among moderates. To the surprise of fellow Republicans who doubted his popularity, he won the presidential nomination over a collection of far more prominent aspirants in 1860. In that event, his tempered anti-slavery stand proved provocative enough to drive eleven Southern states out of the Union and into a bloody civil war.

But how did the largely untested Lincoln achieve this extraordinary political prize at the age of fifty-one, hardly known outside his own region? Valuable clues can be found in some of the campaign biographies issued in 1860 to introduce him to American voters. These were the equivalent of the long-form television commercials that today routinely give voters a glowingly rosy picture of a candidate's background and accomplishments, however mundane or dubious. In Lincoln's case, the emphasis in the 1860 campaign (during which, it might be noted, the candidate himself remained home and largely silent) was not on his anti-slavery credentials or his legal record (a career in the law, then as now, was often seen as something of a liability). Instead, supporters stressed his inspiring rise from a primitive log cabin to the doorstep of the White House. Through hard work, relentless study, and reliable honesty, Lincoln had led an exemplary and inspiring life. That he also liked funny stories, good books, and what today we might call country music only added to the appealing picture. As the *New York Tribune* emphasized:

> Born in the very humblest White stratum of society, reared in poverty earning his own livelihood from a tender age by the rudest and least recompensed labor . . . his life is an invincible attestation of the superiority of a Free Society, as his election will be its crowning triumph. That he split rails is of itself nothing; that a man who at twenty was splitting rails for a bare living is at fifty the chosen head of the greatest and most intelligent party in the land, soon to be the Head also of the Nation—this is much, is everything.

Political cartoons of 1860 offer a revealing glimpse into the "marketing" trends of the day, both pro and con. Hostile caricatures often showed Lincoln accompanied by a cruelly lampooned African American (an obvious allusion to the divisive slavery issue). But sympathetic cartoons inevitably portrayed Lincoln in handmade trousers and open-necked cotton shirt, wielding a large axe or a rail-splitter's maul that reminded viewers of his frontier origins and commitment to hard labor.

One such cartoon showed him being lifted aloft by supporters on the same kind of log rail he supposedly spent his young adulthood splitting—and being carried all the way to the White House. Print portraits designed for home display or as decorations for rallies and parades might show Lincoln steering a flatboat—reminding voters that as a young man he had helped carry goods down the Mississippi to New Orleans (where, fatefully, he had first seen a slave market, turning him forever against human bondage). Supporters were encouraged to play pro-Lincoln campaign music at home, like the example produced for the 1860 race under the title, "Honest Old Abe song & chorus."

Historians have increasingly credited Lincoln's election to the "hullabaloo" of the 1860 campaign rather than to a determination by the electorate that slavery should be abolished or even restricted in its growth. But still to be widely acknowledged is the role that Lincoln himself played in creating what can only be called the cult of personality that made this effort successful. In fact, he consciously contributed to the effort to portray himself as a kind of reluctant celebrity—too modest to take himself seriously, too humble to consider himself superior to other men, but politically shrewd enough to make sure that his homeliness, humility, and work ethic were widely communicated to the public.

From the beginning of his career, Lincoln was fully aware of the importance of what he variously called "public sentiment" and "public opinion." "In this and like communities," he declared in 1858, "public sentiment is everything. With public sentiment, nothing can fail; without it nothing can succeed. Consequently, he who moulds public sentiment, goes deeper than he who enacts statutes or pronounces decisions." In other words, Lincoln considered managing public opinion even more important than laws or judicial decisions! As his contemporary George S. Boutwell marveled, "Lincoln possessed the almost divine faculty of interpreting the will of the people without any expression by them."

Lincoln made that extraordinary observation about "public sentiment" at his first debate with Stephen A. Douglas, in Ottawa, Illinois, back in 1858. Those famous debates themselves, it might be noted, came about in an effort to boost Lincoln's celebrity. Many expert observers that year concluded that Lincoln would never be able to dislodge

Stephen A. Douglas from the Senate, no matter how tirelessly the Republican candidate campaigned. In those days, senators were chosen by legislators, not a direct vote of the people, and, as a result of gerrymandering and the fact that several sitting Democrats were not even seeking re-election, it seemed doubtful from the start that the Republicans could muster enough votes in contested districts to create a legislative majority for Lincoln.

Locked into an all but hopeless race, Lincoln cleverly raised the stakes by challenging his rival to a series of debates. Unable to risk refusing and appearing cowardly, Douglas committed to seven "joint meetings." The debates inspired unprecedented newspaper coverage and produced a book-length transcript that became a best seller. As predicted, Lincoln lost the senate election, but his debate challenge helped transform him into a viable candidate for national office.

Two years later, with similar insightfulness, he accepted an invitation to speak in New York—an opportunity to *dispel* the prevailing notion that Lincoln was *only* a frontier debater and stump orator. Lincoln crafted a scholarly, closely argued, legalistic masterpiece for the occasion. The Cooper Union address further elevated Lincoln's national stature—even though he had won no major elective office since his one successful run for Congress fourteen years earlier. Here was a burgeoning presidential candidacy based on a unique combination of political commitment and celebrity appeal—with the customary stepping stones of previous office entirely bypassed. (By contrast, two of his rivals for the 1860 Republican nomination, William H. Seward and Salmon P. Chase, had served as both governors and US senators, the customary pathway to a national ticket. They lost.)

Lincoln was a willing participant in this transformation from obscure backwoods lawyer to national celebrity. By the time he began to think seriously about the presidency, he had been photographed only a few times, with unimpressive results. While in New York for his Cooper Union appearance, however, Lincoln offered no objections when his hosts ushered him into the gallery of Mathew Brady, America's best and best-known photographer. Brady took one look at Lincoln through his lens and was dissatisfied with what he saw. "I had great trouble," he admitted, "in making a natural picture." Brady did what no such artist had thought to do before: rejecting the customary close-up, he moved his camera back and captured a view of Lincoln's massive upper torso. The photographer placed Lincoln's hands on a stack of books to suggest wisdom, and posed him before a faux pillar to represent power. Then in a moment of inspiration, he asked if he could rearrange Lincoln's shirt collar. "Ah," the subject murmured, "I see you want to shorten my neck." "That's just it," replied Brady, "and we both laughed." Lincoln obligingly tugged up his collar, masking what German American leader Carl Schurz called his "long and sinewy" neck, and Brady quickly snapped the picture.

The result proved a phenomenon. Four weeks later, with more than a bit of homespun modesty, Lincoln told an admirer asking for his latest likeness, "I have not a single one now at my control; but I think you can easily get one at New-York. There I was taken to one of the places where they get up such things, and I suppose they got my shaddow [*sic*], and can multiply copies indefinitely." That is precisely what they did. Engravers and lithographers seized on the handsome "shaddow" and used it as the basis for campaign prints, textiles, buttons, and posters. As artist Francis B. Carpenter well knew, "The effects of such influences, though silent, is powerful." Lincoln himself concluded "Brady and the Cooper Union speech made me President."

A few weeks later, the characteristically self-effacing politician agreed to submit to the unpleasant process of sitting for a wet-plaster life mask, in order to facilitate what its Chicago maker promised would be a heroic statue. Once he won the nomination, he posed for additional photographs in Springfield, copies of which were broadly circulated and inspired prints in other media. He was now actively participating in what passed in 1860 for mass communications.

Beginning in June 1860, an increasingly willing Lincoln also welcomed the first artists assigned to paint campaign portraits. For weeks, he allowed them to work in his cramped temporary office at the Springfield statehouse. At one point that summer, he was surrounded by several easels at one time as these portrait makers struggled to capture his likeness while he was "on the jump"—opening and reading his daily mail from eight to nine each morning. "This is the first time I have had this specific sort of picture made," Lincoln confided to one of these artists, Thomas Hicks of New York. But when Lincoln saw the roman-ticized finished work, he exclaimed, "I think the picture has a somewhat pleasanter expression than I usually have, but that, perhaps, is not an objection." Hicks took the canvas back to New York, where it was im-mediately copied and issued as a campaign print. "It is allowed to be ugly in this world," the candidate reflected to another artist, G. P. A. Healy, "but not as ugly as I am."

Flattering portraits like those created by Hicks and Healy helped dispel the potentially threatening rumor that Lincoln was simply too homely and ill-mannered to serve as president. Throughout the 1860 campaign, while Lincoln maintained his official silence and rarely strayed beyond his Springfield hometown, the attractive results of his enthusiastic cooperation with artists and photographers virtually did the campaigning for him. And successfully. Although Lincoln won less than 40 percent of the popular vote in November, he received more than enough electoral votes to make him president.

After the election, Lincoln showed no inclination to curtail his re-liance on visual media to circulate sympathetic images. Although mak-ing virtually no public statements between his election and the commencement of his inaugural journey more than three months later, Lincoln posed for additional paintings, patiently sat for another sculp-ture, and allowed local photographers to record the slow development of a new beard.

Lincoln's decision to grow those whiskers may have represented his most ingenious embrace of celebrity yet. Back in October, a little girl from upstate New York had written a letter urging Lincoln to begin growing a beard. As Grace Bedell put it, "You would look a great deal better for your face is so thin. All the ladies like whiskers and they would tease their husband's [sic] to vote for you." Lincoln initially replied that people might call it "a piece of silly affect[ta]tion" were he to begin sporting whiskers so late in life, "having never worn any." But soon after his election, Lincoln stopped shaving anyway. One newspa-per joked, "Old Abe is puttin' on [h]airs." But as photographs of the newly bearded Lincoln gained circulation, Americans became increas-ingly fascinated by the question of what the new president would look like when he arrived in Washington.

Lincoln's decision—maybe or maybe not inspired by what his secretary called the "childish prattle" of a young admirer—served for a time to deflect the national conversation away from thoughts of secession and war. And when Lincoln *did* reach the capital for his swearing-in, he no longer resembled a rough-hewn frontier rail-splitter. He had become an avuncular, bearded statesman who looked fully ready to confront the crises awaiting him.

Ever conscious of promoting his subsequent achievements—while taking continued care, like any Victorian-era gentleman, to disguise his outright interest in promulgating his own likenesses—Lincoln went on to become one of the most photographed men of his age. His arrival in Washington neatly coincided with the development of new photographic technologies that allowed multiple-lens cameras to take four images simultaneously, thus speeding rapidly made and widely distributed prints to an eager public. Photographs that inevitably showed Lincoln's alarming physical deterioration during his years in office testified to his tireless devotion to the Union in a time of war and widespread political discontent.

Once he issued the Emancipation Proclamation, moreover, Lincoln made himself available with renewed energy to painters and sculptors. Conceivably he was now as determined to encourage heroic imagery to illustrate his new place in history as he had been eager to enable flattering imagery to widen his appeal to voters. In 1863, the president allowed Philadelphia painter Edward D. Marchant to work in the White House for three months to create a portrait of Lincoln signing the Emancipation Proclamation with a feathered quill. The President cooperated no doubt because the canvas was originally earmarked for Independence Hall, where it would hang alongside portraits of the nation's Founding Fathers. The idea must have appealed to Lincoln enormously.

The following year, Lincoln permitted New York artist Francis Carpenter double the time—six months in all—to create a now-iconic painting of Lincoln's first reading of the draft proclamation to his cabinet. This painting inspired one of the most popular engravings of the entire nineteenth century (though it failed to appear until Lincoln's death—Carpenter was always a slow worker). Marchant's print, on the other hand, appeared in an engraved edition in time for the hard-fought 1864 presidential campaign and stood as one of the few positive references to the controversial emancipation order that season.

By the final year of his life, Lincoln no longer doubted the useful impact of his own personal appearance or his increasingly fragile physical condition. Clad in the signature stovepipe hat that always made him appear closer to seven than to six feet tall, his whiskers now reduced to a near-goatee, he was still raising ceremonial flags, offering encouraging words to visiting regiments, attending the theater, concerts, and lectures, and speaking spontaneously to appreciative crowds gathered on the White House lawn following great events. As much as he acknowledged the dignity of his office and its then-traditional removal from direct electioneering and speechmaking (the Gettysburg Address was a rare exception to his usual determination to "avoid saying foolish things" in public), he continued to show himself before Washington. He visited troops in the field to inspire them into action. When the Confederate capital of Richmond fell to the Union in early April 1861, the Union commander in chief even toured the occupied city—not with a large force of armed bodyguards but grasping the hand of his youngest son on his birthday.

The rail-splitter and autodidact who had risen from obscurity was now the living symbol of the Union and of black freedom—a celebrity magnified into a national emblem. Even the image of Uncle Sam himself—once depicted by cartoonists as white haired and looking eerily like George Washington, now morphed into a tall, thin, bearded fellow with an uncanny resemblance to Abraham Lincoln.

For his time and place, Lincoln was remarkably sensitive to the advantages of emphasizing personality over politics—and would undoubtedly have pushed the envelope in this regard had he lived in our own age. There is little reason to doubt that this lover of technology would have adapted to the modern media with the same enthusiasm with which he embraced new-fangled rifled cannon and ironclad warships to defeat the rebellion, the telegraph to speed communications, the photograph to lay bare his suffering, and the formal painting and statue to cement his place in history. Such an enlightened man would have carried

a Blackberry as routinely as he carried a gold pocket watch—and probably would have used it to keep in close touch with political allies and
supporters in the media.

Astonishingly, Abraham Lincoln missed only one great opportunity
to enhance his personal reputation. The public of his era increasingly
collected images not only of their own families but of celebrities like
Lincoln as well. Yet no one, the President included, ever thought to
arrange a group sitting of the Lincoln family designed specifically for
these family albums. The modern cult of the First Family had not yet
come into existence, and Lincoln failed to recognize its potential—a
rare lapse on his part.

Artist Francis Carpenter did at least come close. While working in
the White House on his emancipation canvas, he frequently observed
Lincoln in loving exchanges with his son. Carpenter became convinced
that if "the worst of his adversaries" could only see the burdened president behind the scenes, it "would have melted their hearts." To Carpenter, "the President never seemed grander in my sight than when,
stealing upon him in the evening, I would find him with a book open
before him . . . with Little Tad beside him."

Thus, when Carpenter took Lincoln and Tad to Mathew Brady's
Washington gallery in February 1864 to pose the President for a series
of pictures meant to serve as models for his main project, he persuaded
Lincoln to sit for one photo together with Tad. He posed them examin-
ing the photographer's oversize sample photograph album as if it were
one of those books he often saw Lincoln reading to the boy. The resulting warm portrait of father and son, which might have served as a
hugely effective campaign tool by softening the prevailing image of Lincoln (at least to his opponents) as a tough warrior and harsh abrogator
of civil liberties, inexplicably remained unpublished that decisive year.
Only after Lincoln's murder did Mathew Brady release the photograph
to the public. Had it been issued earlier, Lincoln's unprecedented personal celebrity might have been spread even further.

One suspects that Lincoln would not have made the same mistake
today.

ACKNOWLEDGMENTS

Thanks, first, to director Steven Spielberg, producer Kathleen Kennedy, historian Doris Kearns Goodwin, and the other creative spirits responsible for the 2012 film *Lincoln*, which provided the happy occasion for this book. Thanks in particular to screenwriter Tony Kushner, whose powerful screenplay captures the spirit of Lincoln for our time.

Next, thanks to the team members at Dreamworks, Disney, and Participant Media who provided essential links to the film project and its creative team, thereby making our companion book possible. The list includes our old friend, Lynn Hirshfield, and new ones like Marvin Levy, Steve Newman, Theresa Cross, and Kevin Campbell.

Thanks to the publishing team at PublicAffairs, which managed the editorial, design, production, and marketing processes for this book in record time and with their usual professionalism, expertise, and good cheer, including Clive Priddle, Melissa Raymond, Jaime Leifer, Emily Lavelle, Joanna Rothkopf, Susan Weinberg, and Peter Osnos. Excellent support work was also provided by the freelance team that Melissa assembled, including copyeditor Carrie Watterson, designer Cynthia Young, art researcher Laura Wyss, proofer Lori Lewis, and indexer Robie Grant.

Special thanks to my long-time colleague Rob Kaplan, who is not only a highly talented editor but a deeply knowledgeable amateur scholar of Lincoln. Rob helped identify the historians and other authors who contributed to this book, offered shrewd and creative suggestions for topics to be included, and provided wise editorial advice that significantly improved my introductory chapter, "The Faces of Lincoln."

Without Rob's help, this project would have taken me much longer, its quality would have suffered, and I would have learned less and had much less fun along the way.

Finally, and most important, thanks to the distinguished writers who contributed chapters to this book. They worked against absurd deadlines, handled an unorthodox editorial process with great flexibility and aplomb, and under these handicaps somehow generated essays that are innovative, insightful, and fascinating. I complete this project filled with admiration for all twelve of these remarkable men and women and with the hope that I may have an opportunity to work with each of them again in the not-too-distant future.

Karl Weber
Irvington, New York
September 2012

NOTES

CHAPTER 1
The Faces of Lincoln

1. Works cited in this chapter include:

Peterson, Merrill D. *Lincoln in American Memory*. New York: Oxford University Press, 1994.

Thomas, Christopher A. *The Lincoln Memorial and American Life*. Princeton, NJ: Princeton University Press, 2002.

Tripp, C. A. *The Intimate World of Abraham Lincoln*. New York: Free Press, 2005.

CHAPTER 3
"A Sacred Effort"

1. I would like to thank John Sellers at the Library of Congress for showing me Lincoln's notebook. The Lincoln comment about the Haitian ambassador is in John R. McKivigan, *Forgotten Firebrand: James Redpath and the Making of Nineteenth-Century America* (Ithaca: Cornell University Press, 2008), 78.

2. Frederick Douglass, "The Claims of the Negro Ethnologically Considered," in *Racial Thought in America: From the Puritans to Abraham Lincoln, A Documentary History*, ed. Louis Ruchames, vol. 1 (New York: Grosset & Dunlap, 1969), 479–492.

3. David Hume, "Of National Characters," 1754/1776, in Emmanuel Chukwudi Eze, *Race and the Enlightenment: A Reader* (Cambridge, Mass.: Blackwell, 1997). For the Agassiz quotation, see Stephen Jay Gould, ed., *The Mismeasure of Man*, rev. and expanded (New York: W. W. Norton, 1996), 76–77.

4. Thomas Jefferson, *Notes on the State of Virginia*, ed. William Peden (New York: W. W. Norton, 1972), 142.

5. Blight, correspondence, August 10, 2008.

6. As Allen Guelzo states: "There is a certain muddling among historians about who, and how many, were freed by the Proclamation, and that hangs on the ambiguous use of the word 'freed.' If we mean de facto, then the number is

indeed vanishingly small, out of the population of 3.9 million slaves; but if we mean de jure, then the Proclamation freed every one of the slaves in the areas it was applied to. Freedom, in the fullest sense, requires both. A fugitive slave may run away and become de facto free, but so can any escapee from prison, and such fugitives are liable to recapture and rendition at any time. But a slave declared de jure free cannot, once an escape is made to Union lines, ever be returned to slavery; and slaves who are overrun by the advance of the Union armies are thus rendered both de facto and de jure free. They would not be, however, without the Proclamation. Any slave who achieved de facto freedom—what Lincoln called 'actual freedom'—was always liable to reenslavement without the change in legal status conferred by the Proclamation. So, just as it is often said that Lincoln's Proclamation freed no one because it did not instantly work de facto freedom, it can just as easily be said that without the Proclamation, no slave who escaped (or was liberated by the Union army) from slavery ever stopped being a slave—except, of course, for the Emancipation Proclamation. I know this sounds tendentious, but it's tendentious, too, to hear people blather on about how Lincoln never 'really' freed any slave. That's like saying the Voting Rights Act and the Civil Rights Act never gave any black person an 'actual' vote" (Guelzo, correspondence, November 13, 2008).

7. Edward Widmer, "Lincoln's Apotheosis," in *A New Literary History of America*, ed. Greil Marcus and Werner Sollors (Cambridge, MA: Harvard University Press, Belknap Press, 2009).

8. Ronald C. White, *Lincoln's Greatest Speech: The Second Inaugural* (New York: Simon & Schuster, 2002), 32.

9. John Stauffer, *Giants: The Parallel Lives of Frederick Douglass and Abraham Lincoln* (New York: International Publishers, 1950–1975), 240–241. For a different perspective, see James Oakes, *The Radical and the Republican: Frederick Douglass, Abraham Lincoln, and the Triumph of Antislavery Politics* (New York: W. W. Norton, 2007).

10. Eric Foner, ed., *Our Lincoln: New Perspectives on Lincoln and His World*, (New York: W. W. Norton, 2008), 156.

11. Douglass, "Abraham Lincoln," December 1865 [holograph], Frederick Douglass Papers, Library of Congress, reel 19; Guelzo, correspondence, October 3, 2008.

12. Stauffer, *Giants*, 66; Douglass to George Stearns, August 12, 1863, Historical Society of Pennsylvania.

13. Stauffer, *Giants*, 24, 311.

14. Lerone Bennett Jr., *Forced into Glory: Abraham Lincoln's White Dream* (Chicago: Johnson Publishing Company, 2000), 509–511.

15. Barack Obama, "What I See in Lincoln's Eyes," *Time* magazine, June 26, 2005, http://www.time.com/time/printout/0,8816,1077287,00.html.

16. W. E. B. Du Bois, *Writings* (New York: Library of America, 1986), 1196–1198.

17. Gopnik, correspondence, December 1, 2008.

18. Adam Gopnik, *Angels and Ages: A Short Book about Darwin, Lincoln, and Modern Life* (New York: Alfred A. Knopf, 2009).

19. David Herbert Donald, *Lincoln* (New York: Simon & Schuster, 1995), 585.

CHAPTER 4
"By No Means Excluding Females"

1. Roy Basler, *The Collected Works of Abraham Lincoln* (New Brunswick, NJ: Rutgers University Press, 1953–1957), 1:48.

2. *Selected Papers of Elizabeth Cady Stanton and Susan B. Anthony*, eds. Ann D. Gordon, Tamara Gaskell Miller, Stacy Kinlock Sewell, Ann Elizabeth Pfau, and Arlene Kriv, vol. 1, in *In the School of Anti-Slavery, 1840 to 1866* (New Brunswick, NJ: Rutgers University Press, 1997), 1:104–105.

3. The residency requirement was increased in the Illinois Constitution of 1848 to one year.

4. Basler, *Collected Works*, 1:65.

5. Ibid., 3:375.

6. *Abraham Lincoln: Tributes from his Associates, Reminiscences of Soldiers, Statesmen and Citizens* (New York: Thomas Crowell, 1895), 20–21.

7. See Daniel Stowell, ed., *In Tender Consideration: Women, Families and the Law in Abraham Lincoln's Illinois* (Urbana: University of Illinois Press, 2002).

8. Basler, *Collected Works*, 2:385.

9. Lydia Hasbrouck to Abraham Lincoln, March 8, 1861, Abraham Lincoln Papers, Library of Congress.

10. Basler, *Collected Works*, 2:281, 260.

11. Ibid., 2:498.

12. Ibid., 7:243.

13. Elizabeth Cady Stanton, Susan B. Anthony, and Matilda Joslyn Gage, eds., *History of Woman Suffrage*, vol. 2 (Fowler & Wells, 1882; reprint, New York: Arno & New York Times, 1969), 2:153, 174.

CHAPTER 5
Lincoln, FDR, and the Growth of Federal Power

1. Works cited in this chapter include:

Donald, David Herbert. *Lincoln.* New York: Touchstone, 1995.

Farber, Daniel. *Lincoln's Constitution.* Chicago: University of Chicago Press, 2003.

Farber, Daniel. "The Story of *McCulloch*: Banking on National Power." In *Constitutional Law Stories*, ed. Michael Dorf, 2nd ed. New York: Foundation Press, 2009.

Heidler, David, and Jeanne T. Heidler. *Henry Clay: The Essential American*. New York: Random House, 2011.

McJimsey, George. *The Presidency of Franklin Delano Roosevelt*. Lawrence: University Press of Kansas, 2000.

CHAPTER 6
"That This Mighty Scourge of War May Speedily Pass Away"

1. Works cited in this chapter include:

Basler, Roy P., ed. *The Collected Works of Abraham Lincoln*. 8 vols. New Brunswick, NJ: Rutgers University Press, 1953.

Braver, Adam. *Mr. Lincoln's Wars: A Novel in Thirteen Stories*. New York: William Morrow, 2003.

Churchill, Winston S. *The American Civil War*. New York: Dodd, Mead, 1958.

Donald, David Herbert. *Lincoln*. New York: Simon & Schuster, 1995.

Fussell, Paul. *Thank God for the Atom Bomb and Other Essays*. New York: Summit Books, 1988.

Harris, William C. *Lincoln's Last Months*. Cambridge, MA: Belknap Press of Harvard University Press, 2004.

Hersey, John. *Hiroshima*. New York: Alfred A. Knopf, 1983.

Kennett, Lee. *Sherman: A Soldier's Life*. New York: HarperCollins, 2001.

McCullough, David. *Truman*. New York: Simon & Schuster, 1992.

McPherson, James M. *Battle Cry of Freedom: The Civil War Era*. New York: Oxford University Press, 1988.

Sherman, William Tecumseh. *Memoirs of General W. T. Sherman*. New York: Library of America, 1990.

White, Ronald C. *A. Lincoln: A Biography*. New York: Random House, 2009.

CHAPTER 7
At the End of Two Wars

1. Works cited in this chapter include:

Addison, Joseph. "No. 69" (May 19, 1711). In *The Spectator, Volume the First*, 278–279. Dublin, Ireland: Wilson, 1755.

Alley, John B., and Henry P. H. Bromwell. Quoted in *Recollected Words of Abraham Lincoln*, eds. Don and Virginia Fehrenbacher. Stanford, CA: Stanford University Press, 1996, 2, 40.

Atack, Jeremy, and Peter Passell. *A New Economic View of American History: From Colonial Times to 1940*. New York: Norton, 1994.

Berry, Stephen. *House of Abraham: Lincoln and the Todds, a Family Divided by War*. New York: Houghton Mifflin Harcourt, 2007.

Beveridge, Albert J. *Abraham Lincoln, 1809–1858*. Boston: Houghton Mifflin, 1928.

Bimes, Terri, and Stephen Skowronek. "Woodrow Wilson's Critique of Popular Leadership: Reassessing the Modern-Traditional Divide in Presidential History." *Polity* 29 (Fall 1996): 29, 32, 53.

Bishop, J. Leander. *History of American Manufactures from 1608 to 1860*. Philadelphia: E. Young, 1864.

Braeman, John. "Albert J. Beveridge and Demythologizing Lincoln." *Journal of the Abraham Lincoln Association* 25 (Summer 2004): 18.

Burleigh, Michael. *Moral Combat: Good and Evil in World War II*. New York, NY: Harper, 2011.

Burlingame, Michael. *Abraham Lincoln: A Life*. Baltimore: Johns Hopkins University Press, 2008.

Croly, Herbert David. *The Promise of American Life*. New York: Macmillan, 1914.

Dana, Charles A. Quoted in *Reminiscences of Abraham Lincoln by Distinguished Men of His Time*, ed. Allen T. Rice. New York: North American, 1886, 376.

Dewey, John. "The Need for a Recovery of Philosophy." In *The Collected Works of John Dewey—Essays on Philosophy and Education: 1916–1917*, ed. L. E. Hahn. Carbondale: Southern Illinois University Press, 1980, 10:46.

Grant, Ulysses S. Quoted in *Around the World with General Grant: A Narrative of the Visit of General U.S. Grant, Ex-President of the United States, to Various Countries in Europe, Asia, and Africa*, ed. John Russell Young. New York: American News, 1879, 2:615.

Hardman, J. B. S., ed. *Rendezvous with Destiny: Addresses and Opinions of Franklin Delano Roosevelt*. New York: Dryden Press, 1944.

Harris, William C. *Lincoln's Last Months*. Cambridge, MA: Harvard University Press, 2004.

Hastings, Max. *Winston's War: Churchill, 1940–1945*. New York: Alfred A. Knopf, 2010.

Hearst, W. R. *The American Almanac, Year-book, Cyclopaedia and Atlas*. New York: W. R. Hearst, 1904.

Herndon, William H. to Jesse W. Weik (January 1, 1886). In *The Hidden Lincoln from the Letters and Papers of William H. Herndon*, ed. Emanuel Hertz. New York: Viking, 1940, 117.

Houck, Davis W. *Rhetoric as Currency: Hoover, Roosevelt, and the Great Depression*. College Station: Texas A&M University Press, 2001.

Jordan, David M. *FDR, Dewey, and the Election of 1944*. Bloomington: Indiana University Press, 2011.

Kershaw, Ian. *Fateful Choices: Ten Decisions That Changed the World, 1940–1941*. New York, NY: Penguin, 2007.

Lincoln, Abraham. "Address before the Wisconsin State Agricultural Society, Milwaukee, Wisconsin" (September 30, 1859), "Address to the New Jersey Senate at Trenton, New Jersey" (February 21, 1861), "Annual Message to Congress" (December 3, 1861), "Annual Message to Congress" (December 1, 1862), "Fragment on Free Labor" (September 17, 1859), "Fragment on Government" (July 1, 1854), Letter to William H. Herndon (February 15, 1848), "Petition for an Increase of the Tariff" (May 12, 1842), "Resolutions of Sympathy with the Cause of Hungarian Freedom" (September 6, 1849), "Resolutions in Behalf of Hungarian Freedom" (January 9, 1852), "Speech at Chicago, Illinois" (July 10, 1858), "Speech at Cincinnati, Ohio" (September 17, 1859), "Speech at Kalamazoo, Michigan" (August 27, 1856), "Speech at New Haven, Connecticut" (March 5, 1860), "Speech at Wilmington, Delaware" (June 10, 1848), "Speech in Independence Hall, Philadelphia, Pennsylvania" (February 22, 1861), "Speech in United States House of Representatives on Internal Improvements" (June 20, 1848), "Speech in United States House of Representatives: The War with Mexico" (January 12, 1848), "Stay of Execution for Nathaniel Gordon" (February 4, 1862), "Temperance Address" (February 22, 1842). In *Collected Works of Abraham Lincoln*, eds. R. P. Basler et al. New Brunswick, NJ: Rutgers University Press, 1953.

Lincoln, Mary Todd. Quoted in *Recollected Words of Abraham Lincoln*, eds. Don and Virginia Fehrenbacher. Stanford, CA: Stanford University Press, 1996, 297.

Lind, Michael. *What Lincoln Believed: The Values and Convictions of America's Greatest President*. New York: Doubleday, 2004.

Moore, John Allphin, and Jerry Pubantz. *To Create a New World? American Presidents and the United Nations*. New York: Peter Lang, 1999.

Peterson, Merrill D. *Lincoln in American Memory*. New York: Oxford University Press, 1994.

Phillips, Wendell. Quoted in *The Radical Republicans and Reconstruction, 1861–1870*, ed. Harold M. Hyman. Indianapolis, IN: Bobbs-Merrill, 1967, 480, 483.

Rietveld, Ronald D. "Franklin D. Roosevelt's Abraham Lincoln." In *Franklin D. Roosevelt and Abraham Lincoln: Competing Perspectives on Two Great Presidencies*, eds. W. D. Pederson and F. J. Williams. Armonk, NY: M. E. Sharpe, 2003, 53.

Robertson, William. "Progress of Society" (1766). In *Commerce, Culture and Liberty: Readings in Capitalism Before Adam Smith*, ed. Henry C. Clark. Indianapolis, IN: Liberty Fund, 2003, 504, 506.

Roosevelt, Franklin D. "State of the Union" (January 11, 1944). In *American Political Rhetoric: A Reader*, eds. P. A. Lawler and R. M. Schaefer. Lanham, MD, 2005, 120–121.

———. *The War Messages of Franklin D. Roosevelt, December 8, 1941 to April 13, 1945: The President's War Addresses to the People and to the Congress of the United States of America*. Washington, DC: Ritten House, 1945.

Schwartz, Barry. *Abraham Lincoln in the Post-Heroic Era: History and Memory in Late Twentieth-Century America*. Chicago: University of Chicago Press, 2008.

Soodalter, Ron. *Hanging Captain Gordon: The Life and Trial of an American Slave Trader*. New York: Atria, 2006.

Stevens, Thaddeus. "Reconstruction" (September 6, 1865). In *The Selected Papers of Thaddeus Stevens: April 1865–August 1868*, ed. Beverly Palmer. Pittsburgh, PA: University of Pittsburgh Press, 1997, 23.

Welles, Gideon. "Lincoln and Johnson." In *Selected Essays by Gideon Welles: Civil War and Reconstruction*, ed. Albert Mordell. New York: Twayne, 1959, 191.

Whitten, David O., and Bessie Emrick Whitten. *The Birth of Big Business in the United States, 1860–1914: Commercial, Extractive and Industrial Enterprise*. Westport, CT: Praeger, 2006.

Wilson, Woodrow. "The New Freedom." In *Woodrow Wilson: The Essential Political Writings*, ed. R. J. Pestritto. Lanham, MD: Lexington, 2005, 121.

CHAPTER 9
President Abraham Lincoln
Confronts the War on Terror

1. Works cited in this chapter include:

Cong. Globe, 37th Cong., 2d. Sess. 2964 (1862).

Donald, David Herbert. *Lincoln*. New York: Simon & Schuster, 1996.

Kent, Andrew. "The Constitution and the Laws of War During the Civil War." *Notre Dame Law Review* 85, no. 5 (2010): 1839–1930.

Lieber, Francis. *Instructions for the Government of Armies of the United States in the Field*. Clark, NJ: Lawbook Exchange, 2005.

Lincoln, Abraham. "Letter to Erastus Corning and others" (June 12, 1863), 6:267; "Letter to Matthew Birchard and others" (June 29, 1863), 6:300; "Proclamation Suspending the Writ of Habeas Corpus" (September 24, 1862), 5:436–437; "Response to a Serenade" (November 10, 1864), 8:100; "Speech to Special Session of Congress" (July 4, 1861), 4:438. In *The Collected Works of Abraham Lincoln*, ed. Roy P. Basler, 8 vols. New Brunswick, NJ: Rutgers University Press, 1953.

Military Commissions Act of 2009, *Pub. L. No. 111–84*, *H.R. 2647*, 123 *Stat.* 2190, (October 28, 2009).

United States v. Hamdan, CMCR 09–002, 2011 U.S. CMCR LEXIS 1 at *135–36 (U.S. Ct. Mil. Comm. Rev. June 24, 2011).

Wedgwood, Ruth. "The Case for Military Tribunals." *Wall Street Journal*, Dec. 3, 2001, A18.

Williams, Frank J., Nicole J. Dulude, and Kimberly A. Tracey. "Still a Frightening Unknown: Achieving a Constitutional Balance Between Civil Liberties and National Security During the War on Terror." *Roger Williams University Law Review* 12 (2007): 675.

CHAPTER 11
"The Almighty Has His Own Purposes"

1. "He's kept alive for 95 seconds! Abraham Lincoln's Corpse Revived." *Weekly World News*, October 5, 1993.

2. Douglas L. Wilson and Rodney O. Davis, eds., *Herndon's Informants: Letters, Interviews, and Statements about Abraham Lincoln* (Urbana: University of Illinois Press, 1998), 346, 348.

3. J. G. Holland, *The Life of Abraham Lincoln* (Springfield, MA: Gurdon Bill, 1866), 239, 542.

4. Wilson and Davis, *Herndon's Informants*, 582–583.

5. Isaac N. Arnold, *Life of Abraham Lincoln* (Chicago: A. C. McClurg, 1884), 81.

6. Wilson and Davis, *Herndon's Informants*, 185, 358, 360; Emanuel Hertz, *The Hidden Lincoln: From the Letters and Papers of William H. Herndon* (New York: Blue Ribbon Books, 1940), 142, 167–168.

7. Wilson and Davis, *Herndon's Informants*, 576.

8. Ibid., 547–550.

9. Ibid., 578–580.

10. Michael Burlingame, ed., *An Oral History of Abraham Lincoln: John G. Nicolay's Interviews and Essays* (Carbondale: Southern Illinois University Press, 1996), 95–96.

11. Wilson and Davis, *Herndon's Informants*, 360.

12. Roy P. Basler, ed., *The Collected Works of Abraham Lincoln*, 8 vols. (New Brunswick, NJ: Rutgers University Press, 1953), 1:319–321.

13. Basler, *Collected Works*, 1:382–384.

14. A. Smith to A. Lincoln, July 20, 1858, Abraham Lincoln Papers, Library of Congress.

15. *New York Tribune*, June 12, 1860.

16. John Locke Scripps, *Life of Abraham Lincoln*, ed. Roy P. Basler and Lloyd A. Dunlap (Bloomington: Indiana University Press, 1961), 165.

17. *Chicago Daily Times and Herald*, October 27, 1860.

18. Victor B. Howard, *Religion and the Radical Republican Movement 1860–1870* (Lexington: University Press of Kentucky, 1990), 71.

19. Basler, *Collected Works*, 2:15–16.

20. Holland, *Life of Abraham Lincoln*, 236–237.

21. Basler, *Collected Works*, 3:204–205.

22. Ibid., 8:154–155.

23. Ibid., 8:332–333.

24. Hertz, *Hidden Lincoln*, 266.

25. Basler, *Collected Works*, 4:482–483, 6:244–245; Burlingame, *Oral History*, 5.

26. Basler, *Collected Works*, 5:278–279.

27. Ibid., 5:278–279, 403–404.

28. Ibid., 6:244–245.

29. Ibid., 5:419–425.

30. Daniel Walker Howe, *What Hath God Wrought: The Transformation of America* (New York: Oxford University Press, 2007), 464.

CHAPTER 12
The Real Lincoln Is the Icon

1. Works cited in this chapter include:

Barzun, Jacques. "Lincoln the Writer." In *On Writing, Editing, and Publishing: Essays Explicative and Hortatory.* Chicago: University of Chicago Press, 1971.

Boritt, Gabor. *Lincoln and the Economics of the American Dream.* Memphis, TN: Memphis State University Press, 1978.

Carwardine, Richard. *Lincoln: A Life of Purpose and Power.* New York: Knopf, 2006.

Charnwood, Godfrey Rathbone Benson Baron. *Abraham Lincoln: A Biography.* Toronto, Canada: Madison Books, 1998.

Goodwin, Doris Kearns. *Team of Rivals: The Political Genius of Abraham Lincoln.* New York: Simon & Schuster, 2005.

Thomas, Benjamin P. *Abraham Lincoln: A Biography.* New York: Modern Library, 1979.

Wills, Gary. *Lincoln at Gettysburg: The Words That Remade America.* New York: Simon & Schuster, 1993.

Wilson, Doug. *Honor's Voice: The Transformation of Abraham Lincoln.* New York: Knopf, 1998.

CHAPTER 13
Lincoln—The Unlikely Celebrity

1. Works cited in this chapter include:

Basler, Roy P., ed. *The Collected Works of Abraham Lincoln*. 8 vols. New Brunswick, NJ: Rutgers University Press, 1953.

Carpenter, Francis B. *Six Months at the White House with Abraham Lincoln: The Story of a Picture*. New York: Hurd and Houghton, 1866.

Dicey, Edward. *Spectator of America*. Ed. Herbert Mitgang. Chicago: Quadrangle Books, 1971.

Fehrenbacher, Don E., and Virginia Fehrenbacher. *Recollected Words of Abraham Lincoln*. Stanford: Stanford University Press, 1996.

Goodwin, Doris Kearns. *Team of Rivals: The Political Genius of Abraham Lincoln*. New York: Simon & Schuster, 2005.

Holzer, Harold, Mark E. Neely Jr., and Gabor S. Boritt. *The Lincoln Image: Abraham Lincoln and the Popular Print*. New York: Charles Scribner's Sons, 1984.

Holzer, Harold. *Lincoln at Cooper Union: The Speech That Made Abraham Lincoln President*. New York: Simon & Schuster, 2004.

Lorant, Stefan. *Lincoln: A Picture Story of His Life*, rev. ed. New York: W. W. Norton, 1969.

Ostendorf, Lloyd. *Lincoln's Photographs*, rev. ed. Dayton, OH: Rockywood Press, 1998.

Rice, Allen Thorndike, ed. *Reminiscences of Lincoln by Distinguished Men of His Time*. New York: North American, 1886.

Turner, Linda Levitt, and Justin G. Turner. *Mary Todd Lincoln: Her Life and Letters*. New York: Alfred A. Knopf, 1973.

Wilson, Douglas, and Rodney O. Davis. *Herndon's Informants: Letters, Interviews, and Statements About Abraham Lincoln*. Urbana, University of Illinois Press, 1998.

INDEX

I believe that a good story well told can truly make a difference in how one sees the world. This is why I started Participant Media: to tell compelling, entertaining stories that create awareness of the real issues that shape our lives.

At Participant, we seek to entertain our audiences first and then invite them to participate in making a difference. With each film, we create social action and advocacy programs that highlight the issues that resonate in the film and provide ways to transform the impact of the media experience into individual and community action.

Forty-one films later, from *An Inconvenient Truth* to *Food, Inc.,* and from *Waiting for "Superman"* to *The Best Exotic Marigold Hotel,* and through thousands of social action activities, Participant continues to create entertainment that inspires and compels social change. Through our partnership with PublicAffairs, we are extending our mission so that more of you can join us in making our world a better place.

Jeff Skoll, founder and chairman
Participant Media

PublicAffairs is a publishing house founded in 1997. It is a tribute to the standards, values, and flair of three persons who have served as mentors to countless reporters, writers, editors, and book people of all kinds, including me.

I. F. STONE, proprietor of *I. F. Stone's Weekly*, combined a commitment to the First Amendment with entrepreneurial zeal and reporting skill and became one of the great independent journalists in American history. At the age of eighty, Izzy published *The Trial of Socrates*, which was a national bestseller. He wrote the book after he taught himself ancient Greek.

BENJAMIN C. BRADLEE was for nearly thirty years the charismatic editorial leader of *The Washington Post*. It was Ben who gave the *Post* the range and courage to pursue such historic issues as Watergate. He supported his reporters with a tenacity that made them fearless and it is no accident that so many became authors of influential, best-selling books.

ROBERT L. BERNSTEIN, the chief executive of Random House for more than a quarter century, guided one of the nation's premier publishing houses. Bob was personally responsible for many books of political dissent and argument that challenged tyranny around the globe. He is also the founder and longtime chair of Human Rights Watch, one of the most respected human rights organizations in the world.

·　　·　　·

For fifty years, the banner of Public Affairs Press was carried by its owner Morris B. Schnapper, who published Gandhi, Nasser, Toynbee, Truman, and about 1,500 other authors. In 1983, Schnapper was described by *The Washington Post* as "a redoubtable gadfly." His legacy will endure in the books to come.

Peter Osnos, *Founder and Editor-at-Large*